EIGHTEENTH CENTURY EXETER

EIGHTEENTH CENTURY EXETER

By

ROBERT NEWTON

UNIVERSITY OF EXETER
1984

First published 1984 by the University of Exeter
© 1984 The Estate of Robert Newton
ISBN 0 85989 255 7

The Publications Committee of the University of Exeter wishes to express its
appreciation of Professor Joyce Youings's generous, patient and expert
attention to the preparation of the typescript of *Eighteenth-Century Exeter* for
publication and for seeing it through the press.

Ivan Roots
Chairman of the
Publications Committee,
University of Exeter
1981–84

Printed in Great Britain by A Wheaton & Co. Ltd., Exeter.

Contents

List of Illustrations

Abbreviations

Act Books	Act (Minute) Books of the Chamber of Exeter
CSPD	*Calendar of State Papers Domestic*
DAT	*Devonshire Association, Transactions of*
DCNQ	*Devon & Cornwall Notes & Queries*
DCRS	Devon and Cornwall Record Society
DRO	Devon Record Office
ECA	Exeter City Archives
FP	*Trewman's Exeter Flying Post*
Gazette	*Woolmer's Exeter and Plymouth Gazette*
HMC	Historical Manuscripts Commission
Luminary	*Flindell's Western Luminary*
PP	Parliamentary Papers
Post-Boy	*The Protestant Mercury or the Exeter Post-Boy*
Post-Master	*The Exeter Post-Master or the Loyal Mercury*
WT	*Western Times*
Weekly Journal	*Brice's Weekly Journal*

Foreword

ROBERT NEWTON

Dr Robert Newton CMG died on 10 December 1983 knowing that, as he himself had wished, his last book would be published by the University of Exeter, with whose department of History and Archaeology he had been associated, both as student and teacher, for some twenty years.

Born in Newcastle-upon-Tyne in 1908, he read History at Pembroke College, Cambridge and in 1931 entered the Colonial Service, serving in Nigeria, Palestine (where in 1946 he survived the terrorist attack on the King David Hotel) and Jamaica, retiring in 1961 as Secretary in Mauritius. Soon after taking up residence in Exeter he became a member of the City Council and later one of its Aldermen. He also enrolled as a postgraduate student, completing under the guidance of the late W.D. Handcock a very substantial doctoral dissertation which was published by the University of Leicester in 1968 as *Victorian Exeter*. There followed a diversion to the history of his native county and in 1972 *The Northumberland Landscape* was published as a contribution to the series edited by his friend and mentor Professor W.G. Hoskins. Papers on urban history followed, including one on middle-class housing in Exeter between 1770 and 1870, but his main energies thereafter were devoted to the study of Exeter society and politics from the Glorious Revolution to the Great Reform Act.

As in his earlier work on the city's Victorian politics Robert Newton wrestled with voluminous source material, including the fine series of early local newspapers, knowing from his own experience not only what was likely to be revealed in City Chamber minutes but also their limitations. Clearly his eighteenth-century city councillors had much in common with those he had known in the flesh. Though himself a loyal member of the established Church he applauded the struggles and achievements of Exeter's early Dissenters, not least in the improvement of the city and its suburbs, and indeed his own attachment was to the Liberal Party.

But for all his political and scholarly pre-occupations Robert Newton was at heart an outdoor man. Never one to use a motor vehicle if it was possible to walk, he had an intimate knowledge of Exeter's streets and gradients and he found the time and energy to spend long hours walking with his dogs exploring Devon's woods and moors. To the very end of his life he was a keen ornithologist.

Even in failing health he did not spare himself in meeting the University's requests for cuts in his book, the necessity for which he accepted philosophically if somewhat ruefully. He would gladly, no doubt, have been spared, or have accepted help with, the final checking of references and bibliography, the reading of proofs and the compilation of the Index. Except for the tidying up of some loose ends the text is published as he left it, the illustrations, including that on the wrapper, being largely those he had selected. Permission to reproduce photographs of two portraits in the Guildhall was given by Exeter City Council and of the interior of George's Meeting House by the Royal Commission on Historical Monuments (England). Plates 5 and 6 are Crown copyright by permission of M.S.C. The map of Exeter in 1700 was prepared from Dr Newton's draft by Sean Goddard of the department of History and Archaeology and John Saunders of the University Library did some of the photography. Others who helped to provide illustrations were Jane Baker, Ian Maxsted, Frederick Nicholls and Michael Stocks. The author would undoubtedly have wished to express his thanks to Margery Rowe and her assistants at the Devon Record Office, to the staff of Devon Library Services and of the University of Exeter Library, and in particular to Sheila Stirling and Geoffrey Paley, the librarians of the Devon and Exeter Institution of which he was a much-loved and respected President. Publication of the book owes much to the support of Professor Ivan Roots, Chairman of the University's Publications Committee and its production to the interest, care and efficiency of Barbara Mennell, the University's Publications Officer. Last but by no means least the University wishes to acknowledge on Dr Newton's behalf a loan towards the cost of publication by the British Academy.

JOYCE YOUINGS

Introduction

Exeter's eighteenth-century history can justifiably be taken as beginning in 1688 and ending in 1835. It begins with the dramatic arrival of the Prince of Orange in 1688 and the subsequent 'Glorious Revolution' of the Whigs, both accepted by Exeter so unwillingly but the latter eventually, and until 1835, staunchly defended by Cathedral and Guildhall against Jacobins, Radicals and Dissenters. In November 1688 Exeter's lord lieutenant, the Earl of Bath, explained to James II's secretary of state, that Exeter, the Ever-Faithful City, *Semper fidelis*, was outraged by the association of the city's sword with a Dissenters' meeting-house.[1] In 1833, during the investigations prior to the enactment of the Municipal Corporations Act of 1834, the parliamentary commissioners were informed that the objection to Dissenters was as strong as ever despite the removal by Parliament of legal disabilities.[2] The first election to the new city Council in December 1835, under the provisions of the Act, admitted Protestant Dissenters, or Nonconformists as the Victorians called them, to the Guildhall. It was the end of an era, hailed by Reformers, unrestrained by eighteenth-century scepticism, as the dawn of a new age of enlightened and incorrupt local government.

Throughout the whole period from 1688 to 1835 traditional attitudes in the city on Church and State persisted, although the century and a half saw changes profoundly affecting the development of the city and the lives of its citizens. Exeter both reached and passed the peak of its national importance as a commercial and industrial city. Its economic foundations based on the cloth trade crumbled. No efforts to maintain the Exe Canal could restore the importance of a port that once had challenged Bristol. But for a generation after 1800 the city prospered as a provincial capital, priding itself on its climate, its cheap living and amenities, its schools and its many churches.

In 1688 the Earl of Bath, seeking to impress Whitehall with Exeter's significance in the South West, described the city as 'our London'. Some twenty years later Daniel Defoe emphasised Exeter's combination of trade, industry and 'good company' in an era when, as W.G. Hoskins has written,

Exeter was synonymous in contemporary pamphlets with woollen cloth. The cloth trade dwindled and died, good society flourished, partly on the profits of war. In late-Georgian Exeter an imposing company of the 'gentlemen of England' met at assize balls and assemblies and settled the affairs of the county at quarter sessions. Exeter offered cheap living and congenial society to retired officers of the armed forces, especially to those who had been in the service of the Honourable East India Company. The requirements of a consumer society inspired from about 1770 some sixty years of distinguished building and largely offset the consequences of the decline of the cloth industry. It was this society, and the amenities it required, that led Richard Ford, traveller and author, in 1835 to liken Exeter to London, as the Earl of Bath had done before him.[3] But Richard Ford's Exeter was a city of good society rather than trade, a city created largely in response to the demands of members of the professions and of county families, and of persons whom the census reports have classified as annuitants and persons of independent means.

For E.A. Freeman, Regius Professor of Modern History at Oxford, whose *Exeter* was published in 1887, the year of Queen Victoria's Golden Jubilee, Exeter's importance as an historic town ended with the drama of 1688. It was at that moment that he closed his main narrative; nothing remained but to sketch 'purely local history' down to his own time. Yet Freeman, looking back from the commanding heights of Victorian power, and conceding pride of place in 'modern greatness' to Manchester and Birmingham, was moved by the long continuity of Exeter's existence as a city. The years 1688 to 1835 were in fact a crucial period since it was then that the city had to adapt to the fundamental changes caused by the far-reaching economic and technological development of the nation as a whole. The conditions that had fostered the growing prosperity and importance of Exeter in earlier centuries no longer existed by the end of the eighteenth century. The city had to seek a new role with the assistance of one unchanging factor, its key situation in the communications of the South West, aided by its prestige and attractions as a provincial capital, protected, before the advent of the railways, by its distance from London.

Other ancient provincial capitals found themselves left on one side by economic change in the eighteenth century, the city of York being one. Victorian Exeter would lament its vanished glories. Yet to Exonians of the 1830s there was cause for pride. Dr Thomas Shapter, a member of the Chamber and mayor of the reformed corporation, contributed his survey of Exeter to the report on the *State of Large Towns and Populous Districts* of 1845. Describing the city he knew, he found, instead of 'decline and ruin' after the loss of the cloth industry, an increasing population, 'their personal comforts publicly considered and provided for, and the whole aspect of the city undergoing a change for the better'.[4] If Exeter could no longer claim a major role in the national economy as it had in 1688, it could claim that its subsequent history had been a record of progress; and in carrying into the Age of Reform an attitude to the problems of Church and State that had survived the Glorious Revolution of 1688 Exeter remained *Semper fidelis,* the 'Ever-Faithful City'.

W.T. MacCaffrey, in his *Exeter 1540-1640* (Cambridge, Mass., 1958), and W.B. Stephens, in his *Seventeenth Century Exeter* (Exeter, 1958), have told the story of Exeter's rise to its commanding position in the hierarchy of English towns and cities. My own *Victorian Exeter* (Leicester, 1968) is a portrait of the city between 1837 and 1914 when, on the national scale, it reached its nadir. W.G. Hoskins's *Industry, Trade and People in Exeter 1688-1800* (Manchester, 1938) is an indispensable authority for the period, to which I am deeply indebted, but Hoskins's book is deliberately limited in its scope and ends at the point when Exeter began to live on its social attractions as a provincial capital.

This book is a portrait rather than an analysis. Over forty years ago Hoskins pointed out what an abundance of material exists for monographs on many aspects of Exeter's eighteenth-century life. A detailed study of the family and business relationships of members of the Chamber alone would be particularly illuminating for it would involve a study of local power confined to a small circle but on the whole exercised conscientiously. This book cannot claim to be more than a preliminary survey.

NOTES

1. *CSPD James II,* iii, pp. 304-5: Bath to Sunderland, 9.10.1688.
2. DRO, ECA, Commissioners for Municipal Corporations, proceedings at Exeter, 1-6 November 1833.
3. R.E. Prothero (ed.), *Letters of Richard Ford,* p. 135.
4. PP *State of Large Towns* H.C. 610 1845 xviii, Appendix, part II, pp. 351-80.

Chapter One

Exeter in 1688

'Our London which gives laws to all the rest'
(The Earl of Bath, describing Exeter, 9 October 1688)

Exeter entered the eighteenth century in 1688 with a roll of drums and a
flourish of trumpets. It was the final, and unwilling, appearance of the city
in the historical drama in which Exeter had so often played a leading role
since Dane and Saxon had fought over possession of its strategic site nine
hundred years before. Hesitantly accepting the so-called Glorious
Revolution of 1688 Exeter in due course came to uphold that event as the
palladium of Church and State. It was not until December 1835 that the
city formally abandoned its dominant eighteenth-century tradition, and its
governing body, the Chamber, appropriately placed on record at its last
meeting its appreciation of the ties that had existed between Guildhall and
Cathedral. These ties had been established in the days of the Cavalier
Parliament of 1661-79.

On 5 November 1688 the Prince of Orange landed at Torbay, bringing
with him an impressive professional army under a banner proclaiming 'The
Liberties of England and the Protestant religion'. It was an auspicious date
for all good Protestants, commemorated in the Book of Common Prayer of
1662 as the anniversary of 'the happy Deliverance from the most traitorous
and bloody intended Massacre by Gunpowder' of 1605. In the city of 1688
memories and fears of the persecution of Protestants had been revived by
the recent arrival of Huguenot refugees fleeing from the Most Christian
King, Louis XIV of France, and by the widely held belief that Britain's
own Catholic monarch, James II, was seeking to reimpose his religion on
his subjects by force with the support of Louis XIV and the Catholic Irish.
Providence, it seemed, had once more intervened, as against Spain exactly a
century earlier, and a 'Protestant wind' had carried the invasion safely
down the Channel and then, equally providentially, had changed direction
to allow a safe anchorage in the sheltered waters of Tor Bay.

The November weather in 1688 was vile. Heavy rain and strong winds
followed the brief lull that had enabled the Prince to land his army on the
open beach of Brixham. By military convention the campaigning season
was long past. Conditions in Devon were rough and primitive for
professional soldiers accustomed to the excellent communications of the

Low Countries. The army struggled eastwards towards Exeter by tracks deep in glutinous mud, by sunken lanes negotiated with difficulty even by the sure-footed local packhorses. It crossed a Haldon which was bare and sodden, a brown and rainswept wilderness. On 9 November the main body descended into the valley of the Exe, 'the foot soldiers sorely weather-beaten and much dabbled in Dirt and Rain'.[1]

The Exeter that first appears today to the traveller descending from Haldon is the suburban growth of the twentieth century. The followers of the Prince of Orange would have seen nothing until on their descent towards the flood plain the city was suddenly revealed, a compact cluster of houses across the river, crumbling towers and walls useless against cannon, in a misty setting of pale gold and yellow autumn leaves on the elms which were long an admired feature of the city. The tracks from the west through the hamlets of Ide and Alphington converged upon the small village of St Thomas where they joined the Okehampton road at the approach to the medieval bridge with its crumbling little church of St Edmund. Beyond, to the east, was a fringe of alluvial islands with willow groves and ample grassy spaces largely occupied by the drying racks of the cloth industry or leased by the Chamber for grazing. Beyond again lay the mill leats and water channels, the mills, dyehouses, warehouses and dwellings of the industrial area below the city wall, buildings of the red local stone or of cob, many of them thatched. Upstream, to the west, lay Exe Island, still showing traces of its original marshy environment in Frog Lane and Rosemary Lane. The tiered roof tops of the city drew the eye up to the climax, the great grey cathedral unchallenged by secular buildings and reducing to insignificance the little city churches at its feet. Even to the professional soldiers of the Prince's army, men who knew Bruges, Amsterdam and Namur, the distant prospect must have been impressive. In comparison with Exeter, James II's Secretary of State had recently been informed, all other boroughs in Devon and Cornwall were no more than minor country towns. The city, explained the Earl of Bath,

> is the Bishop's seat, the residence of the Dean, Canons and Prebendaries. . . . and it has always been true to the Church and consequently to the King. Its motto is *Semper fidelis*.[2]

Exeter at that time was indeed one of the four or five leading cities of the kingdom, an important port and a major commercial and industrial centre. On closer inspection, however, the city showed its age. Its narrow streets offered an inadequate stage for the carefully devised military pageantry designed to impress both its citizens and the kingdom. From the West Gate facing the end of Exe Bridge the direct route to the centre of the city passed the church of St Mary Steps and ascended the narrow defile described half a century later by Andrew Brice as,

> A descent called Stepcote-Hill, to which the Butcherow leads, [whereby] the Guts, Blood, Litter, Ordure and a variety of Nastiness are, in hard showers of rain, rapidly carried . . . into the River.[3]

By modern standards South Street, or South Gate Street as it was called in 1688, was little better; when the street was widened in 1830 the old carriageway, excluding the footpaths, was reported to have been only some ten feet in width. And yet at the time of the arrival of the Prince of Orange, and for a century and a half thereafter, South Street was the centre of the carrier trade of the city, and the site of a notable concentration of inns, the still existing White Hart, the Bear, the Dolphin, the Mermaid and the Sun. The South Gate itself, a grim and imposing structure, was used as a prison. It contained the Shoe, a notorious debtors' ward where inmates without friends or resources were allowed to seek alms from the benevolent in the street below. From outside the gate the roads outside the city walls led down to the Quay and Exe Bridge by way of Quay Lane and Westgate Street, by Holloway Street the way lay open to the port of Topsham, and, by way of Magdalen Street, to the suburb of Heavitree and the London road.

Circumstances had brought the Prince to Exeter, a necessary stage on the route to London, but the city was the key to the communications system of the South West. The genius of Roman military engineers had seized upon the significance of the city's site at the lowest practical crossing of the Exe and on the dry and level ridge-top above the river. With a population of some 13,000 people, Exeter in 1688 ranked fourth or fifth among English cities.[4] It comprised twenty-two parishes proper and three extra-parochial precincts, Bedford Precinct, Bradninch Precinct and the Cathedral Close. The castle area of Rougemont, where the Devon magistrates held their meetings and members of parliament for the shire were elected, was administratively part of the county of Devon. Wealth, social status and authority were concentrated in the seven small parishes and three precincts occupying the level crest of the ridgeway, and in close proximity to the closely-allied symbols of spiritual and temporal power, the Guildhall and the Cathedral.

Five of the six wealthiest parishes comprised a total of less than twelve acres and all were densely populated. In St Stephens fifty persons were assessed for the poor rate in 1699, twenty-six of them at the higher weekly rates of 6*d*. and over. The far larger and more populous parish of St Mary Major on the slope towards the river contained only twenty-three individuals assessed at the higher rates. There were only three paupers in the central parish of St Pancras in 1699, while there were one hundred among the artisans and labourers of St Mary Major and seventy-six in St Edmunds. With St Mary Steps, which had little more than its parish church within the city walls, the totally extra-mural parish of St Edmund had grown out of the industrial colonisation of the riverside in medieval times. Sir Thomas Jefford, dyer and briefly mayor in 1687-8, still owned a large house there, but his fine new mansion, Great Duryard in the northern suburbs, was nearing completion.[5]

The large parishes of St Sidwell and St David to the north of the city, the former wholly extra-mural, the latter largely so, together comprised some two-thirds of the whole area under the jurisdiction of the Chamber. St Sidwells was a parish of farms, market gardens and orchards, with a population of smallholders and labourers who lived for the most part in the two short rows of largely thatched cottages outside the East Gate. By the 1690s its population was finding a major source of employment in the developing brickfields, and later would work in the various branches of the communications industry such as coach-making and in house building. It was the stronghold of the 'Grecians', the name given to the eighteenth-century mob stimulated by free food and drink to intimidate respectable voters at parliamentary and mayoral elections. St Davids too was primarily a rural parish, its parish church standing alone in the fields in the vicinity of a handful of houses and inns for carriers. A farmhouse of the period, with a gabled porch, still survives today in Lower North Street. There were fulling and grist mills down by the river, willow groves, and grazing grounds such as the 'great marsh' near Cowley Bridge which the Chamber sold for £250 in 1700.[6] In the north of the parish the hills rise steeply to some five hundred feet in the angle of the Exe, where the river turns seawards below its junction with the Creedy; this area was well-wooded, a source of timber for building and bark for tanning. In 1691 the Chamber, owner of the ancient manor of Duryard which comprised a great part of the parish, sold five hundred oaks for £900, a very large sum, to Mathew Frost, tanner, of Shobrooke near Crediton.[7] Below the woods were fields of rough pasture with much gorse and thorn, a valuable source of fuel, and the cob and thatched linhays of the countryside of Devon.

The heart of the city was the Carfax, from the French *carrefours* or crossroads, which knotted together the strands of the communications, by road, lane and trackway, from which Exeter derived its being and its prosperity. It was the meeting place of the High Street, and its extension, Fore Street, with South Street and North Street. Fore Street, very steep and hazardous for traffic, ended at the West Wall overlooking the river, direct access to Exe Bridge through the West Gate being provided via Smythen Street and Stepcote Hill. South Street in particular marked the westward limit of the select residential and business zone of the city. Below it lay the dwellings and industrial premises of fullers and sergemakers with their warehouses, dyehouses and drying linhays. This was the West Quarter, notorious, according to Andrew Brice, for the stink of urine collected by women for use in the fulling mills. It was also a stronghold of the butchers, the 'rugged chieftains of the Mob' as Brice described them, with their journeymen, 'rugged, beastly fellows',[8] who throughout the eighteenth century supplied toughs armed with clubs, usually in the Whig interest, to intimidate voters at parliamentary elections. As late as 1911 the medical officer of health reported that the inhabitants of the West Quarter were 'a terror to landlords and a continual source of trouble to the sanitarian authorities'.[9]

From the Carfax, North Street too dropped steeply to the North Gate between houses that leaned towards each other across what was little more than a lane. Beyond the Gate this plunged even further to the crossing of the Longbrook whence it climbed through the fields and orchards of St Davids to Cowley Bridge and thence to Crediton and the little clothing towns of mid and north Devon. The Iron Bridge, a masterpiece of nineteenth-century ironwork, constructed in 1835, and the general smoothing of the gradients at that period, have made it difficult to appreciate the earlier difficulties of the northern approach to the city, especially as experienced by the great wagons of the eighteenth century; the obstruction caused by the gate itself was such that this was the first of the city gates to be demolished. Today the original condition can be best appreciated by the pedestrian descending under the Iron Bridge by the former St Anne's Well Brewery, where the steep slope on either side of the now concealed Longbrook is a reminder of the natural defences on the north side of an earlier Exeter, before they were slighted in the interests of modern traffic, first the wagon and coach, and later the automobile.

The approaches to the East Gate had no difficult gradients and the neighbourhood became the focal point of the coach trade when roads and vehicles alike were improved in the course of the eighteenth century, and the fine inns for which Exeter became noted were here in close proximity. From the East Gate the London road led through Honiton, Dorchester and Salisbury with the first stage, to Honiton, providing one of the easiest sections of the route. Northwards the roads ran to Tiverton and Bampton, to the clothing towns of the Culme valley and to Taunton, Bath and Bristol.

Within the gates, High Street alone in the Exeter of 1688 justified the description by Celia Fiennes in 1698 of a city with 'well-pitched, spacious and noble streets'.[10] In 1724 the antiquarian William Stukely recorded, more temperately, that 'the beauty of the place consists mainly of one long street, broad and straight.'[11] Along the line of the High Street, on the broad and level crest of the ridge, were concentrated the dwellings and business premises of the ruling oligarchs, and the town houses of county families such as the Bampfyldes, Walronds and Rolles, dominated by the great house, stables and gardens of the Russells who, as pillars of the new regime, were soon to become dukes of Bedford. Only in the High Street and within the Cathedral precinct was there any semblance to the spaciousness or nobility which would be approved by later classical taste. Exeter's leading Whigs, John Elwill and Edward Seaward, owned houses in Bedford and Bradninch precincts respectively and five aldermen owned houses in the Cathedral Close. But even the main streets were muddy or dusty, unpaved and unlit. Pedestrians were at risk of being crushed by great wagons struggling behind teams of four to six horses amid the congestion caused by livestock from the country, dealers with stallions and unbroken ponies and drovers with their dogs. Until 1694 the cattle and pig markets were held in the High Street itself. Country women with their baskets of dairy produce and produce and vegetables sat in the shelter of overhanging storeys and washed their goods at the Carfax. The life of the countryside, its pace and its customs, prevailed throughout the city.

Exeter had evolved as a medley of medieval, Tudor and Jacobean architecture. Houses were constructed largely of the soft local stone, or were timber-framed, infilled with cob, lath and plaster. The poor lived in cottages of one or two rooms or, a family to a room, in medieval houses abandoned by more prosperous citizens. Brick was just coming into fashion, and also sash windows, such houses in Gandy Street being described as 'new built' when advertised for sale in 1724.[12] One belonged to a mercer's widow and another to an attorney. But the houses of the wealthier merchants as seen by the Prince of Orange still resembled those surviving today, though with many modifications, near the junction of High Street with Queen Street. Timber-framed and plastered, with their gables and internal galleries, bay windows and leaded panes, the houses themselves contained the business premises of their owners as well as their domestic apartments, and many, even the congested parish of St Mary Major, had gardens and even small orchards.[13] The larger ones were surrounded by a warren of little courts.

The parish churches, though of ancient foundation, were small, undistinguished and inadequately maintained. The church of Allhallows on the Walls at the bottom of Fore Street was in ruins. Allhallows Goldsmith Street, though in one of the wealthier parishes, was disused, St Olaves had been handed over for the use of the Huguenots, refugees from the *dragonnades* of Louis XIV, and was long known as 'the French Church'. The churches of the congested little parishes of St John and St George were served by one incumbent.

In many respects, however, the parishes were still close-knit village societies, administrative as well as ecclesiastical units. Conformity and social discipline were maintained by vicar or rector, church-warden, constable and beadle, by the rich merchant and alderman whose virtues and achievements would be proclaimed for posterity on a mural tablet in the church. The congregation testified to its orthodoxy in Church and State by taking the sacrament; failure to do so was unlikely to escape notice. Strangers and vagrants came under scrutiny, and paupers from elsewhere were swiftly removed before they became a charge on the rates.

Law and order depended on the tradition of active citizenship, particularly on the energies — or acquiescence — of the property-owning classes, merchants, professional men and shopkeepers. Scarcely a generation had elapsed since citizens had been required to defend their city with arms. The prevention of crime and the apprehension of offenders was the ancient but often reluctantly assumed common law duty of the parish constables, shopkeepers and artisans who wielded the white staves of office provided by the Chamber. They were elected annually after the Michaelmas mayor-choosing and were subject to the authority of the aldermen-magistrates, who in many respects were the equivalent of the land-owning justices of the countryside, and were in charge of the four quarters of the city. Their duties included the supervision of ale houses where, in the conditions of the 1680s, they might stumble on talk of treason and plot. In practice the exercise of authority was tempered by moderation. Riotous behaviour and demonstrations were long tolerated, and were an accepted feature of such special occasions as the annual mayor-choosing. At elections the unfranchised, in particular the apprentices and journeymen of the butchers, demonstrated the rights of 'free Englishmen' in contrast, in the popular view, to the 'Popery and Wooden Shoes' of France. If riots became a serious threat to property the better off citizens were enrolled as special constables. In the last resort the only recourse was to use troops. By contemporary standards, however, riots in Exeter were never serious, none ever likely to involve the burning of the Bishop's palace or of Rougemont Castle.

Exeter remained a close-knit, neighbourly city. Many of its inhabitants met death in the gutter or the debtor's gaol, but there were no 'Two Nations' in the sense that would be dramatised in Disraeli's *Sybil*, not even physical segregation, economic or social, such as was experienced in the later industrial England. Throughout the city, business and industrial activities, the latter sometimes nauseous and dangerous, were intermingled with private dwellings. Rich and poor rubbed shoulders as they walked on their affairs. Aldermen-magistrates were familiar figures in the streets. They might have offenders whipped at the cart's tail or placed in the stocks outside the Guildhall but they were not yet remote guardians of the social order. Not until the reign of George III did the prosperous businessmen and the professional classes of Exeter withdraw into their sanctuaries, and by that time it was clear that Exeter was not to be exposed to the full force of the social consequences of economic growth. The decisive division in the Exeter of 1688 was religious, which involved political differences between the Dissenters and their sympathisers and the Anglicans.

Rich and poor alike suffered from the discomforts of an old city. Thatched roofs were to be found inside as well as outside the walls. Fire risks accordingly were serious and householders whose chimneys caught fire were liable to prosecution and fine. In the Guildhall were kept leathern fire-buckets and the hooks used for pulling down burning thatch and timber, the buckets also being lent to the butchers whose prerogative it was to throw dirty water over spectators during the saturnalia that accompanied the annual mayoral elections. Sanitation was minimal, as it was throughout Europe until the death rate in towns in the nineteenth century demonstrated that the habits of medieval society could no longer be tolerated. Old houses still used the medieval 'garderobe', an aperture within the stone wall giving access to a cesspit, which was always difficult and sometimes, on account of the accumulation of gas, lethal to clean. The chamber-pot and the close-stool were regarded, without embarrassment, as normal furniture and were emptied wherever and whenever convenient. It was not till 1740 that the Chamber ordered that doors should be provided at either end of the narrow passage of Parliament Street near the Guildhall 'to prevent people from emptying close-stools there to the nuisance of the neighbourhood'. Public latrines of a sort had existed at Exeter since at least the second half of the sixteenth century; in the eighteenth there was one at the ruinous Snail tower, in the south-west angle of the walls overlooking the river, which in 1775, by order of the Chamber, was removed to the field below. Andrew Brice, writing of the Exeter of the 1730s, said that the public also used the wall of the church of St Lawrence in the High Street.

Water supplies were good by the standards of an age not remarkable for personal cleanliness, but cures for 'the itch' and other skin disorders abounded in the local newspapers of the eighteenth century. Most of the large houses had their own wells and it was not till well into the nineteenth century that seepage from cesspits into wells was recognised as a serious hazard to health. Some piped water had been available at a few distribution points since the Middle Ages, notably at the Great Conduit in the Carfax, which was not removed until 1819. In 1693 the Chamber embarked on an expensive scheme by which water was pumped up from the river to a cistern behind the Guildhall. Celia Fiennes admiringly described the cistern as 'vast' and as holding something of the order of 40,000 gallons of water for the use of the whole city.[14] But as demand grew, with higher standards of living and an increasing population, the supply was palpably inadequate; the pressure was fickle, the pipes wooden and badly laid and its limitations were demonstrated all too drastically by the cholera epidemic of 1831. The majority of the population, however, still depended on water obtained from the river which, despite the mills and the filth flowing down from the streets, was still pure enough to satisfy the exacting requirements of salmon. In 1698 Celia Fiennes described the Exe as a fine river where 'they catch the salmon as they leap with spears.'

Diseases, including typhus, typhoid and smallpox flourished amid the poverty and malnutrition, the inadequate water supplies, the flies and the heaps of offal and foetid matter among which pigs scavenged in the streets. In 1695 a local correspondent wrote graphically of a 'terrible fever' advancing west 'like a great shower, having some droppings before and after it'. In that year burials in the largely working-class parish of St Sidwell numbered 145 in contrast to the average of 42.5 of the four preceeding years. In Holy Trinity, an 'industrial' parish, they were twice the average.[15]

Life still moved in harmony with, or in subjection to, the weather and the seasons. Darkness and daylight rather than the clock and the machine regulated hours of work. Bad weather brought much work to a standstill. For fuel the city had outrun the resources of the nearby countryside, even with the assistance of furze and loppings. Coal imports were increasing, but the cost for cooking and heating, and certainly to provide hot water for washing, was well beyond the resources of the poor. Cheap coal became a regular feature of public assistance by the end of the eighteenth century. Bad communications as much as bad harvests resulted in serious food shortages and even starvation.

The harshness of daily life was to some extent mitigated by the traditional pageantry. The city had turned away with relief from the enforced decorum of the Commonwealth, though quiet behaviour in the streets at the time of Sunday church services was strictly enforced. Not till the early nineteenth century would the religious revival and the influence of Evangelicalism frown upon the relaxations of the masses and seek to substitute lectures for cakes and ale. The birthday of Charles II, Oakapple Day, was commemorated by decorating houses with sprigs of oak; the members of the Chamber walked in procession to the Cathedral, and wine and ale were dispensed to freemen in the Guildhall. The Chamber maintained its own band of musicians, the waits, who were provided with fine cloaks and ornamental chains. They performed in the streets and outside the mayor's residence at Christmas and on such occasions as coronations, victories and royal anniversaries. There was pageantry mixed with horseplay and some disorder to celebrate mayor-choosing, and annual processions round the walls and the wider bounds of the county of the city. On such occasions the Incorporated Trades, that is the guilds, marched with their traditional finery and banners: the fullers, weavers and shearmen, the barbers, the apothecaries, the carpenters and the butchers, as well as the councillors and aldermen, sergeants at mace and staffbearers, all testified to the historic past of the city, its achievements and privileges.

Exeter was not however a parochial city, if by parochial is implied preoccupation with life within the walls. The fortunes of its merchants, and of the city itself, depended on the devious foreign policy of Stuart kings, on the fortunes of Holland or the ambitions of Louis XIV. Religious issues involved not only passionately debated questions of eternal salvation but pressing political and constitutional problems. When the Recorder, Sir Edward Seymour, was entertained by the mayor it may be assumed that the Chamber became at least as well informed about the political situation at Whitehall as any later city council; information would be sought out and digested with the more care when property and personal survival could depend on distant events. Merchants such as John Sandford and Gilbert Yard had received the questionnaire by means of which, in April 1688, James II had sought prior agreement to support his policies in Parliament; like Sir Edward Seymour and most of the gentlemen of Devon they had refused commitment.[16]

As one of the foremost industrial and trading cities of England, Exeter in 1688 was sharing in the economic growth that had marked the national economy since the 1670s. The city was self-confident and expansionist at a time when the ancient cloth industry of Devon was attaining its maximum importance in national trade. Since the turn of the sixteenth century, and especially since 1660, the serges of Devon had found ready markets. Exeter, with its client port of Topsham, was outstanding in that trade. Exports to the ports of continental Europe, especially to the Netherlands, Germany and Spain, were expanding rapidly, and there was an increasingly important flow of cloth to London for finishing.[17] Purely as an industrial town Tiverton may have outranked Exeter, but Exeter was also a political, social and financial centre, a provincial capital and a centre of distribution to a well-populated and prosperous hinterland. Grocers, that is wholesale importers of valuable commodities such as sugar, rice, coffee, tea and tobacco, were prominent in the Chamber, the governing body of the city, but formal descriptions of occupations, such as merchant, grocer, fuller and even ironmonger, concealed wider financial interests, the burgeoning banking activities of men who had accumulated wealth and had used it not only to finance trade and the various processes of local industry but also to lend, on good security, to the Chamber itself. John Elwill, grocer, already a Whig Member of Parliament and in due course to be a baronet, evidently increased his great wealth from financial enterprises. As one of the Receivers General for the Revenue he had the opportunity to employ large sums on his own behalf before they were remitted to London. In 1699 he was informed that if he did not remit his receipts and close his accounts he would be ordered into custody. The Tory alderman Christopher Bale, also a member of the governing merchant class, enjoyed similar perquisites.

Exeter's rulers, the twenty-four members of the Chamber, had consolidated their position since Tudor times as a select oligarchy watching over and shrewdly promoting the interests of the city. Although in 1642 the Puritans, a powerful minority, had brought the city into the Civil War on the side of Parliament, King Charles had later found a warm welcome in Exeter and the Chamber of 1660 was staunchly royalist. A close-knit group linked by kinship and business, its members since 1660 had been whole-hearted supporters of the Stuart monarchy. In the troubled decades of the 1670s and 1680s, amid plots and counterplots, they had firmly supported the Crown, organised the militia, watched the ports and kept a wary eye on mysterious Irishmen who swore 'incredible and ridiculous things'.[18] Since the 1670s, when the term Tory came into use for the party of the Crown, the Chamber had been Tory and a firm upholder of the Church of England. The Chamber, Bishop Sparrow (1667-76) once reported, formally resolved 'to come constantly in their formalities to our quire on Sundays, resolving by all the waies they can express their conformity to the Church and to countenance the service'.[19]

Plate 1. Benjamin Heath, Town Clerk 1752–66, oil painting by R.E. Pyne, Exeter Guildhall. Photo Vosper Arthur.

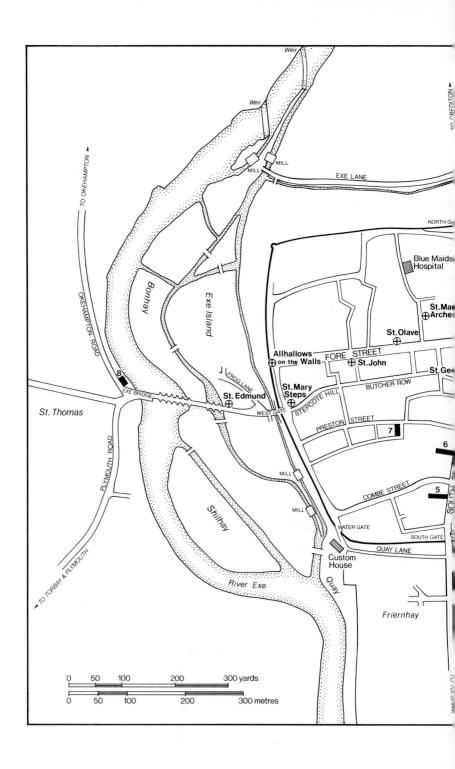

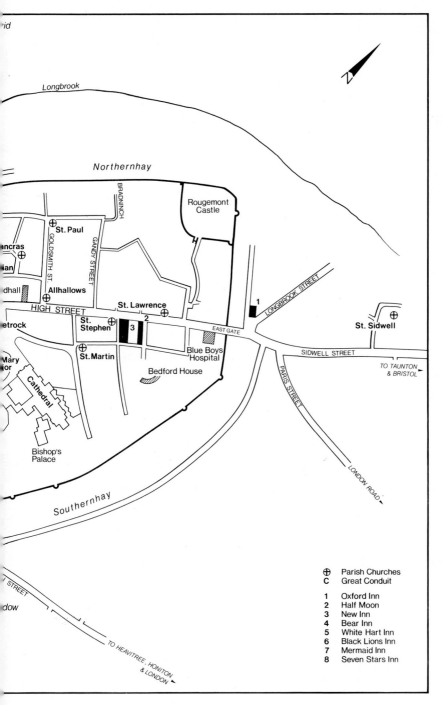

id

Longbrook

Northernhay

BRADNINCH

Rougemont
Castle

St. Paul

GOLDSMITH ST

GANDY STREET

ncras

ian

dhall

Allhallows

St. Lawrence

HIGH STREET

etrock

St.
Stephen

2

3

LONGBROOK STREET

1

EAST GATE

St. Sidwell

SIDWELL STREET

Mary
ior

St. Martin

Blue Boys
Hospital

TO TAUNTON
& BRISTOL

Cathedral

Bedford House

PARIS STREET

Bishop's
Palace

Southernhay

LONDON ROAD

STREET

dow

TO HEAVITREE, HONITON
& LONDON

⊕   Parish Churches
C   Great Conduit

1   Oxford Inn
2   Half Moon
3   New Inn
4   Bear Inn
5   White Hart Inn
6   Black Lions Inn
7   Mermaid Inn
8   Seven Stars Inn

EXETER IN 1700
Based on map by Sutton Nicholls, 1723

Plate 3. John Tuckfield of Shobrooke, MP for Exeter 1745–76 and donor of site of Royal Devon and Exeter Hospital in Southernhay, oil painting, artist unknown, Exeter Guildhall. Photo Vosper Arthur.

Between 1670 and 1680 over one thousand men and women, almost all of them Presbyterian, appeared before the aldermen-magistrates of Exeter for breaches of the Conventicle Act of 1664 which prohibited religious gatherings other than those of the Established Church.[20] With the Tories as the Church Party and hence associated with the Penal Laws against Dissent, the Dissenters were necessarily Whig, the party of religious toleration (except for Roman Catholics) and they provided an enduring Whig vote throughout the eighteenth century. Later still they became supporters of reform in Church and State. According to a statement made in 1716 the authority of the wealthier Dissenters was exercised widely over their employees, and there is every reason to assume that wealthy Anglican employers did the same. The occupations of those arrested in the 1670s included goldsmith, spicer, grocer and merchant, but over one-third of the men were connected with some branch of the cloth industry. In elections at this time the Dissenters were reported to have borne a major share of expense in conjunction with the 'Low Church', those who, without leaving the Church of England, had little patience with religious ceremony or with the status and authority of bishops and for whom a plain man's religion was sufficiently explicit in the Bible. For the Dissenters of 1688 the Prince of Orange appeared as the leader who would bring them into the promised land of religious toleration.

The Exeter Dissenters of the 1680s included substantial citizens fully capable of playing a role in public life. When, in 1687 and 1688, royal agents 'regulated' the Chamber in the hope of securing the return of amenable members of Parliament, the men they chose, though not among the wealthiest, were not men of straw. The new mayor, Thomas Jefford, reputedly a particularly skilful dyer, was not himself a Dissenter, but among his colleagues nine had been fined by Tory magistrates for offences against the Conventicle Act. Three, Thomas Crispin, John Boyland and Andrew Jeffrey, had been Masters of the Exeter Company of Weavers, Fullers and Shearmen.[21] Three others, Thomas Sampson, John Pyne and Jerome King, though previously barred from the Chamber by law and, more efficaciously, by sentiment, had had no difficulty in being elected by vote of the ratepayers as members of the Corporation of the Poor. The reaction of the displaced Exeter establishment, the wealthy Tory merchants, was expressed by the Earl of Bath, writing in October 1688 to the Earl of Sunderland:

> You may easily imagine it to be a great mortification to them to see the most substantial, rich, loyal citizens turned out of the government for no offence and never so much as asked any questions . . . It cannot choose but be grievous to them to be domineered over by a packed Chamber of Dissenters, and to see the sword, which was never known in the memory of man in this city, carried every Sunday before the mayor in state to a conventicle.[22]

The King reversed his policy as the fast-moving crisis reached its climax with the invasion of the Prince of Orange. On Saturday 4 November 1688 the Earl of Bath as Lord Lieutenant received the order-in-council restoring the former members of the Chamber. The Earl took immediate action. On the Sunday, while the Prince of Orange was disembarking in Tor Bay, the old order was restored at a ceremony in the Cathedral. Crowds thronged the streets to watch the hastily organised procession from the Guildhall, 'to see', as the earl expressed it, 'the Sword rescued from a Conventicle and carried once more, after the ancient manner, to the Cathedral Church'. The King, he wrote, had 'given great satisfaction to every person in the great and populous city'.[23] The celebrations over a return to the good old days of Charles II were abruptly terminated. For the Prince of Orange and his army were marching upon Exeter.

Neither the city, nor the South West generally, had had any preliminary share in the plotting that preceded the invasion. The members of the Chamber, with their authority and *amour propre* restored, were sensible, it was reported, of the 'King's great Goodnesse and Prudence'.[24] Now they were to be invited to plunge without warning into the cold waters of treason. Moreover they lacked the independent counsel of the territorial magnates whose privilege it was to risk their heads and estates in such matters, for they, as elsewhere in England, rallied support for the Prince of Orange. In these difficult circumstances the Chamber displayed a prudent hesitation. The first, unauthorised, contact with the Prince, in the person of an obscure country gentleman, was promptly, but with tactful courtesy, confined in the Guildhall by Mayor Brodridge.[25] Here he was well treated and was no doubt sustained by the sound of demonstrations of support from members of the populace. The official emissaries of the Prince of Orange arrived on the following day. Both were men of high rank and reputation but they too were unsuccessful in persuading the mayor to provide an official welcome. Christopher Brodridge pleaded his oath to James II and begged to be relieved of any commands prejudicial to his conscience. When the Prince of Orange himself entered the city on 9 November only two members of the Chamber had the hardihood to welcome him, doing so at the South Gate. It is true that when the Prince entered the city he was greeted by the masses with enthusiasm but Dr Burnet, the Prince's chaplain and advisor, noted that the lay and ecclesiastical leaders of the city were 'very fearful and backward'. The Bishop and the Dean had fled. Among the welcoming crowd there must have been many who had acclaimed the Whig hero, the Duke of Monmouth, in 1680 when, as in 1688, the Chamber had held aloof. But it could not have been entirely forgotten that Monmouth had lost his head in a messy execution on Tower Hill. It was very different at Salisbury three weeks later when the Prince was welcomed by the mayor and aldermen in all their finery: but by that time King James was in retreat, the aristocracy and gentlemen of England were flocking to support the Prince of Orange, and adherence, with success in sight, was ceasing to be treason.

Despite the weather, and the coolness of the city authorities, the entry of the Prince of Orange into Exeter was impressive, and was accompanied by all the panache and high ceremonial of international military society, a fitting theme for Lord Macaulay. It was the opening move in an enterprise which was crowned with eventual success. For a few days Exeter, unprepared and unrehearsed, stood forth on the national stage, called upon to play a leading part in high drama, and, though the days when armed citizens could be called upon to man the walls had passed, it was not impossible that the ever-faithful city could have influenced events by delaying the eastward march of the Prince's army as the Catholic insurgents had been delayed in 1549. In 1688, however, the city authorities had neither the means nor the will for effective opposition. The city settled down to meet the needs of an army held under tight discipline, there being 'such civil behaviour among them, without swearing or damning and debauching of women'.[26] Much-needed provisions were paid for in good coin and horse-dealers made the most of the urgent need for remounts.

The Prince left Exeter on 17 November. He had waited anxiously for evidence of effective support from the territorial magnates of the kingdom and had been heartened by the arrival of Exeter's Recorder, Sir Edward Seymour, who brought the support of the Tory gentlemen of the South West. Seymour (1633–1708) was a member of a family long accustomed to playing for high stakes in politics and to paying the penalty for misjudgement on the scaffold. In Macaulay's words 'beyond comparison the foremost among the Tory gentlemen of England', a former Speaker of the House of Commons, he had been Recorder of Exeter since 1683, except when he had lost his position in the purge of 1687–8. A man of resolution and courage he was fitted to confirm the feeble knees of city dignitaries in a perilous crisis. Head of the senior branch of an ancient family noted for its pride he did not truckle to kings, still less to Dutch princes, and his popularity with the masses was not endangered by his ability to swear and swagger among the seamen of the South West, or even by his scandalising a cathedral canon to whom he expressed unsound opinions of the Resurrection.[27] As Recorder Seymour had cultivated good relations with the Chamber and in return had been entertained at the mayor's table, 'having obliged this city in many public affairs'.[28] In the critical days of mid-November 1688 he organised the collection of signatures of the nobility and gentry then in Exeter to a pledge of support for the Prince, and was appointed by him governor of the city. On 8 December the restored Chamber resolved that 'Mr maior, all the aldermen and Mr Pyne doe attend on Sir Edward Seymour, baronet, our Recorder' about the sick soldiers left behind in the city by the Prince of Orange'.

Sir Thomas Jefford and his colleagues quietly departed, their last meeting to discuss routine affairs having been held on 1 November. There was no proscription of the defeated, though there was a passing disposition on the part of their successors to seek evidence of irregularities in their administration. On 23 November, after the Prince of Orange had left Exeter, regular meetings of the Chamber were resumed with fourteen former members present, all of them Tories. In the chair was Christopher Brodridge, merchant, already twice mayor in the days of the Tory ascendancy in the reign of Charles II. Among his colleagues was John Snell, grocer, a High Tory evicted from the mayoralty in the purge of 1687 who was to be Sir Edward Seymour's colleague as Tory MP for Exeter in 1702. A kindred spirit was Christopher Bale, merchant, also a Tory and described as a creature of Sir Edward Seymour by that fervent Presbyterian Whig Mr Justice Rokeby[29] who regarded the Whig cause as that of 'God and Christ against Satan and Anti-Christ'. (There were, of course, Tories who claimed similar divine sanction for Toryism.) Bale too became Seymour's colleague as MP for the city after a rough by-election in 1689 and was subsequently returned, unopposed, in the election of 1690. All were men of substance and of high standing locally, confident in themselves and in their city.

The Chamber lost no time in bringing its membership up to strength. Seven members were 'elected' on 22 November: Nicholas Brooking, merchant, John Bankes, merchant, Christopher Cook, brewer, Christopher Mayne, merchant, John Gandy, brewer, John Elwill, grocer and George Pyle, fuller. All, except perhaps the last, were members of Exeter's wealthy governing class. They included a strong Whig element derived from the city's Puritan group in the previous generation. John Bankes, owner of Polsloe manor, was the son-in-law of Richard Crossing, mayor during the Commonwealth. Nicholas Brooking, merchant and also fuller — he took a lease of the fulling mills outside the West Gate in 1697 — was brother-in-law of the prominent Whig merchant, Edward Seaward. John Elwill, whose father had left money to 'godly ministers' in the city, later won recognition by the Whig party managers for his political influence in the South West. After experiencing some of the vicissitudes of party warfare he secured a baronetcy when the Whigs controlled the government in 1709. A correspondent on local politics of the influential Whig Sir George Treby, attorney-general in 1689, Elwill later fell victim to Edward Seymour when the latter purged the Devon magistracy of Whigs. Seymour, so Speaker Harley was informed, 'threw out Sir John Elwill, worth £50,000, the most necessary justice in the county'.

Among the other new councillors elected in November 1688 the two brewers, Christopher Cook and John Gandy, were dismissed by Mr Justice Rokeby as 'Tory' and 'Tory bigot' respectively. Three more members were elected to the Chamber on 11 December: John Curson, merchant, and the grocers Thomas Hill and Gilbert Yard. Yard's name had appeared on the list of Devon gentlemen declining to be committed to royal policy in response to the questionnaire of 1688. John Curson was remarkable in he had been appointed to the Chamber by the Crown in 1687 and had retained his position when the Chamber was again purged in March 1688. He must, therefore, have been regarded as a reliable supporter of James II, yet he was the sole member of the 1687–8 Chamber to retain his seat after the Revolution and in 1697 become mayor. The Chamber was brought up to full strength on the last day of December with the election of another grocer, Edward Dally, who had been apprentice to William Sandford, mayor in 1678 when the Chamber was strongly Tory.

By the end of 1688, therefore, the Chamber had been reconstituted with remarkable expedition and apparent unanimity. It included both Whigs and Tories, thus reflecting the Convention Parliament at Westminster, where the two parties with conflicting principles met to decide the future of the monarchy. But the consensus imposed by the political crisis on Exeter was as ephemeral as it was at Westminster. A laconic minute in the Act Book on 15 January 1689 recorded that 'whereas Mr Bankes, Mr Broking, Mr Elwill, Mr Mayne and Mr Pyle were of late elected to be members of this society, for some reasons best known to this house they are all dismissed and freed of and from the same.' It was customary at the time for the Act Books to record the reasons for the dismissal of members of the Chamber. Robert Hutchings, tailor, was dismissed on 21 September 1690 because he had 'become *non compos mentis*'. On the same day George Saffin, woollen draper, was dismissed and the record in the Act Book was explicit: 'George Saffin esquire, late mayor and still one . . . of the common council of this city, for refusing the oaths of allegiance and supremacy, is thereby become disabled and so dismissed of the said society.' To ease acceptance of the regime of William and Mary the oaths of allegiance and supremacy had been redrafted in order to meet the conscientious scruples of the Tory High Flyers; to some, such as George Saffin and, on a higher level, the saintly Bishop Kenn of Bath and Wells, the ingenuity of human draughtsmanship could not remove scruples over the withdrawal of allegiance sworn to an anointed king.

Except briefly in 1687–8 the Chamber had been consistently Tory since the party labels Whig and Tory had come into general use in the reign of Charles II. The 'Glorious Revolution' of 1688 had been accepted by Exeter after much hesitation. It had not changed the views of Exeter's ruling class. Four out of five of the members of the Chamber dismissed in 1689 were Whigs and had connections with Dissent. Their immediate replacements in February 1689, Richard Perriam, mercer, and John Burrell, apothecary, were certainly Tory, Burrell being also a High Churchman. The facts suggest that there was a purge of the Whigs, with the important exception of Edward Seaward who had been elected sheriff on 26 November and in 1691 would be mayor.

In the crisis of 1688, and during the political conflicts of its aftermath, the city's Toryism was sustained by two masterful grandees, one being Sir

Edward Seymour and the other the new bishop, Sir Jonathan Trelawny, Vice-Admiral of Cornwall and a sound, though moderate, Tory. As Bishop of Bristol Trelawny had been one of the Seven Bishops tried, and acquitted, for seditious libel in June 1688. As an influential landowner and moderate Tory his value to the government included his ability to secure the return of his friends and followers in a parliamentary election. Trelawny himself reported in 1692 that the citizens 'express a great reliance they have on my integrity and on any occasion they apply to me'.[30] Certainly the Bishop's forceful personality could be relied upon to check the Whigs in his city and diocese, as well as to curb the high-flying Tories among his clergy.

Thus, as Exeter relinquished its last leading role in historical drama and the Glorious Revolution was brought to its peaceful conclusion, though not without challenge, the city was made safe for Toryism for over one hundred and forty years, a Toryism that changed in course of time but, in Exeter at least, retained certain characteristics to the end. In the meantime, in 1688, the nation escaped civil war. The flowing tide of seventeenth-century economic expansion resumed its course and Exeter sailed on the flood.

NOTES

1. Contemporary sources are *The Expedition of his Highness the Prince of Orange*, written at Wincanton and published in 1688, and John Whittle, *The Exact Diary of the late Expedition*, 1689. Macaulay's account makes a dramatic story and among modern books J.R. Jones, *The Revolution of 1688 in England* and J. Carswell, *The Descent on England* are excellent studies.
2. *CSPD James II*, iii, pp. 304-5: Bath to Sunderland, 9.10.1688.
3. Andrew Brice, *The Mobiad*, 1770, but written in about 1735, p. 62, footnote.
4. The exact size has been much debated: see W.J. Harte and W.G. Hoskins in *DCNQ*, xx, 1939, pp. 210-14 and 242-7 and R. Pickard, *The Population and Epidemics of Exeter*, 1947. Professor Hoskins suggests a minimum figure of 13,000 in 1689.
5. W.G. Hoskins, *Industry, Trade and People in Exeter* and *Exeter in the Seventeenth Century*.
6. DRO, ECA, Receivers' Accounts, 9/10 – 11/12 William III, sale of property in the manor of Duryard.
7. DRO, ECA, Act Books, 17.12.1691.
8. Brice, *The Mobiad*, p. xvi.
9. *Report of the Medical Officer of Health*, Exeter, 1911, p. 77
10. C. Morris (ed.), *The Journeys of Celia Fiennes*, p. 245.
11. R. Pearse Chope (ed.), *Early Tours in Devon and Cornwall*, p. 138.
12. *Postmaster*, 9.10.1724.
13. D. Portman, *Exeter Houses 1400-1700*, passim and S.D. Chapman (ed.), *The Devon Cloth Industry in the Eighteenth Century*, pp. 51-88.
14. Morris, *op. cit.*, pp. 247-8.
15. Pickard, *op. cit.*, p. 61 and table xviii.
16. G. Duckett, *Penal Laws and the Test Act*, i, pp. 373-6.
17. Hoskins, *Industry, Trade and People*, passim.
18. *CSPD Charles II*, July-September 1683, p. 171: Secretary Jenkins to the mayor of Exeter, 19.7.1683.
19. J. Simmons, 'Some letters from the bishops of Exeter, 1668-88', *DCNQ*, xxii, pp. 73-4.
20. A.A. Brockett, *Nonconformity in Exeter 1650-1875*, passim and the Appendix to his M.A. thesis (University of Exeter 1960) for details of Dissenters prosecuted.
21. Joyce Youings, *Tuckers Hall Exeter*, pp. 124-9 and Appendix 1.

NOTES *continued*

22. *CSPD James II*, iii, pp. 304-5: Bath to Sunderland, 9.10.1688.
23. British Library, Add. MS 41805: Bath to Preston, 5.11.1688.
24. *ibid.*
25. Gilbert Burnet, *History of His Own Times*, 1723-4, passim and Macaulay, *History of England*, vol. II, chapter 9. Burnet accompanied the Prince from Holland.
26. *Expedition of his Highness*, p. 5.
27. HMC 29 *Portland* iv, p. 134: Richard Duke to Robert Harley, 20.9.1704.
28. S. Izacke, *Remarkable Antiquities of the City of Exeter*, 1724, p. 63.
29. From *The Diary of Mr Justice Rokeby*, edited by W. Boyd, in *Devon and Cornwall Notes and Gleanings*, ii, 1889, p. 172.
30. HMC 71 *Finch* iv, p. 143: Trelawney to Nottingham, 11.5.1692.

Chapter Two

The Augustan City, 1700–1740

Ten years after the crisis of 1688 Celia Fiennes visited Exeter and recorded her impressions. She rode into Exeter from Cullompton, and it was from Beacon Hill to the north that she obtained her first view of the city and beyond it 'the River Exe which runs to Topsham where the ships come up to the bar'. On closer acquaintance she found 'a town very well built, with spacious streets, flourishing markets full of good country produce, a great serge market and a yarn market'. Exeter, she wrote,

> does exceedingly resemble London . . . there is an Exchange full of shops like our Exchanges are . . . there is also a very large space railed in by the Cathedral, with walks round it, which is called the Exchange for Merchants, that constantly meet twice a day just as they do in London.[1]

Only Newcastle, besides Exeter, reminded her of the metropolis. A Londoner, she appears not to have noticed that Exeter was a 'city in a grove'. The term was applied by Dr Thomas Shapter to the city of 1800 but it would have been even more appropriate in the early eighteenth century. Preeminently it was city of elms, growing in profusion outside the wall in Southernhay, in the Cathedral Close, between Holloway Street and the river and on Northernhay. The big trees in the Close were blown down by the famous storm of 1703 and were replaced by limes, which did not flourish, so elms were replanted. The Chamber took good care of its trees, endeavouring to prevent unauthorised felling, in 1728 enclosing part of Northernhay within a cob wall as a nursery for young trees, and in 1733 giving the Receiver *carte blanche* 'to plant as many trees upon the city's land as he thinks fitt at the expense of the Chamber'.[2] John Hooker, the city's Elizabethan Chamberlain, had made it his business to do likewise.

Daniel Defoe, who toured Devon in 1724, a few years after Celia Fiennes, was similarly impressed by the beauty and prosperity of Exeter, 'a rich, beautiful [and] populous' city, 'full of gentry and good company, and yet full of trade and manufacturers also.'[3]

Devon itself, populous and prosperous, was an important industrial area by the standards of the day, having enjoyed more than its share of the

18

expansion which had been a feature of the national economy since about 1670. In 1690 the number of houses in the county assessed for Hearth Tax was exceeded only by those of Yorkshire and Norfolk. Clothmaking employed, full or part time, many hands. Spinning, weaving and some fulling were carried on in most of the Devon towns and villages. The fertility of East Devon in particular was much admired, Celia Fiennes noting the 'large tracts of ground full of enclosures, good grass and corn, beset with quicksets and hedgerows'.[4] But Exeter was the unchallenged capital, the centre for society, politics and business. Merchants, shopkeepers, innkeepers, booksellers, millers and milliners throve on the demand engendered by a prosperous hinterland. And from the hills above Exeter the sea was visibly linked to the city by the Exe and the canal, offering access to the markets of Europe and the New World.

The city commanded the main-road system of the South West. For the carriage of goods and materials the pack-horse was ubiquitous, sure-footed, sturdy and with a fast gait, usually moving in trains of six animals. That medieval conveyance, the horse-litter, was still in use and was manufactured by Thomas Holmes, the coachmaker of Palace Gate, who also built coaches and the more modish chariots. But increasingly the great hooded wagons of the carriers laboured up and down the hills. In very favourable conditions carriers between Exeter and London might complete their journey in a week, though to the West the pace was slower. They worked from the inns, particularly those in the neighbourhood of South Street. John Welch, the Cornish carrier, 'inned' at the Mermaid and moved, in 1726, to the Bear. From the Bear his wagons set out twice a week to take goods and passengers to Lifton, Launceston, Liskeard and Camelford. George Hatchell, the Taunton carrier, after using pack-horses, had invested in wagons by 1727. Hatchell's base was the Black Lion, near the Bear, whence his wagons set out twice a week on Wednesday and Saturday, to reach Taunton the same night, a good day's journey of some thirty miles. He undertook to carry goods and passengers bound for Cullompton, Wellington and 'any place on the road' as far as Bristol.[5] By such means news and gossip, and out-dated copies of London newspapers, percolated into the rural areas.

Coaches for the carriage of passengers were slow, heavy and uncomfortable vehicles. It was not till the reign of George II that substantial improvements were made in their construction. In 1727 Newcombe's Bath and Bristol stage coach, with six horses, set out each Monday morning from the Sun near the East Gate, and was advertised as arriving at Bath on the following Wednesday.[6] By this coach ailing Exonians were enabled to visit the 'Hot-Well Waters' of Bath and Bristol. From the Half Moon, in High Street, the Exeter Stage Coach left for London on Mondays, Wednesdays and Fridays, going by way of Dorchester and Salisbury and taking three days over the journey in summer if all went well. By this route came the London mail bringing the London newspapers and other periodicals. The single fare from Exeter to London in the 1720s was £2 5s., representing well over a month's wages for a craftsman in full employment; in addition passengers had the expense of meals and tips. The service was sometimes vexatious. In 1728 the proprietors of the Exeter Stage Coach acknowledged that they had received complaints against their coachmen 'not only for their tedious and too frequent stoppings, but their treating passengers with ill-manners and abusive language'. Coachmen accordingly were strictly charged to be civil and obliging on pain of instant dismissal.[7] As the creator of Jorrocks pointed out over a century later the romance of the road could be overdone.

Dignity and status required ownership of a coach though many must have been in the position of Squire Western whose wife enjoyed the status but could make little use of it owing to the state of the roads. Citizens who were not what the nineteenth century would term 'carriage folk' could hire their transport. In 1725 a coach with six horses and a good coachman was advertised for hire 'for any part of England'. Robert Newcombe, at the sign of the Sun, supplied for hire 'a very commodious and genteel coach' as well as chariots, horse-litters and single horses.[8] Mourning coaches were required to lend dignity to funerals and could be hired for the purpose. Members of the Chamber usually hired mounts when on business trips, the horse-hire for three days' Chamber business at Taunton costing twelve shillings.[9] The poor, as they were to do till the coming of Mr Gladstone's 'parliamentary train', walked or travelled by carrier. Among them were the ubiquitous pedlars finding their way to remote farms, men like John Boyd, a Scot, who, on a December evening near Exeter in 1727, was robbed not only of £47 in cash, but also of hollands, muslins, lace and handkerchiefs.[10]

According to a report of 1696 the inns of Exeter could provide accommodation for 866 guests and 1,037 horses, the city coming second in this respect to Bristol but surpassing Norwich, Gloucester, and even York, and implying a substantial number of inn-servants, grooms, ostlers and postboys.[11] The main concentration of inns lay in close proximity to the main residential and business areas. The largest inn at Exeter at this period was the New Inn, adjacent to St Stephen's church in High Street. This belonged to the Chamber and was rebuilt in 1688 at a cost of £755. The ground landlords were the dean and chapter. In 1690 the Chamber spent £50 on a new ceiling. In 1692 a further £30 were spent on painting the dining-room, and substantial improvements were completed in 1697 when the painter Charles Stannaway adorned the dining-room with the royal arms. It was insured for £1,000 in 1729 when it was leased for a rent of £200 a year.[12] The New Inn was the social centre of the city, its Apollo Room being much used for concerts during assize week. The adjoining stables, part of the Bedford estate, were leased to the Chamber, who paid a fine of £175 when the lease was renewed in 1727. In 1723, when the stables were damaged by fire, the Chamber found it necessary to counter rumours 'industriously spread abroad by certain designing or malicious persons' that the stables had been completely destroyed. The public were informed that, while some damage had occurred, the New Inn could still provide as much accommodation as any other inn in the city with room for coaches and over one hundred horses.[13] Next in importance to the New Inn were the Bear in South Street, the Half Moon in High Street and, in a strategic situation at the point where the Taunton and London roads converged outside the East Gate, the Oxford Inn.

Though the road system was of cardinal importance in the rise and future development of Exeter, the sea offered greater opportunities to trade. The salt water ebbed and flowed past Topsham, three miles from the city, where in 1688 the Prince of Orange landed his heavy cannon. Below Topsham the Exe flowed through marshes and grazing grounds, its mouth protected by the sand-hills of Dawlish Warren. Beyond the Warren the open water gave to Exeter entry to the high seas: to London; to the ports of Europe from Hamburg to Leghorn; across the Atlantic to Madeira and the Azores, the sugar islands of the Caribbean, the fisheries of the Grand Banks and the North American continent with its rice, tobacco and timber. At that time, an age of vigorous commercial enterprise and expansion, the sea seemed to offer Exeter prospects rivalling even those of Bristol.

In the 1560s the Chamber had undertaken the hazardous and expensive task of constructing a canal, the first pound lock canal in England, to circumvent the worst obstructions on the river between Exeter and Topsham. About two miles in length, and at best suitable for vessels of only eight to ten tons, this canal had been badly neglected during the Civil War. Improvements were made in the 1670s but only to enable lighters of eight tons to reach the Water Gate. Between 1691 and 1693 the Chamber spent £648 on repairs to the canal banks, sluices and weirs, but these were expensive palliatives.[14] King William's War (1689–1697), and especially the campaign in Ireland, was opening up new possibilities of commercial expansion, despite the hazards of privateers and French frigates. In 1689 Exeter was required to supply stores for two battalions sent to Ireland as well as ammunition and stores for Londonderry.[15] Imports of coal were continuously rising, but profits were reduced by the need to use Topsham, more easily accessible for shipping, and long Exeter's rival as a port. Towards the end of the seventeenth century the charges for breaking bulk and transporting cargoes overland from Topsham to Exeter were estimated to cost the Exeter merchants £3,000 per annum.[16] In 1697 the thirteen members of the Chamber present agreed unanimously that it would be 'for the city's advantage to make the river Exe navigable for ships of 100 tons to come to the said city'.[17]

Civic pride rallied to the canal project. The whole Chamber was constituted a committee to supervise the work; its members advanced £50

£50 each towards the initial expenses. Merchants, chandlers, dyers, fullers, apothecaries and others lent £25 to £50 each on short-term loan.[18] The city had already embarked on an expensive plan to improve the city's water supplies, and the improvement of the canal, technically a very difficult operation, stretched its financial resources to the utmost. The contract was awarded to William Bayley, the contractor for the water supplies, who absconded, taking with him some of the funds raised for the canal. The Chamber persevered. The mayor, Alderman Bale, went to London accompanied by the sheriff to give evidence before the committee of Devon and Cornwall MPs appointed to examine the draft act required to authorise the necessary works. Funds were raised on mortgage. The greater part of the manor of Duryard, valued overall at £5250 2s. 6d., was sold for £4,622, though after claims against the Chamber had been met only £2,706 reached the chest.[19] Most of this sum went to the master carpenter Gilbert Greenslade for work on the Haven, the anchorage below the city.

By 1701 the new canal, running from Exeter to a point below Topsham, was substantially completed, and henceforward on a favourable tide vessels of 200–300 tons could reach the Exeter quay. The work was completed in time for the phenomenal expansion of Exeter's seaborne trade in Queen Anne's reign. Exports climbed steadily to reach their peak in 1710, the year of Malplaquet.[20] The profits from the city's own quay formed a major item of revenue, amounting to £800 in a normal, and good, year such as 1712–13. In the financial year 1728–9 the revenue amounted to £1,000. But the technical difficulties and cost of maintaining the canal as a first-class waterway proved to be beyond the resources of the city. In the financial year 1752–3 the profits from the quay were shown as nil, having been set off against expenditure of £871 on new sluice gates.[21] Exeter could never seriously challenge Bristol. The estuary of the Exe presented navigational problems which the Chamber could never solve with the available financial means and technical skill. In contrast, the Avon, though not without difficulties, could more easily bring vessels into the heart of Bristol. Beyond the Avon was the Severn providing an easy waterway to Wales and the Midlands. On land the roads provided Bristol with much easier communications with London than Exeter enjoyed and also with growing economic developments in the Midlands and the North. But for a space Exeter appeared to have opened at last a practicable passage to the sea.

By the end of the seventeenth century serges, more hard-wearing than the traditional kerseys, dominated the cloth industry of Devon. It was the manufacture and sale of serges which made such a deep impression on Celia Fiennes during the reign of William III:

> There is an incredible quantity made and sold in [Exeter] . . . The whole town and country is employed for at least twenty miles round in spinning, weaving, dressing and scouring of serges. It turns the most money in a week of anything in England.[22]

These were the years remembered long afterwards in local pageantry as the era of the Golden Fleece. The cloth 'made', that is woven, in the Devon countryside was mostly 'finished', that is fulled, dyed and packed, in the city before being exported. In 1698 Celia Fiennes was entertained in Exeter by the agent of her brother, a London merchant, who was buying cloth for export.[23] The weekly serge market in South Street excited the admiration of Defoe, and indeed the value of Exeter's cloth exports had in 1710 reached £463,000 a year, exceeding that of London.[24] Thus were the pack-horse trains traversing the lanes of Devon linked with the great cities of Europe, Rotterdam, the gateway to the Rhine, Amsterdam, Hamburg, Cadiz, Oporto and Leghorn. The city's reputation attracted Protestant immigrants from Germany such as John Baring and John Duntze and Dutch gables appeared on new merchants' houses on Topsham's waterfront.[25]

Cloth was only the most important constituent of an extensive and varied trade. Ships convoyed by Anglo-Dutch squadrons carried to Rotterdam not only serges but tin, pewter and calf-skins and re-exports such as tobacco, rice and tea. From Newfoundland came dried cod in exchange for Mediterranean salt. From the West Indies and North American colonies came, besides tobacco, sugar, molasses, log-wood, beaver skins and various naval stores. From Spain and Portugal Exeter's ships brought fruit, olive oil, indigo and wines, her shops sold pipe staves from Rotterdam and Carolina rice. Leghorn straw hats, wide-brimmed with ribbons under the chin, gave a touch of modish rusticity to the ladies of Augustan Exeter and Devon. Oranges, 'directly from Seville', were available at 14s. a hundred and jars of olives at 3s. Thomas Clutterbuck, merchant, had for sale at his premises on Stepcote Hill lemons 'just imported' and fresh lime juice at 5s. per gallon. In High Street in 1727 Joseph Trobridge sold chocolate and 'London' teas, the latter at a price which he claimed was 'very little above what they usually give for that insipid adulterated trash generally carried about the country'.[26] The West Country was notorious at this time for smoking and while Bideford was more prominent in the American tobacco trade, Exeter imported 'fine, pleasant, prepared Tobacco for the Head, Stomach and Weak or Dim Eyes'. The landlord of the Blackamore's Head near the West Gate, who sold stout, ale and beer at 2d. a quart 'without doore' and 3d. inside, also presented customers with pipes and tobacco.[27]

Exeter's merchants, shopkeepers and craftsmen provided the country gentry and wealthy citizens with the means both of enjoying a rising standard of living and of displaying social status. James Braddick, 'late of London', sold hunting saddles. Alderman Wood, mayor in 1706, in part derived the wealth which contributed to his influence in the city from the sale of muskets, bayonets, swords, cartouche boxes, halberds and gloves at the sign of The Sword and Glove. Near the East Gate George Light sold kettle drums and other musical instruments. In the High Street opposite

Martins Lane Mrs Pring was displaying, just before Christmas 1724, 'Fine Calicoes sprigged with Silk, . . . Printed Linens, Silk and Holland Handkerchiefs, Silk Gloves, Silk and Worsted Thread and Cotton Stockings'.[28]

Household furniture was available to satisfy the eighteenth-century taste for exquisite craftsmanship. Nicholas Williams, joiner, of South Street, supplied clock-cases, cabinets, commode tables, book cases, looking-glasses and veneered work in walnut. To his shop at the top of Fore Street Hill Humphrey Wilcocks brought from London beds and hangings, 'chiney watered and damasked', painted linen for hangings, coach-glasses, sconces, and for the new fashion of making tea, tea-tables and salvers. Wine cellars provided 'Canary, Tent, Red Port, White Lizbone and Sherry by the Butt, Hogshead or Gallon'; while for the improvement of gardens Nicholas Hooper of Northernhay supplied fruit trees, wall or standard, and 'evergreens of the most curious and fashionable cuts'.[29]

The reveillé each morning on Rougemont proclaimed a garrison city with officers requiring accommodation and entertainment. Markets, fairs and assizes brought the country into the city. George Greenslade of the Dolphin in High Street drew attention to the convenience of his establishment both for 'Town Customers' and 'Country Lodgers'. During the assizes the sheriff of Devon entertained at the New Inn whose Apollo Room was also used for displays of conjuring and sword dancing or for performances by travelling players of works by Vanbrugh, Farquhar and Steele.[30] In the suburb of St Thomas south of the river the Seven Stars Inn provided a stage for an early performance of *The Beggars' Opera* by 'the ingenious Mr Gay' of Barnstaple and for Mrs Centrilivre's comedy, *The Busy Body*, with a prologue by Andrew Brice. Visitors to the summer fair in Southernhay in 1726 were treated to the spectacle of Troy in flames, 'agreeable to history', and the plunder-laden Achaean fleet.[31]

In the centre of the city in the vicinity of the Guildhall and the Cathedral, and not far from the inns in South Street used by the important carriers, coffee houses had sprung up to provide facilities for both business and pleasure. The Chamber accounts for 1700–1 include such items as 'expenses at coffee houses at various times, 8s. 5½d.', from which it may be inferred that city affairs were not always conducted at the Guildhall.[32] Mol's Coffee House in the Cathedral Yard sold tickets for concerts and at Lewis Jones's coffee house nearby in the 1720s sales of house property were negotiated, debtors met their creditors and the Commissioners of Chancery met to settle an estate. In such establishments catalogues of book sales were made available. Indeed book sellers were concentrated in the same part of the city, John Murch at The Sign of the Bible in High Street near the entrance to Martins Lane, Nathanial Thorn in the Close, and James Lipscombe in Martins Lane itself. Marjery Yeo in her shop in the Close was selling Defoe's *Compleat Tradesman* very soon after its first appearance in

London in 1725. It probably sold well in a commercial city with a strong element of Dissent. Bibles, prayer books and books of devotion were conspicuous but account books, charts, works on navigation and mathematical instruments pointed the interests of a trading community, and also to be found among the books were the popular nostrums of the day, 'Daffey's Elixir', 'Stoughton's Elixir Magnum Stomachum', 'Spirits of Scurvy-Grass', 'Toppin's Famous Liquor for Gout, Stone and Gravel' and 'Liquid Snuff of Padus'.[33]

In the Cathedral Close members of the new profession of newspaper editors awaited the London papers which carried a wide selection of news items ranging from Philadelphia to Constantinople, the movement of shipping, the price of stock, government appointments, social gossip and rumours. Enlivened by gory crime reports and tales of pirates and buccaneers and popular metropolitan heroes such as Jack Sheppard who was hanged at Tyburn in 1724, the London papers were read aloud and discussed in inns and coffee houses. Andrew Brice would await them until dawn, often in vain, to extract material for his own local paper.

Early eighteenth-century England, with lively politics and a prominent role in continental war, provided an insatiable market for news. In 1695 the development of the press was stimulated by the lapse of the Licensing Act, which had sustained a political and religious censorship and limited the number of printing presses. Journalists and pamphleteers now had a free hand for publication; only after publication were they subject to the drastic law of seditious libel used as a political weapon. The modern provincial press had its origins in the *Norwich Post* of 1701, followed by the *Bristol Post-Boy* in 1702, and in 1704 by the *Exeter Post-Man*. The *Bristol Post-Boy* and the *Exeter Post-Man* were both launched by Samuel Farley of Bristol, member of a family which in Anne's reign founded newspapers in Bristol, Exeter, Salisbury and Bath. In 1715 the *Exeter Post-Man* was acquired by Philip Bishop, who changed its name to *The Exeter Mercury*. Bishop, a freeman of Exeter, died in gaol in 1716 while awaiting trial for publishing a libel on George I. In 1715, the year when the Hanoverian regime faced the first test of Jacobite rebellion, a second newspaper was founded in Exeter by Joseph Bliss, who began printing *The Protestant Mercury or The Exeter Post-Boy* at his house outside the East Gate near the London Inn. His venture came to an end by 1718 but his apprentice Andrew Brice made a more lasting mark.[34]

Brice, the son of a shoemaker, had been intended for the Dissenting ministry and, like his fellow Exonian, Lord Chancellor King, had received the admirable education available in the Dissenting academies of the period. He broke his articles of apprenticeship with Bliss (according to the latter he 'roguishly absconded and deserted'), and founded *The Exeter Post-Master or the Loyal Mercury* in 1717. The following year he achieved the distinction, shared by both Bliss and Bishop, of falling foul of the House of Commons for printing their proceedings. *The Post-Master* came to an end in

1725 and was replaced by *Brice's Weekly Journal*. Brice was a prolific writer, fortified by wide reading and leavened by a sardonic sense of humour. A staunch Whig, he wrote of that dour Hanoverian George I that 'the loftiest and even extravagant Panegyrick of a Pliny could not reach his exalted Character and Virtues',[35] a comment designed to exalt Whiggery rather than the King. Brice had the courage and pertinacity essential for survival. Apart for incurring the displeasure of the House of Commons over the publication of debates, his campaign on behalf of the debtors lodged in the gaol of St Thomas involved him in prosecution and a fine for libel. Brice also wrote poetry and prologues to plays and published translations from Horace. His *Mobiad*, written in about 1735 but not published till 1770, owed much to the conventions of social satire of his day: it is a Hogarthian portrait in verse of early Georgian Exeter. His 'Predictions for Christmas Morning', written within the shadow of the cathedral and appearing on Christmas Eve 1725, must have caused raised eyebrows in the Close. The description of the cathedral bells chiming six o'clock was followed, not by appropriate moral sentiments, but by a vignette of Betty Wagtail stealing 'slyly from the Prentice's bed, to unmake her own, before she dares to venture to Morning Prayers'.[36]

Graver representatives of life in the Cathedral precinct were the doctors, both those of divinity and those of medicine, among them several men of considerable erudition as well as wealth. Dr John Bidgood, who had studied in the medical schools of Padua, was said to have been 'vastly rich', being worth 'between five and twenty and thirty thousand pounds' when he died at his house in the Close in 1690. One of his neighbours, Dr John Osmond, physician, owned an impressive library containing books on divinity, physics, history and philology.[37] Men such as these, lay and clerical, were active in charity. It was a period distinguished by the foundation of hospitals. At Exeter the inspiration came from the Cathedral Dean, Dr Alured Clarke, who had previously been instrumental in the foundation of the County Hospital at Winchester in 1736. The prestige of Dean Clarke's office and his personal initiative enlisted the support of county society. Subscribers met in the Chapter House and John Tuckfield, later Tory MP for the city, presented land in Southernhay. The outcome was the elegant Georgian building of the Devon and Exeter Hospital, opened in January 1743.[38]

The medical profession had yet to become a profession in the modern sense with approved standards rigorously enforced. There were less-qualified practitioners offering their services in Exeter, men such as Andrew Parsons, 'Licensed Practitioner in Physick and Chysurgery', an Exonian who returned from Scotland in 1716 to attend at the New Inn three days a week with 'honest advice on any Distemper incident to Men, Women and Children'. Parsons claimed to have a new and safe method for curing venereal diseases and also offered to treat 'Teeth or Stumps, altho' broken by unskilfull Performers'. William Lily, who settled in North Street in the same year, specialised in the treatment of cataract but also undertook to remove 'Cancerated Breasts, Large Wens and to cure Hare-lips'.[39] The people of Augustan England were too-often callous to man and beast but, like George II's queen, they stoically endured agonies at the hands of fashionable doctors and quacks alike.

Exeter was not a city where men could accumulate vast fortunes such as were made by the great merchants, the war contractors and the financiers of contemporary London. Nevertheless there was solid wealth. Among members of the Chamber, the merchant John Bankes left £6,400 in 1699 to be distributed among his family, in addition to real estate, and Christopher Mayne's will provided for settlements amounting to £8,000.[40] Sir John Elwill, variously estimated to be worth £20,000 and £80,000, left extensive landed property. Grocers such as George Saffin and John Newcombe were in a position to lend sums of £1,000 or more at interest to the Chamber. In 1694-5 the ironmonger Joshua Hickman was receiving interest on £5,000 lent to the Chamber. Phineas Cheeke the brewer had the resources to take over a mortgage of £8,000 on the Chamber's property originally advanced by the wealthy High Tory Sir William Portman. Thomas Jeffery, Dissenter, owned substantial landed property and investments. He was a member of a group of five, all Dissenters, who invested £1,199 each in South Sea stock in 1720.[41]

An incomplete tax assessment of 1699 lists fifty individuals assessed at £500 and over, and seven at £1,000. Twelve of these were at various times members of the Chamber, including the Dissenters Thomas Atherton, assessed at £500, and Edmond Starr at £1,000, both nominated to the Chamber by James II.[42] Such wealth, based on the cloth trade or on overseas ventures, including the import of luxuries by grocers, was reinforced not only by financial operations, loans, purchases of land, mortgages and other investments, but also by prudent marriages. This prosperous class was, however, a very small percentage of the population, numbering perhaps not more than 150 out of a total population of 15,000 or two per cent. It was reinforced by the rising professional classes, particularly medical men and lawyers, but not by landowners. Indeed the gentry were losing interest in town houses. In 1726 Bampfylde House was to let and the Walrond house was for sale.

The select society of merchants who administered the affairs of the city had only a short step from their combined dwellings and business premises to the Exchange in the Cathedral Close where Celia Fiennes saw them discussing affairs with their fellows. Humphrey Bawden, mayor in 1724, lived in the High Street where he also sold his hose of fine silk, worsted and yarn.[43] The house of Alderman Rowe, fuller, was situated at the top of Fore Street hill, near the Carfax. It contained a shop and warehouse in addition to a large dining room and eight good 'lodging chambers'. It also provided a good view from the top room extending over the quay and the river, 'and all ships passing and repassing the bar'; or so claimed the advertisement in 1716 when the alderman wished to let part of his house.[44]

In this heyday of Exeter's cloth industry the large and rambling establishments of the businessmen who did not aspire to the Chamber were to be found throughout the city, with their communities of family, apprentices and servants under a patriarchal authority. A house in South Street, 'very commodious for a Merchant, Sergemaker or Tucker', included four large cellars, a dye house, eleven lodging rooms, a large dining room, kitchen and shop.[45] A similar establishment in Holy Trinity contained four lodging rooms, three closets, two garrets, parlour, kitchen, cellars, press-chamber, counting-house, shop, outhouses and had two gardens with fruit trees. The house of the fuller Benjamin Bawden, off Fore Street, contained domestic premises, packing chamber and drying shed, all constructed of stone, timber and slate. Even in the congested neighbourhood of Stepcote Hill, Nicholas Dark, fuller and hotpresser, owned a dwelling house and packing chamber constructed of brick, timber and slate, a garden in which he was about to build a press-shop; the whole, together with household goods, stock and tools, was insured in 1740 for £1,000,[46] the same sum for which the Chamber had insured the New Inn in 1729.

In the seventeenth century the Puritan fathers and grandfathers of this prosperous minority had laid the foundations of an educational system which was to endure until the reform of the endowed schools in the 1870s. The parable of the talents equated successful hard work with godliness. By education man developed the potentialities bestowed on him for the divine purpose. Prompted by a bequest, the Chamber, in the reign of Charles I, had begun the adaptation of the medieval Hospital of St John occupying an extensive area inside the East Gate. Here was established the Exeter Free Grammar School, originally intended as a school for the instruction of the sons of freemen in the Latin tongue, and also the Blue Schools, also in the hospital premises, where the sons of the poor between seven and fourteen years of age might receive food and clothing, instruction in reading, writing and arithmetic, and a premium of £6 on being bound as apprentice.[47]

In the ensuing hundred years the grammar school received over £3,000 in cash donations besides extensive endowments in real estate.[48] By the early eighteenth century it was providing a sound conventional education for the sons of Exeter's middle classes, merchants, professional men and successful shopkeepers, fitting them for the widening opportunities in business and the professions and for entry to the universities, especially to Oxford. The school provided, too, a firm grounding in the culture associated with eighteenth-century gentility. As 'young gentlemen' the boys displayed their talents before the mayor and city dignitaries in performances of fashionable plays by Richard Steele, or, in Latin, by Terence.[49] The Blue Boys too played their part in civic ceremony, beating

beating the bounds and walking in mayoral processions; payments for 'apples for the boys' and 'Blue Boys walking before the mayor' appeared in the Chamber's accounts. By the mid-eighteenth century the proliferation of private schools offering instruction in such useful skills as surveying, navigation, accountancy and the like suggests that the grammar school curriculum was failing to meet the needs of a business community. Many sons of Exeter merchants picked up languages in their early excursions abroad but in a city with a substantial Mediterranean trade it is not surprising to find a learned Jew of Padua offering instruction in Hebrew, Italian, Spanish and Portuguese. Huguenot settlers taught French to boarders and day-girls and offered instruction in 'all manner of works fit for gentlewomen' such as painting on glass, silk transparencies and embroidery.[50]

The ancient High School, administered by the Dean and Chapter, was in decline. By 1750 it was closed. But the Church was turning away from the transcendental issues of heaven and hell towards the inculcation of rational social behaviour and discipline. So, in 1709, Bishop Offspring Blackall founded his Episcopal Schools for boys and girls. The boys were taught reading, writing, arithmetic and accounts; the girls sewing and knitting. All received religious instruction on Sundays. To these schools Councillor Nathanial Rowland bequeathed £200 and the goldsmith William Ekins gave £50 for instruction in navigation.

Only a small minority of parents could contemplate either paying for education or obtaining for their children instruction of any kind. The great majority of the population were poor. Many were among the very poor whose very survival seems a statistical impossibility. For a full day's work to the satisfaction of his employer an unskilled labourer received from 12*d.* to 1s. 2d. a day, but to earn £20 he had to work for 300 full days a year. Skilled men got little more, their wages in Exeter ranging from 1*s.* 2*d.* to 1*s.* 4*d.* a day. Masons, carpenters, plasterers, paviours and helliers were paid about 1*s.* 8*d.* a day. Master craftsmen received 1*s.* 8*d.* to 2*s.* and by 1740 some received 2*s.* 8*d.*[51] Andrew Brice, advertising for an apprentice in 1725, claimed that a journeyman printer, 'in full business', would earn 20*s.* to 30*s.* a week, or 3*s.* 4*d.* to 3*s.* 6*d.* a day.[52] For artisan and labourer alike everything depended on good health and regularity of employment, and also, since one-third to one-half of income might be spent on food, on weather and crop prospects. In the main, however, Exeter experienced abundant employment and stable prices throughout the first half of the century. Of the earnings of women there is virtually no evidence. In 1725 Ann Hutchins, upholsterer, offered to work in any house, in town or country, for 12*d.* a day.[53]

By the standards of the day the subordinate officers of the Chamber were well paid and they enjoyed regularity of employment and all the perquisites, licit and illicit, of eighteenth-century bumbledom. Short of abusing an alderman they appear to have retained their posts until their incapacity could no longer be ignored. The sergeants-at-mace received £10 per annum, increased to £16 in 1739, the staff bearers £3 10*s.*, increased to £5 in 1746. In addition these officers were provided with uniforms, they all received perquisites (food and drink on ceremonial occasions) and pay for miscellaneous duties and when they were no longer capable of performing their duties they were eligible for accommodation in an alms house. The officers of the newly formed Corporation of the Poor were even better off, the housekeeper and master workman appointed in 1701 each receiving £20 per annum with accommodation for themselves and their families, diet and household washing. The beadle, 'appointed to suppress beggars without the house and to keep the poor in good order within the house', was paid £18 per annum, with free accommodation and washing, livery and the all-important staff of office.[54]

By the end of the seventeenth century it had become impossible for each city parish to maintain its poor from its own resources. The wealthier parishes such as St Kerrian and St Petrock, and the extra-parochial areas such as the Close and Bedford Precinct, were already contributing to the poor relief of other parishes. In 1698 Exeter, followig the example of Bristol, obtained an act of parliament constituting the Corporation of the Poor, comprising the mayor, eight aldermen and forty elected guardians, to organise poor relief on the basis of the whole city. The poor, stated the preamble to the act, were increasing — in 1699 poor relief was costing £2,163 a year — and, reflecting the usual lively concern of the property owners for the morals of the lower classes, idleness and debauchery among the meaner sort, it was claimed, were also increasing.[55]

The court of guardians of the new Corporation assembled at the Guildhall for its first meeting in August 1698, attended by its *ex-officio* members, the mayor and eight aldermen. The governor, Sir Edward Seaward, presided. The two treasurers were William Ekins, goldsmith, who in 1704 was to pay a fine of £100 rather than accept election to the Chamber, and Benjamin Hawkins. Several of the guardians, such as Nathaniel Rowland and Francis Lidstone, later became members of the Chamber. There were at least seven Dissenters, among whom was the grocer Jerome King, who became deputy governor to Seaward in 1700.

The Corporation promptly settled to work. Bricks were made and stock-piled before the brick-making season ended in October. A committee was appointed to inspect the rate books of parishes and precincts in order to raise an initial £1,000 towards the construction of a workhouse. In 1701 a delegation was despatched to Bristol to obtain advice from a city which had recently pioneered centralised relief of the poor. And since it was agreed that 'spinning in worsted-wool' was the primary employment of the poor it was decided to employ a master workman skilled in the 'Art and Mistery of Cloathing'. To ensure that relief was strictly limited to inhabitants of the city the Corporation's beadle and other officers were issued with warrants to search out from among the poor in the city those 'not having a right to be there' and to bring such persons before the mayor and justices 'to be moved, punished or otherwise dealt with'.[56]

Whig-inspired, and including men who, as Dissenters, were excluded from traditional governing circles, the new Corportion at the outset met with palpable hostility from the Chamber. Tory aldermen-justices refused to sign and confirm the new poor rates. Alderman Bale, twice MP for the city, and his deputy, Alderman Newcombe, obstructed arrangements for an election to fill a vacancy. Mayor Joshua Hickman was blandly unhelpful when the Corporation was locked out of a meeting arranged in the Guildhall and was in no hurry to use his authority to encourage co-operation from the parochial officers. The exasperated Corporation formally resolved that the behaviour of these gentlemen was 'notorious contempt' of an Act of Parliament and injurious to the Corporation.[57] The church-wardens and overseers, however, complained that they were exposed to affront and assault when attempting to perform their new duties. The Corporation in its turn prepared to distrain the property of the parochial officers to enforce collection of the rates. The argument with the Chamber was settled by an appeal to the court of King's Bench which cost the Corporation of the Poor over £60 but did result in an order instructing the mayor and aldermen either to confirm or alter the rate required to raise the first £1,000. By 1701 the new mayor, John Snell, had given the requisite instructions to the parochial officers, and in September of that year the Corporation despatched a delegation to thank Snell for 'his Justice and Friendship' and to establish good relations with his successor.[58] In that year the rate was fixed at £2,900, based on the average paid by the parishes over the years 1695–97, and it remained at this figure for the first half of the century. In fact the revenue was inadequate and fell short by an average of about £82 a year. The cost of furnishing the workhouse, a project completed in 1707, also exceeded the £3,000 which the Corporation was originally empowered to raise for this purpose. In consequence, it had to be empowered, in 1753, to raise a further £3,669 to meet debts of close on £3,200.[59] The site chosen was in open country on what was then called the London Road although it led to the village of Heavitree. Due provision was made for religious instruction. The Bishop authorised Anglican services and preaching in the chapel and non-Anglicans were escorted by the Corporation's officers to attend services in 'Meetings allowed by Law'.

Those who received assistance from the poor rate were the fortunate few. No local authority was willing to dispense charity except to its own people; accordingly those who could not establish proof of domicile were dealt with as rogues, vagabonds and beggars. The officers of the Corporation, in conjunction with the parish officials, were therefore authorised to search for poor persons residing in any house without a right to be there. Pious and humane individuals continued to leave money for the support of the poor, but most testamentary distributions of charity were limited to the indigenous poor of individual Anglican parishes.

Though prices on the whole remained stable the poor suffered severely in bad weather, such as in the cold winter of 1715–16 when the Exe was frozen for six weeks and much business came to a standstill, and again in the bitter winter of 1739–40 when, according to an Exeter historian, 'the fowls and fishes were frozen to death' and many of the poor 'perished through the severity of the season'.[60] In January 1740 the Chamber ordered the distribution of £100 for the relief of the poor, and this was followed by a further distribution of £500 ordered in February 1741 but with the proviso that action should not be taken until after the general election held in May. But it was not till the end of the century that Exeter, having lost its former industrial base, and with a growing population, was faced with really serious problems of social distress and starvation. There was considerable justification for later generations regarding the early eighteenth century as Exeter's golden age.

NOTES

1. Morris, *Journeys*, pp. 245-8.
2. DRO, ECA, Act Books, 6.11.1733.
3. Cole, *Tour through Great Britain*, i, pp. 222-3.
4. Morris, *op. cit.*, p. 244.
5. *Weekly Journal*, 24.3.1727, 16.6.1727.
6. *ibid.*, 3.3.1727.
7. *ibid.*, 31.1.1728.
8. *ibid.*, 26.11.1725, 29.3.1728.
9. DRO, ECA, Receivers' Accounts, Book 52, 1700/1701.
10. *Weekly Journal*, 15.12.1727.
11. W.G. Hoskins, 'The Inns of Exeter 1686-1708', *DCNQ*, xx, pp. 266-7.
12. DRO, ECA, Receivers' Accounts, 1684/5-1687/8; Act Books, 18.2.1689, 19.1.97 and 4.11.1729.
13. *Post-Master*, 31.5.1723.
14. DRO, ECA, Receivers' Accounts, 1692/3. See also E.A.G. Clark, *Ports of the Exe Estuary*, chapter II.
15. E.B. Powley, *The Naval Side of King William's War*, p. 57.
16. Clark, *op. cit.*, p. 35.
17. DRO, ECA, Act Books, 12.1.1697.
18. *ibid.*, 4.7.1699, 18.7.99, 25.7.99.
19. DRO, ECA, 'Fines for land sold of the manor of Duryard', a survey dated 4.10.1700; Receivers' Accounts, 1698/1700. The largest sum (£1,480) was charged to George Gould, a Dissenter, but this was reduced to £701 by various liabilities of the Chamber. Sir Thomas Jefford paid £241, and Duryard Mills were sold for £550 gross, £309 net.
20. Hoskins, *Industry, Trade and People*, p. 154, App. B1.
21. DRO, ECA, Receivers' Accounts, Book 29, 1712/13; Book 52, 1727/28; Book 56, 1728/9; Book 95, 1752/53.
22. Morris, *Journeys*, p. 245.
23. *ibid.*, p. 271.
24. Hoskins, *ibid.*
25. *ibid.*, p. 42.

NOTES *continued*

26. *Weekly Journal*, 26.7.1728, 23.5.1729; *Post-Master*, 7.6.1723; *Weekly Journal*, 30.6.1727.
27. *Weekly Journal*, 11.2.1727.
28. *ibid.*,   9.12.1726;   *Exeter   Mercury*,   13-17.1.1716;   *Post-Boy*,   2.12.1715;   *Post-Master*, 18.12.1724.
29. *Post-Boy*, 18.5.1716; *Post-Master*, 8.1.1725; *Post-Boy*, 30.3.1717, *Weekly Journal*, 4.8.1727.
30. *Weekly Journal*, 21.3.1729, 31.3.1729, 7.2.1729, 20.12.1728, 17.1.1729.
31. *ibid.*,15.11.1728, 3.3.1727, 29.7.1726.
32. DRO, ECA, Receivers' Accounts, 1700/1701.
33. *Weekly Journal*, 21.3.1729; *Post-Master*, 21.6.1723, 15.9.1721, 6.11.1724, 17.9.1725.
34. G.A. Cranfield, *The Development of the Provincial Newspaper*, passim and T.N. Brushfield, *The Life and Bibliography of Andrew Brice*.
35. *Weekly Journal*, 23.6.1727.
36. *ibid.*, 24.12.1725.
37. J. Prince, *Worthies of Devon*, p. 76 and *Post-Boy*, 16.7.1716.
38. P.M.G. Russell, *History of Exeter Hospitals*, pp. 22-4.
39. *Post-Boy*, 28.10.1715, 16.12.1715.
40. West Country Studies Library, Typescript Wills.
41. Francis Wood, 'The Social Identification of Merchants in Exeter, 1680-1760', pp. 50, 186-7; DRO, ECA, Act Brooks, 8.9.1692, 24.10.1721; Receivers' Accounts, Book 58, 1729/30; Act Books, 7.11.1727, 7.4.1730; Receivers' Accounts, Book 70, 1735/6.
42. DRO, ECA, Book 159A. Rate assessment, March 1690. I am indebted to Profesor Hoskins for drawing my attention to this document.
43. *Weekly Journal*, 24.12.1725.
44. *ibid.*, 13-17.1.1716.
45. *Exeter Mercury*, 23.3.1717.
46. S.D. Chapman, *Devon Cloth Industry*, pp. 64, 68.
47. H. Lloyd Parry, *The Founding of Exeter School*, pp. 39-58 and *Endowed Charities (County Borough of Exeter)*, H.M.S.O., 1909.
48. W. Carwithen (ed.), Samuel Izacke et al., *Account of the Legacies left to the Poor of the city of Exeter*, 1820, passim.
49. *Weekly Journal*, 29.12.1727.
50. *Post-Master*, 25.9.1724; *Exeter Mercury*, 20.10.1725.
51. E. Gilboy, *Wages in Eighteenth Century England*, pp. 107-21 and DRO, ECA, Receivers' Accounts.
52. *Weekly Journal*, 20.8.1725.
53. *ibid.*, 3.9.1725.
54. DRO, ECA, Corporation of the Poor, Court Books, 31.7.1701, 10.2.1702.
55. Hoskins, Industry Trade and People, p. 142.
56. DRO, ECA, Corporation of the Poor, Court Books, 12.10.1698, 24.9.1698, 15.4.1701, 13.5.1701, 16.12.1701.
57. *ibid.*, 9.11.1698, 7.11.1699, 2.12.1699.
58. *ibid.*, 4.5.1700, 12.7.1700, 11.1.1701, 4.7.1701.
59. Private Act, 31 George II, cap. liii.
60. A. Jenkins, *History and Description of the City of Exeter*, 1806, p. 203.

Chapter Three

The Chamber: 'the most wise and gravest'

In theory the Twenty-Four, the sixteen common councillors and eight aldermen who governed Exeter, were, in the words of John Hooker, the Elizabethan Chamberlain of the city, 'a selected and chosen company of the most wise and gravest citizens'.[1] No longer subject to the imperious commands of a Tudor Privy Council, or to the less effective directions of the Stuarts, the Chamber in the eighteenth century was virtually left to itself. Liberty for local authority to govern or misgovern was one of the fruits of the Glorious Revolution. The eight aldermen, 'gentlemen who met upstairs in black coats to transact the business of the Chamber and came down in red gowns to act as magistrates',[2] enjoyed as JPs even more security of tenure than their colleagues the country gentry. The former were appointed by their fellow councillors, the latter by the lord lieutenants and the Crown. Many of the aldermen-magistrates of Exeter remained in office to a ripe old age, with a weighty thirty or forty years of experience; amid the party struggles of Queen Anne's reign they were safe from a political purge of magistrates not belonging to the party in power, accused of 'poisoning the minds of the people' and of coercing voters.[3]

Like Parliament itself the Chamber jealously maintained its independence on the grounds that free and rational debate should be protected from exterior pressures and members wisely attempted to ensure that they themselves should be spared embarrassment or hostility if their views on delicate local issues became public knowledge. When, in 1769, it was divulged that there had been opposition within the Chamber to the grant of the freedom to the wealthy clothier John Duntze, it was resolved that

> if any Member of this Body shall have revealed or made known any Motion or Proposal which he shall be minded to make to this Body with an Intent to destroy the freedom of Debate or to contravene our Free Determination or to raise any Enmity or Ill Will against this Body or any of its Members from Dissenting to such Motion or Proposal such Member shall be Deemed to be a Disturber of the Publick Peace.[4]

While, however, the Chamber usually closed ranks against the criticism of of outsiders, the majority decisions recorded in the Act Books testify to the fact that the Chamber was not, despite its control over membership, lacking differences of opinion. Doubtless groups assembled before formal meetings of the Chamber, as in modern corporations, to discuss the line to be taken on important issues; but Exeter was rarely monolithically Tory and the hard-fought mayoral elections of the 1730s in particular were accompanied by divisions in the Chamber which were reflected in the votes cast for rival candidates. It was these elections that inspired Andrew Brice's *The Mobiad,* and from his satire there emerges a vivid picture of the tumult of local government in the days of George II, when the populace, with or without votes, were given the opportunity to voice their pungent opinion of the idiosyncracies of their rulers whose characters and foibles were well-known within the confines of a small community. *The Mobiad,* however, was published a generation after the events it satirises. The contemporary local newspapers, restrained by the severe libel laws, usually confined their comments on mayoral elections to a brief and polite reference to the abilities of the incoming or the outgoing mayor.

The rivalries and ambitions of aldermen and councillors, their business interests and associations, their network of family relations, must have influenced the conduct of affairs and these could not have been always harmonious. They would have been given ample space in the great days of Exeter's early Victorian press. The conception of informed citizens enlightened by a vigilant press was unknown to Georgian Exeter, but the members of the Chamber were not out of touch with public opinion. Business was conducted behind closed doors but members discussed affairs when, as seen by Celia Fiennes, they strolled with their peers in front of the Cathedral, or conducted the Chamber's business over a pipe and a drink in the inns of the city. They met prominent citizens outside their own circle at the feasts in the Guildhall and at the mayor's table.

While the Chamber administered the affairs of the city as a private estate and resented interference, it was always prudent in sounding public opinion, that is the opinion of the more substantial citizens, on matters which lay outside the boundaries of prescription and charter. It was essential to do so if it appeared necessary to raise funds in addition to the traditional dues and rents that were the Chamber's normal source of income. Public meetings were an occasional but often effective means of obtaining wider support. In 1747 the government's limited proposals to facilitate the naturalisation of Jews aroused heated controversy and prejudice, and the Chamber accordingly requested the Mayor to consult a meeting of citizens in order to decide what instructions should be sent to the city's Members of Parliament. In 1750 the Mayor was desired to call a meeting 'to consider of proper Methods for the lighting, repair, cleansing and watching of the city'. Expenditure on these objects could not be financed from the Chamber's traditional income; a rate levied for this purpose required an Act of Parliament and no Private Act would be obtained without the concurrence of at least a major portion of the citizens. In 1752 the Chamber appointed a special committee to attend a public meeting summoned to discuss proposals for a turnpike act.[5] The mayor and aldermen also met some of the principal citizens, including, on several occasions, representatives of the Company of Weavers, Fullers and Shearmen, to discuss the attitude to be taken on the question of imports from Ireland since Exeter businessmen were as opposed to the import of Irish yarn as to the closure of Exeter, since 1693, to the import of Irish wool.[6] The dignity and traditional authority of the Chamber were maintained, with tact, and it was not till the early years of the nineteenth century that the role of the Chamber was seriously questioned by influential citizens.

The foundation of Exeter's government was the body of freemen. 'The freeman', wrote Hooker, 'is the chiefest and principle Member of the Commonwealth of the city and, as it were, out of his loins do proceed all such as be Officers, and have any Government or Charge of the same.'[7] By the eighteenth century the freedom had long since ceased to provide most of its original economic advantages. Many prominent citizens did not trouble themselves to claim the privilege, with the consequence that some of those who were elected to membership of the Chamber had to be admitted to the freedom in haste, at times on the very day of their election. Many of the freemen were poor; for them the freedom gave a claim on charity or admission to an almshouse and, since it also gave the right to vote, it conferred a share in the cash, free food and drink lavishly distributed at parliamentary elections. Among the artisans, and even husbandmen and labourers, who flocked to claim the right by succession and apprenticeship, were many earnest men, Dissenters and bible-readers, but also others who welcomed an opportunity to make up for the hardships of daily life at the expense of candidates.

> Shall to be freely drunk the Right be lost,
> That best of annual Rights Shab-Freemen boast?
> Rather come on no free Election more . . .

At such times men whose property was little more than the right to vote had the satisfaction of seeing wealthy merchants and aldermen submit to unaccustomed good fellowship with one and all, when

> The Master-Tradesmen courtly condescend
> To call a simple Working-Man 'my Friend . . .'
> Druggist to Founder tips obliging wink
> And Mercer asks his Errand-Man to drink.[8]

In 1725 the Chamber ordered that none but freemen should be admitted to 'the benefactions belonging to this body'. In 1733 it was resolved that no tradesman should be employed in any work undertaken by the Chamber,

The Chamber's subordinate officers and employees, appointed and reappointed each Michaelmas, were all freemen: the sergeants-at-mace and the staff-bearers, the waits and the grave diggers, the lock keepers and the bellman or town-cryer, the keeper of the Bridewell, the gaoler of the South Gate prison and their assistants. But with the development of party politics, the right to vote conferred by the freedom led to an increase in the number of country gentlemen and clergy, usually sound Tories, admitted 'by order of the mayor and council'. Between 1688 and 1760 those admitted to the freedom comprised no less than 110 different occupations, including the nobility, gentry and high officers of the Crown.

From the ranks of the freemen came the Twenty-Four, the members of the Chamber. Apart from any limitations imposed by the need for wisdom and gravity, the field of choice was restricted by law, habit and prejudice. Dissenters were excluded by law which Exeter, unlike Bristol, never circumvented, for instance by the practice of occasional conformity which accepted token appearances at an Anglican service despite more regular attendance at a Dissenters' chapel. Membership of the Church of England was essential. Wealth was highly desirable for, since the Chamber was invariably short of ready cash, members were often expected to advance large sums on loan, at interest, or, having disbursed money on the Chamber's behalf, to wait a long time for repayment. It may be assumed that in return they had a weighty voice on policy and received sympathy in the furtherance of their own ambitions and business interests. Joshua Hickman, ironmonger, lent substantial sums to the Chamber and was twice mayor, in 1699 and 1711. The wealth of Nicholas Wood, cutler, certainly contributed to the prestige of the Chamber and in 1706 supported the dignity of the mayoralty. He also reached the summit of local ambition by securing his unopposed return as Member of Parliament for the city in 1708. The early eighteenth-century Chamber certainly represented the more prosperous citizens. Financial embarrassment among its members was rare.

Between 1688 and 1760 no less than 128 individuals were elected to the Chamber and these, with five unidentified, represented twenty-six occupations. However, five occupations, druggist, fuller, goldsmith, merchant and grocer comprised about three-quarters of the total membership of the Chamber. Grocers predominated with twenty-seven members, and between 1688 and 1715, the years of Exeter's economic heyday, grocers and merchants together comprised forty-five per cent of the membership of the Chamber. Under the early Hanoverians, grocers continued to form the largest occupational group and numbered fourteen in all among the sixth-three members elected during this period. In second place between 1715 and 1760 were the seven druggists, and there were also three apothecaries. Having regard to the indeterminate status of the various branches of the medical profession at this period druggists and apothecaries together may be regarded as foreshadowing the role of doctors and surgeons in the early nineteenth century. Robert Dabynott, apothecary, was evidently wealthy enough to maintain the prestige of the mayoralty as early as 1694, but he had no successor until John Phillips, apothecary, became mayor in 1721. No druggist appears to have reached the chair before 1709, but five became mayors between 1709 and 1760, one of them, Samuel Simmons, holding the office twice. The legal profession was not represented among the elected members of the Chamber, despite its standing in Exeter, until 1833 when one of the two elected that year, John Carew, claimed exemption on the grounds that he was a practising attorney. It was not till the post-Reform era, after 1835, that lawyers assumed a prominent role in Exeter's local government.

The speed with which the Chamber was brought up to full strength in the winter of 1688–9 was exceptional. There was usually no hurry to fill vacancies — the Chamber was almost permanently under strength — and even when the first step was taken with the formal resolution that a new member or members should be chosen 'this day fortnight or the next meeting of the Chamber' in practice the decision was often repeatedly postponed. The politics and religious views, personal standing and connections of the prospective candidate all had to be considered. In 1725 it became necessary to provide against disputes by resolving that if more than one candidate was proposed for a vacancy 'neither of them shall be looked upon to be elected but as he shall have a majority of the votes of the Chamber.' Prospective candidates were not necessarily consulted, with the consequence that in 1809 the election of Bartholomew Parr, doctor of physic, had to be declared invalid after he had explained that, as a Dissenter, he was ineligible. To avoid similar embarrassment in the future the Chamber then resolved that 'the names of persons nominated for election should be communicated to the Chamber at the meeting previous to the meeting at which such Election is intended to take place and that a Memorandum of such names should be taken down by the Town Clerk.'[10]

Family connections were weighty qualification for membership of the Chamber. Alderman John Newcombe, the grocer, was followed by his son John Newcombe Jr and his son-in-law Humphrey Bawden, mercer, in 1725 and 1717 respectively. Another son-in-law was the druggist Robert Lidstone who, like his father-in-law and brother-in-law, became mayor and alderman, as Andrew Brice duly noted.[11] A close genealogical study would undoubtedly establish in detail a family network that persisted in Chamber circles throughout the century. Apprenticeship to members was also a strong recommendation. Between 1690 and 1760 twelve new members can be identified with certainty as former apprentices of aldermen and mayors.

Not all citizens, however, even if they could face the financial liabilities, were anxious for inclusion in the ranks of 'the most wise and gravest'. Some were virtually shanghaied into office despite their objections. Membership of the Chamber involved much time-consuming work, much of it such as in a later age would be the duty of full-time officers. Many found it well worth their while to pay a heavy fine to escape the honour. It was 'absolutely inconvenient' to take office, wrote William Pitfield, apothecary, in 1759, declaring himself 'ready to submit to any fine that might be imposed'. In 1704 William Sandford Jr was fined £100 for refusing election, though his father had been a member. Subsequently he accepted. Nicholas Arthur, plumber, who did much work for the Chamber in his business capacity, similarly refused in 1747, was fined and then changed his mind. Both men eventually became mayor. Two goldsmiths, William Ekins in 1704 and Benjamin Brown in 1712, were among those who were fined, and who paid, for refusal of office. Pleas on the grounds of poor health were accepted with reluctance. In 1755 Robert Prowse claimed exemption on the ground of his infirmities; nevertheless he was fined £100 subject to the customary abatement of twenty per cent for prompt payment.[12]

The Chamber was usually reluctant to release its members unless they become financially embarrassed. Insolvency was a potential liability since office holders were apt to retain credit balances for months, or even years. Hugh Palmer, merchant, was promptly discharged from membership of the Chamber in 1713, 'being reduced to a state of poverty'. Edward Spicer, goldsmith, and mayor in 1708, was 'removed, dismissed and discharged' on his bankruptcy in 1718. But James Taylor, grocer, had to pay a fine of £50 when in 1710 he sought to retire on account of 'the straightness of his circumstances'.[13]

In later years the Chamber gave some assistance to members who resigned for financial reasons. In 1813 John Balle, silversmith, received a grant of £30 per annum after his resignation. William Bate, haberdasher, who had resigned in 1808 'in an ill state of health and reduced circumstances', received a grant of £20 per annum in 1814.[14] Retirement from public life or private business on account of age was not a widely accepted practice in the eighteenth century and the only formal concession made to age, even for aldermen, was the exemption for 'those who were beyond the age of three score years' from the penalty of 12*d.* imposed for neglect to wear the black woollen gown prescribed for meetings of the Chamber. Only one member of the Chamber, Robert Hutchings, was so palpably inadequate that he had to be removed from the Chamber on the grounds of his being *non compos mentis,* and that was in 1690.[15]

Once elected a new member was promptly appointed to one of the *ad hoc* committees by means of which the Chamber conducted most of its detailed work. After four to six years he could expect election to the onerous office of Receiver. The Receiver was the linchpin of the Chamber's administration. His primary duties, according to Hooker, included the collection of all revenues, ordinary and extraordinary, and the payment of all 'Charges, Expenses, Fees, Rents, Annuities whatsoever due and payable by the

Chamber'.[16] The Receiver was assisted by an accountant, who was also in private business, and employed members on his own staff on his work for the Chamber. The work was detailed and demanding. In 1774 the hatter Thomas Scott preferred to pay a fine of £150 rather than undertake the burden.[17] There were some perquisites such as the sale of old materials and the loppings from trees, a privilege withdrawn in 1816. By custom the Receiver was expected to entertain his colleagues, though not infrequently he found it less trouble, and perhaps cheaper, to compound with a fine of £10 or £15, 'my fine for not keeping the feast as Receiver', as John Newcombe recorded in his accounts for 1727.[18] The breakfast provided by the Receiver on the convivial occasion of a mayoral election was discontinued in 1776 and with it the token reimbursement of 13s. 4d. The Receiver's major role corresponded to that of the modern city treasurer and for this he received no salary. He was responsible for income and expenditure fluctuating between £3,500 and £8,800 a year. Robert Lidstone, in 1722–3, had to account for revenue amounting to £1,275 13s. 6¼d. and expenditure of £1,284 4s. 8¼d. Nicholas Wood, in 1704–5, accounted for revenue of £4,088 16s. 10d. and expenditure of £4,082 9s. 11d. but this was an exceptionally high level, and until 1760 the figures were usually below £3,000 on both sides of the account.

The accounts themselves were audited and certified by a committee of aldermen, all of them past Receivers, and usually after a delay which could amount to as much as twenty years. The accounts of the then Alderman Vivian, Receiver 1725–6, and Alderman Simmons, Receiver 1726–7, were not fully discharged until December 1747. If Receivers, or any other members of the Chamber in possession of its funds, died before their accounts were finally settled the Chamber had to embark on even more prolonged negotiations with their widows and executors. But while credit balances often remained for long periods in the hands of the Receiver he, on the other hand, often had to advance funds from his own resources at need. The accounts of 1695 include the payment of the then large sum of £757 to Daniel Ivie, clothier, as the balance due to him on his account of the previous year.[19] In 1699 the Chamber, not having sufficient cash available, had to give a bond for £283 to John Munckley, goldsmith, for sums due to him from his receivership.[20] On occasion the Chamber requested the Receiver to advance money in return for a lien on future revenue. Thus Emmanuel Hole scribbled breathlessly in his account book for the year 1721–2:

> Sometimes I was out my office as receiver I was pretty much in advance of the Chamber. The Chamber promised if I would continue to take care of the Mills I should receive the rents for them until I was paid and have interest for what I was in advance till that time.[21]

Hole had advanced funds for the repair of Head Weir Mills for which the Chamber later received a rent of £140 per annum.

It was therefore prudent for the Chamber to insist that its members, all potential Receivers, should be men of substantial wealth and good credit. For the Receivers themselves there was compensation in the fact that, on the occasion of a surplus being available, they could employ it at interest in their own businesses until their accounts were finally made up.

By the 1730s it had become customary for the Receiver to be elected sheriff at Michaelmas in the year in which his receivership had ended. The duties, though less demanding than those of the receiver, could be troublesome and expensive. They involved him in the risk of legal proceedings, as in 1749 when the Chamber resolved to defend the sheriff and his officers, and to meet their costs, when they had broken down a door during the uproar that accompanied a mayoral election.[22] Like other office-holders the sheriff was expected to advance cash at need, subject to eventual repayment in the leisurely eighteenth-century manner. Nicholas Lee, as sheriff, had to pay the constables from his own pocket and was assured that the claim would be allowed by the Chamber in his receiver's accounts for the previous year. Sheriff Manley, in 1746, was requested to pay out £120 in rewards on the conviction of three persons for burglary, the Chamber undertaking 'to stand and be a security to Mr Manley and to pay him interest at five per cent until he shall be paid by the Crown or otherwise'. For Alderman Medland, drug-gist, in 1744, the financial implications were evidently chilling. The Chamber therefore:

> to induce him thereto have proposed to bear the Expense of the Execution of the Office and to indemnify him against all Incidents and Accidents that may possibly attend that Office, and Mr. Medland having upon these terms accepted the Office this Body do agree to bear all the Expense except the Expense of passing his Account and to execute a Bond under their Common Seal for that purpose.[23]

Some ten years after election as common councillor, and after holding the offices of receiver and sheriff, a candidate with suitable qualifications, including wealth, interest and influence, might expect election as 'The Worshipful this City's Mayor, Lieutenant of his Majesty the King'. There were other factors to be considered, questions of personal suitability and also political considerations on which the eighteenth-century press perforce was silent. Arthur Culme, grocer, waited twenty-one years for the mayoralty; according to Brice he was deliberately shelved and then adopted only to block a more unpopular candidate. John Haddy, a prominent alderman and a receiver-general of taxes never attained the mayoralty, though Brice considered that Haddy had filled all the subordinate offices of the Chamber with distinction and claimed that he was ambitious to become mayor.[24] Brice was a Whig and the Chamber was predominantly Tory;

but it would be naive to imagine that merit was the sole determinant for election as mayor.

The mayor's brethren in the Chamber jealously watched for any extension of the authority of his office at their expense while at the same time they rallied to support his dignity as representative of the Chamber. It was Mayor Thomas Dodge who in 1769 nominated as a freeman John Duntze, son of one of the several German Lutherans who had settled and prospered in early Georgian Exeter. The Chamber censured the mayor because he had insisted on his 'particular right of nominating a Freeman which this Body in no wise allows'. Furthermore, he had made public his intention, thus infringing the 'Dignity and Independence of the Chamber'. Records were examined and disclosed no precedent. On the contrary it was confirmed that 'the Mayor for the time being hath no Right as Mayor separate and distinct from the right of every Member of this Body to nominate or recommend a Freeman'.[25] At the close of the century, in 1795, a similar situation arose when Mayor John Balle gave a casting vote in a tied election of an alderman. On that occasion the Recorder advised, after a protest by supporters of the defeated candidate, that the mayor had no such right. The election was accordingly declared void, though the candidate supported by the mayor was in fact chosen at a new election.[26]

To the authority derived from 'great trade and generous living', allied with the connections and relationships which the eighteenth century summarised as 'interest', the mayor added the formidable authority of a magistrate. By the 'governing' charter of Charles I the mayor, recorder and aldermen had powers of gaol delivery with an extensive jurisdiction, mayor, recorder and one alderman forming a quorum. At quarter sessions the mayor, recorder and two of the eight aldermen formed a quorum. For these purposes, if not already alderman and therefore JP, the mayor was sworn as a justice immediately after his election and could look forward to election as alderman at the next vacancy. In his own court, held twice a week, the mayor in theory still shared with the provost's court jurisdiction over all real and personal actions arising within the city, though the mayor's court's main activity had been reduced to such matters as the electorally-important admission or disfranchisement of freemen.

The mayoral election at Michaelmas was a rampageous mixture of ceremonial and violence, an opportunity for the roughest elements of the population to remind gowned and be-wigged dignitaries that they were but human. On the day before the election 'Young Exeter', as Andrew Brice termed them, enjoyed freedom to pelt more sobre citizens and visitors, men and women, with the ammunition provided in abundance by the streets, mud, dead cats and offal. Rival mobs, stimulated by drink, fought with fists and clubs for their favoured candidates. The proceedings in the streets terminated on the day after the election with bull-baiting outside the house of the new mayor, bystanders and passers-by, by ancient custom, being soaked by buckets of dirty water, an amusement in which the butchers by tradition were prominent.

Within the Guildhall the proceedings were more decorous, requiring the attendance of the Recorder or his deputy, and the town clerk. The prescribed oaths were administered. The votes of the Chamber were scrutinised. Two members of the Chamber were then 'reported to be duly nominated to the Freemen in the Hall below for their election of a mayor for the year ensuing'. By the eighteenth century the choice by the freemen was usually a formality, an opportunity for drinking and horseplay rather than for expressing the will of the citizens. The mayoral elections of 1735, 1736 and 1738, however, were conducted with all the sound and fury of a parliamentary election and the Chamber itself was at odds.[27] In 1735 Mathew Spry, mercer, defeated John Haddy, receiver-general of taxes and proprietor of the water-works, by a majority of fifteen in a poll of 1,253. Haddy was a Tory who received the votes of the outgoing mayor John Newcombe, all the aldermen and five councillors. Mathew Spry on the other hand was supported by the leading Tory gentlemen among the freemen, William Courtenay, Edward Drewe, Andrew Quicke and John Rolle. This was the time when as Andrew Brice noted, 'Country Esquires and Gentlemen . . . very politely mingled with the common Townsmen at elections for Mayor, as much as for members of Parliament, *as honourary Freemen.*'[28] In the mayoral election of 1737 thirteen members of the Chamber voted for Thomas Heath, who was defeated, and four for Samuel Simmons, but Heath was successful in the following year when he was supported not only by his former opponent but also by prominent Tories such as Sir Henry Northcote, MP for the city, and Henry Rolle, son of John Rolle of Stevenstone who was MP for Exeter in 1713 and 1722.

These were the rowdy mayoral elections that provided material for *The Mobiad* in which the Whig Andrew Brice sang 'Of Mobs and Mischiefs which from Mobbings spring'. Every effort was made to recruit voters. On 23 November 1735 the Chamber resolved that:

> Every son of an Alderman and the eldest son only of every common Council Man being of age have each a right to his freedom and may demand accordingly, likewise every person marrying an Alderman's daughter.[29]

The election of Thomas Heath as mayor, at Michaelmas 1738, was preceded by over seventy admissions to the freedom on one day, 18 September, all on the grounds of succession or apprenticeship.[30] These were the years when, with unprecedented lavishness, the Chamber was conferring the freedom 'by order' on 'the most zealous gentlemen, clergy and attornies of the Tory party'.

It is difficult to perceive any real pattern from the extant mayoral voting lists. In his notes to *The Mobiad* Andrew Brice hints at personal rivalries and manoeuvres of the kind which the editors of the early Victorian press would have described in graphic detail. There were also, no doubt, many local issues playing some part in the outcome. By the 1730s, however, Whig fortunes were reviving in Exeter while the unscrupulous and well-organised national campaign to bring down Walpole was affecting every borough in the country and would achieve success with the minister's fall in 1742. With the Chamber divided against itself and the Whigs showing vigorous life, mayoral elections were seized upon as an opportunity to express the never wholly-extinguished hostility towards the city's Tory establishment.

Once elected, however, the mayor embodied the traditions, dignity and authority of a virtual city-state that was rarely troubled by interference from London. On ceremonial occasions, to celebrate Marlborough's victories, or, in George II's reign, victories of the Seven Years War, royal anniversaries, weddings and births, the mayor paraded in solemn procession attended by the constables with their staves of office, the staff-bearers and sergeants-at-mace 'in gorgeous robes, and Hats superb of lace', the swordbearer, the aldermen in scarlet robes and the councillors in black walking two by two, and the city trade organisations with their insignia and banners. At the Cathedral the mayor maintained the dignity of the city, and of his own person, with the backing of his colleagues, insisting on a suitable chair of state and in 1708 securing the removal of doubts 'concerning the wearing of the Cap of Maintenance and bearing the Sword before the said Mayor and his Successors'.[31] He entertained lavishly and expensively, his official entertainments consisting of eighteen 'Monday Dinners' and four 'Great Dinners', until these were slightly reduced in 1812 to 'two Great Dinners, four smaller dinners, six Chapel Dinners, Qualification Dinner, Magistrates' visits and two small Assize Dinners'.[32]

The Chamber insisted on these functions which, together with expensive private hospitality, contributed to the city's prestige and the mayor's influence. In 1707 Lord Poulett commented on the 'generous living' which contributed to Alderman Wood's prestige in the city. Failure to maintain the standard of hospitality expected of the mayor was resented. The receiver's accounts for 1737–8 include an item of £4 15s. 11d., equal to eight weeks' wages of a master craftsman, for a dinner 'provided at the mayoralty house for the Chamber, they not being invited to dinner by Mr Culme, the present mayor, as is customary'.[33] Arthur Culme, grocer, had been elected to the Chamber in 1716; that he was not chosen mayor till 1738 may perhaps have been due to his reluctance to provide 'generous living'. But the Chamber, in its turn, contributed generously from it funds towards the mayor's expenses. In 1734 the mayor's salary was raised from £100 to £150, a substantial item when total expenditure amounted to only £2142. The seven aldermen on that occasion made sure of their *quid quo pro* and received retrospective increases of £50 for the years of their own mayoralties, 'they having received not more than one hundred pounds each in their respective years'.[34] In December 1738 the mayor received another increase of £50 per annum though at that time there had been no marked rise in prices; by 1753 he was being paid £250 or approximately nine per cent of the Chamber's total expenditure for the year 1753–4.

Entertaining on prestigious occasions was financed directly by the Chamber, as in 1703 when £20 was paid for the mayor's dinner in honour of that powerful High Tory nobleman, Lord Rochester, uncle of the Queen. A collation for the third Duke of Marlborough, which cost £7, was also paid for by the Chamber and handsomely supplemented by a present of wine costing £38. The Chamber paid the butler who functioned at mayoral entertainments and also the wages of the mayor's official cook. The domestic cost of a year of office involving high standards of hospitality was also evidently daunting. In 1797 the merchant John Brake, on being informed that he was to be the next mayor, required, and received, not only a guarantee of the then usual salary of £250 but also £30 in lieu of plate, £24 for china and a further £75 to cover expenses in fitting up his house for the mayoralty.[35] Between 1688 and 1760 only one member of the Chamber found it possible to accept the mayoralty three times, and this was Nicholas Lee, grocer. In the hard times of 1802 when Charles Collyns, the banker, became mayor, the Chamber, then in financial trouble itself, had the satisfaction of accepting the mayor's refusal of a salary, but agreed in return to meet incidental expenses.

The mayor, of course, was expected to head subscription lists and to distribute traditional perquisites to his officers. In 1797 the swordbearer received twelve guineas and the staff bearers six guineas each, 'in compensation for not having received the usual hospitality of the mayor'.[36] And since the Chamber was frequently hard put to find cash it was convenient to turn to a wealthy mayor, as in 1753 when mayor Nicholas Lee advanced £1,000 on loan to meet extraordinary expenses. In 1814 the town clerk reported that he managed to remit £2,000 to London only because 'the mayor had kindly assisted him with the loan of a considerable sum'.[37] As the eighteenth century wore on it is clear that some members of the Chamber, for understandable financial reasons, required considerable persuasion to accept office as mayor.

As a group the eight Aldermen ruled Exeter and were formidable in their accumulated experience derived from years both of business and of city administration. Alderman Copplestone, elected in 1709, died in 1754 and had been mayor in 1719. Alderman Westlake died in 1833, fifty-two years after his election to Chamber, forty-eight years after his mayoralty. Even under pressure from their colleagues, aldermen were difficult to remove. Alderman Brooke, though his bankruptcy was admitted, was not removed in 1782 until he had been represented by counsel, the delivery of the mayor's summons to each member of the Chamber had been proved on oath, and copies of the proceedings authenticated. In 1801 Alderman Dennis, a habitual absentee from meetings, was at last persuaded to submit a request to resign, though the Chamber insisted on a legal instrument surrendering his offices. Dennis then withdrew his request on the grounds that the Chamber's resolution approving it had not been 'sufficiently explanatory of his motives'. The Chamber gave up, merely fining him one guinea for failing to attend meetings.[38] In 1808 John Balle and Joseph Greenway, both former mayors and at the time close to insolvency, fought attempts to remove them with writs of *mandamus* until eventually allowed to resign on the grounds of ill-health and non-residence.[39] Touchy aldermanic voices still speak from the records: Alderman Bale in Dutch William's time, obstructing the whiggish Corporation of the Poor and 'saying withal that he did not sit in Parliament seven years for nothing';[40] Alderman Dennis, when Napoleon was supreme in Europe, grumbling about discourteous treatment despite 'near forty years in the Chamber'.

Aldermen sat on all committees, executive and inquisitorial. They lent distinction to official occasions, in 1689 attending that noted toper Admiral Herbert, 'floating in Torbay', and presenting him with a pipe (126 gallons) of canary. In 1740 they waited on the Duke of Cumberland, also in Torbay, to present the future victor of Culloden with 'an Hogshead (63 gallons) of Red Port, an Hogshead of White Lisbon wine and a box of sweetmeats'.[41] They gave weight to the occasion when a clergyman received the Chamber's thanks for a congenial sermon. In the aldermen, as they walked the streets, the authority and traditions of the Chamber were embodied; for the majority of the citizens their power over daily life was more to be courted or feared than that of remote govenment in London.

The Chamber worked within a rigid frame of law and tradition under the guidance of the Town Clerk, who was necessarily an attorney and also a member of one of the prominent local families. Henry Gandy, town clerk from 1733 to 1752, was succeeded by Benjamin Heath who, though not a practising lawyer, had been intended for the bar. Heath came from a Dissenting family of fullers and merchants, one of several during the century who took with them the virtues of Dissent into the social respectability of the Church of England. He was a sound but conventional scholar but he acquired fame in the South West by his organisation of opposition to the hated cider tax. His orthodoxy in Church and State was endorsed when Oxford conferred upon him a doctorate of law. In return he felt it his duty to 'enter upon a Refutation of Mr Hume's philosophy' which, in Heath's view, 'overthrew all truth and knowledge, all Religion and Morality'.[42] David Hume (1711-1766), the distinguished philosopher and historian, was much attacked in orthodox circles for his scepticism. His 'refutation' by Exeter's town clerk was in itself a mark of the long persisting and deep-rooted conservatism of respectable circles of the city. Heath's younger brother Thomas, businessman and scholar, was elected to the Chamber in 1730 and was twice mayor, in 1738 and 1749. Much respected for his integrity Thomas Heath was evidently more successful as a scholar than in business and died relatively poor. His son John followed Benjamin Heath as town clerk in 1766 and resigned in 1775 as Mr Serjeant Heath, with a handsome present of plate and a retainer of 20 guineas a year. He later became recorder of Exeter but relinquished his position in 1780 on his appointment as judge.

The Heaths were a gifted family, a fine provincial product of the Augustan England shaped by Addison, men of wide-ranging, though conventional, intellectual interests, respectable in their private lives and public conduct. On Benjamin Heath's death in 1766 the Chamber ordered a full-length portrait to be placed 'in the most conspicuous part of the Guildhall'.[43] Their careers in local government must be set against an over-facile acceptance of Hogarth's pictures, or the accusations of 'swilling and guzzling' by nineteenth-century reformers. In the post-Reform era, John Gidley, town clerk from 1835 to 1865, was to continue in his interests and publications the tradition of dry and meticulous eighteenth-century scholarship.

In the eighteenth century the role of the town clerk resembled that of an attorney managing the business and political interests of a large estate, advising on precedents and procedure, managing legislation in the form of private Acts of Parliament, drafting loyal addresses to the Throne and arranging advertisements in the press. For all these activities he received remuneration at the current rate like any attorney in private practice. He prepared mortgages, was paid for their copying and engrossing, and enjoyed a host of minor receipts, such as 6d. for a summons to an army corporal charged with assaulting the staff-bearers. For parliamentary business, too, which was frequent and expensive, the town clerk received his legal fees and costs.

The swordbearer Andrew Brice described as:

> Be-crowned with Cap of an Umbrella's size,
> Rich velvet, richer in embroideries
> Comes burley He, who, as of Spades the King,
> Bear Sword erect . . .[44]

Not only did he represent the authority of the Chamber on ceremonial occasions but he was also employed as a dignified emissary of the Chamber, a major-domo attending on an alderman 'to know his mind, whether he will continue as a member of the Chamber or not',[45] conveying to new councillors formal notice of their election and, if they were not overjoyed at the prospect, reminding them of the penalties of refusal. He was responsible for the comfort of the judges at assizes and, in 1774, received ten guineas for his 'extraordinary trouble and expense in entertaining the judges for a week beyond their usual time'. In the early nineteenth century the swordbearer, then by profession an accountant, undertook more onerous duties such as investigating, together with the chamberlain, the highly unsatisfactory accounts of the wharfinger, for which he received £42 in consideration of his 'great pains and trouble'. Besides fees and the usual perquisites he received a salary which was increased from £20 to £40 a year in 1738, and to £60 a year in 1774;[46] it remained at £60 till the Municipal Corporations Act of 1835 when the then holder of the office, a survival of archaic ceremony regarded by the Reformers as fit only for the nursery, became, briefly, an unsatisfactory superintendent of police.

The chamberlain's office was a creation of the sixteenth century and the holder was usually an attorney. The duties included the care of the Chamber's records, the making of surveys of city property and, in general, to help and advise the Receiver. Like the swordbearer, the chamberlain was required from time to time to undertake special enquiries. Swordbearer and chamberlain were senior officers of the Chamber, members of the higher ranks of city society and of unimpeachable Tory sentiments and Anglican orthodoxy.

The Recorder strictly was the city's principal legal officer whose function was to advise the mayor and Chamber on all matters of law and to act as the Chamber's chief agent and representative in the politico-legal world of London. As such the Recorder had to have a good social background; it was an additional advantage if he carried some weight in politics as a Member of Parliament. Sir Edward Seymour's career was unique in that as Recorder of Exeter from 1681 to 1684 and from 1689 to 1707, he placed at the disposal of the city his immense influence as a leading politician and landowner, twice Speaker of the House of Commons and repeatedly holder of one of the great offices of state. Exeter could not expect its subsequent recorders to equal Seymour's eminence and had to be content with their connection with respectable landed families. John Belfield, who became recorder in 1727, was a protégé of Seymour's at Totnes and, briefly, represented Exeter as a Tory after the by-election of 1728. John Cholwich of Farringdon, an undistinguished member of a West Country county family, followed Belfield in 1751 and retired in 1764. Cholwich was followed by John Glynn, serjeant-at-law and a far more individualistic character than the general run of Exeter's eighteenth-century recorders. Glynn was a supporter of John Wilkes and was Wilkes's colleague for the great constituency of Middlesex, a stronghold of popular feeling against governments and for demonstrations that set London in a turmoil. Glynn resigned in 1772 to become recorder of London. In his day Exeter too became Wilkite, though rather as a mark of provincial dissatisfaction with 'Courtiers' and the policies associated with Lord Bute than as a breach in the city's basic conservatism.

Each year, at Michaelmas, the Chamber appointed and formally re-appointed its officials and employees: not only the aldermen allocated to the various wards and quarters of the city, but also the warden of the poor and the warden of Exe Bridge, the constables and porter of the city gates and the scavengers. The Chamber on these occasions gave at least formal approval to the employment of the whole range of artisans paid from the general account: joiners, helliers, smiths, masons and the like, and also those paid from the funds of St John's Hospital and other charities under the Chamber's control. Inevitably the Act Books of the Chamber do not record discussion on the merits of any individual employee but the system must have contributed to the influence that could be exercised by the Chamber, its 'interest', the instruments by which it exercised political influence according to the generally accepted practices of the period. As freemen the Chamber's employees voted under the eyes of their employers. Some of them were substantial employers themselves, for instance the 'plumber for the whole work of this body' (in 1764 this was Mr Alderman Arthur), and for them the loss of an important contract might be serious. On the other hand some were substantial creditors of the Chamber. There was therefore ample scope for arriving at mutually advantageous agreements over the price of a vote. The parish constables, too, according to Andrew Brice, were all members of the Blue Party, that is Tory, in contrast to the turbulent Whig 'Grecians' of St Sidwells who fought under yellow colours.[47]

In such circumstances the influence of a united Chamber might be overwhelming, but at times it was hesitant or divided and while individual members exercised their considerable influence on behalf of one parliamentary candidate or another there were times when little could be achieved by the Chamber as a whole. The members of the Chamber were not autocratic proprietors of boroughs, like a Lowther in Westmorland or a Russell in Devon. In the last resort they had to live with their fellow citizens.

NOTES

1. John Hooker, *The Antique Description . . . of the City of Exeter,* p. 159.
2. *Western Times,* 15.6.1835.
3. HMC 29 *Portland* iv, p. 579: Bishop Warburton and E. Cholmondeley to Harley, 30.8.1710.
4. DRO, ECA, Act Books, 30.9.1769.
5. *ibid.,* 22.12.1747; 20.11.1750; 1.9.1752.
6. *ibid.,* 6.2.1753 and Youings, *Tuckers Hall Exeter,* pp. 102-8.
7. Hooker, *op. cit.,* p. 159.
8. Brice, *The Mobiad,* pp. 69, 163.
9. DRO, ECA, Act Books, 19.1.1725, 14.8.1733.
10. *ibid.,* 23.3.1725; 27.6.1809; 18.7.1809.
11. *Weekly Journal,* 27.9.1728.
12. DRO, ECA, Act Books, 13.3.1759; 7.11.1704, 21.11.1704; 3.11.1747, 17.11.1747; 17.10.1704; 12.8.1712; 9.9.1712; 13.3.1755.
13. *ibid.,* 3.3.1713; 29.10.1718; 28.10.1710; 20.2.1711.
14. *ibid.,* 10.4.1813, 2.6.1818.
15. *ibid.,* 4.2.1696, 21.9.1690.
16. Hooker, *op. cit.,* p. 166.
17. DRO, ECA, Act Books, 3.10.1774.
18. DRO, ECA, Receivers' Accounts, Book 60, 1727/8.

NOTES *continued*

19. *ibid.*, 1694/5.
20. DRO, ECA, Act Books, 9.5.1699.
21. DRO, ECA, Receivers' Accounts, Book 39, 1721/2.
22. DRO, ECA, Act Books, 21.11.1749.
23. *ibid.*, 17.1.1738; 6.10.1746; 1.10.1744.
24. *The Mobiad*, p. 162, footnote; p. 77, footnote.
25. DRO, ECA, Act Books, 30.9.1769, 20.10.1769.
26. *ibid.*, 3.11.1795, 17.11.1795.
27. DRO, ECA, Box 13: Polls of Elections of Mayors, 1735, 1736, 1738, 1740, 1760, 1768.
28. *The Mobiad*, p. 4.
29. DRO, ECA, Act Books, 23.11.1735.
30. M. Rowe and A. Jackson (eds), *Exeter Freemen*, pp. 259-61.
31. DRO, ECA, Act Books, 14.9.1708.
32. *ibid.*, 15.12.1812.
33. DRO, ECA, Receivers' Accounts, Book 75, 1737/8 and Act Book, 12.12.1738.
34. DRO, ECA, Act Books, 21.5.1734.
35. *ibid.*, 24.8.1797.
36. *ibid.*, 19.9.1797.
37. *ibid.*, 19.6.1753, 23.6.1814.
38. *ibid.*, 19.5.1801, 15.9.1801, 27.10.1801, 3.11.1801.
39. *ibid.*, 21.11.1808, 3.5.1809, 2.6.1809, 18.7.1809.
40. DRO, ECA, Corporation of the Poor, Court Book 1698-1702, 2.12.1699.
41. DRO, ECA, Act Books, 7.9.1689; 12.8.1740.
42. Sir William Drake, *Heathiana*, p. 13.
43. DRO, ECA, Act Books, 22.9.1766.
44. *The Mobiad*, p. 95.
45. DRO, ECA, Act Books, 23.2.1697.
46. *ibid.*, 12.3.1774, 3.9.1817; 12.12.1738, 24.6.1774.
47. *The Mobiad*, p. 88, footnote.

Chapter Four

Party Politics 1688-1760

Parliament, noted an observer in 1690, was 'divided into Tories, Whigs, Court Whigs and Tory Whigs'.[1] The Whigs had derived from the opponents of the Court in the reign of Charles II and included an element of republicanism as well as religious dissent. Among their supporters, after vacant sees had been filled by the new regime, was an influential group of bishops. The Tories derived from the supporters of Charles II and the older generation of Cavaliers, squires who clung to old loyalties and old habits, country parsons bound by conscience and faith to the Lord's Anointed in the person of the crowned king. Their principles were reaffirmed by the annual commemoration of Charles I, Martyr and King. Among them were the men who became known as 'High-Flyers' and 'Tantivy parsons', some of whom tended to regard Whig bishops as heretical.

Toryism shaded into Jacobitism. For some sixty years Devon was a potential invasion area for armed intervention on behalf of James II and his heirs with the support of a French fleet. Jacobitism, at least in spirit, lingered long in old manor houses between Exmoor and the Quantocks, in North Devon and around Exeter itself. Known or suspected Jacobites among Exeter's neighbours included a Courtenay of Powderham, a Bampfylde of Poltimore and Stephen Northleigh of Peamore.[2] In 1715 the West Country came to the verge of armed rebellion when the country gentlemen rode armed to meet Sir William Wyndham at Bath and the church bells of that city rang for the Pretender.

Exeter's businessmen, however, were unlikely to have welcomed the prospect of armed rebellion, which would have been bad for trade. In a loyal address to George II in 1727 the Chamber explained that Exeter was a trading city, for which peace was essential, though on this occasion, with an appreciation of commercial interests in the Mediterranean, it was ready to support a war over Gibraltar. Few relished the prospect of another Catholic monarch, ecpecially a monarch restored by French arms. Local Jacobitism rapidly became a nostalgic sentiment and, as in Squire Western's case, a robust provincial suspicion of Whig lords and Hanoverians. It was also an excuse for letting off steam against the government. As late as 1754 the white cockade appeared in the city streets on the occasion of the Pretender's birthday. Its removal by troops from the Poltimore Inn in St Sidwells provoked a lively riot though this incident was caused by traditional dislike of interference by soldiers rather than by any inclination to die for the son of James II. Exeter's Toryism was not Jacobite: in great measure it was a form of conservatism that long prevailed in the city. The Liberal *Western Times* complained with justice in 1868 that 'The tone of the city, what is called its respectability', was predominantly Tory.[3]

The city's Whigs were the heirs, by birth or in spirit, of the men who had once held the city for Parliament; and in 1688 there were still among them men and women who had been subjected to arrest, fine and imprisonment when the city was held for King Charles I. Exeter moreover was still an influential centre of Presbyterianism, with ministers of learning and ability. Dissenters formed a powerful minority, mustering perhaps five hundred votes for the Whig cause out of a total electorate of between 1300 and 1500.[4] They included men of wealth and public spirit, such as those whose appointment to the Chamber in 1687 had been so keenly resented. In 1688 Exeter's community of Dissenters entered upon its golden age which lasted for some thirty years, and occupied a respected position among England's Dissent. In due time its social respectability declined. The path to wealth and power led through Anglicanism, as the history of Lutheran immigrants would demonstrate. The spirit of seventeenth-century Dissent, however, lived on in the city, surviving the doctrinal disputes which split the old Presbyterian core. In the end the Unitarians, inheriting the worldly success and moral rectitude of their Presbyterian predecessors, would storm the Guildhall on behalf of Reform, and Dissenting ministers would be toasted at Whig political banquets in the city. Their allies, anti-clerical in sympathy and, like them, excluded from local office, would be described as Low Church and would include the smaller businessmen and artisans.

The Whig leaders in Exeter in 1688 were merchants and financiers who, as their successors failed to do, earned their reward in government honours lists. Edward Seaward, son-in-law of the Presbyterian Nicholas Brooking (mayor under the Commonwealth in 1656) but not himself a Dissenter, was a wealthy man with the resources to advance £500 on loan in 1698 towards the cost of improving the city's water supply.[5] Mayor in 1691, he was the moving spirit in the institution of the Corporation of the Poor and presided at its first meeting. In 1700, when he was governor for the second time, his deputy was the Dissenter Jerome King, grocer, father of Sir Peter King who turned to the Established Church, bringing with him the intellectual talents nurtured by a sound Dissenter's education and becoming in 1725, as Baron King of Ockam, Lord Chancellor of England. Though a staunch Whig Seaward was not a fanatical party man, one of those whom Samuel Butler described as 'A Sect whose chief Devotion lies in odd perverse

Antipathies'. He was sufficiently tolerant of political differences to stand security for that strongly Tory alderman Christopher Bale when the latter applied successfully for the position of receiver general of taxes. He successfully contested one of the Exeter parliamentary seats in the momentous election of 1695 and his services to his party were rewarded with a knighthood.

John Elwill, like Seaward a grocer's son, also had a background of Dissent. He evidently played a significant part in Whig party organisation in the South West and he kept in touch with important Whig politicians at Westminster, such as Sir George Treby who became Attorney General in 1689. One of the many for whom success in business gave entry to landed society he married a Bampfylde of Poltimore. Despite his dismissal from the Chamber in 1689 his standing and interest in the South West were substantial and though unsuccessful in Exeter he was returned as Member of Parliament for the tiny borough of Bere Alston in 1691 and 1695. Elwill was a good party man; in the elation following the Whig victories in the general election of 1695 he urged the dispossession of all Tory office holders, the 'Tantivy men' who, he suggested with evident relish, should be left to 'fret and foam until they see how little good they do thereby'.[6] In 1704, however, when the High Tories had an opportunity to install their own partisans in power, Elwill had a taste of the draught he had prescribed for his opponents; he lost his place on the county commission of the peace, although, according to old Richard Duke of Otterton, he was 'the most necessary justice in the county'. Elwill received recognition for his political services in 1709, when, in the ebb and flow of party strife, the Whigs again secured control of patronage. He became a baronet and his fees, over £1,000, were paid by the Crown.[7] At Exeter he worked with Edward Seaward on the Corporation of the Poor, and thus in association with prominent Dissenters; but he never received recognition by the Chamber nor, despite his wealth and influence, the honour of support by the Chamber's votes and interest in an election for the parliamentary representation of his native city. His fine brick house, in the style of Queen Anne's day, still stands today by the Pin brook as a memorial to a man who, of all Exeter's merchant class at this time, came closest to some prominence in national politics. Other merchants, members of the Chamber, became Members of Parliament in the early eighteenth century but they were no more than cyphers. None of them received recognition in the form of a knighthood or a baronetcy; all were Tory. The brief and modest eminence of Seaward and Elwill was the last effective local expression of the once powerful element of opposition represented in the seventeenth century by Puritan, Dissenter and Whig.

The passion of party politics in these years was engendered by strongly held and opposing views on the Fundamentals of Church and State, including the succession to the throne. But fervour was maintained at boiling point by frequent elections. The Triennial Act of 1694 required a general election every three years, apart from elections consequent on the demise of the Crown; between 1689 and 1715 there were twelve general elections, practically one every two years. At Exeter, between 1688 and 1715, there were only eleven general elections, but there were three by-elections, for a total of twenty-five parliamentary seats, Exeter being represented by two members. Twenty of the twenty-two seats contested in general elections were won by Tories. Fourteen Tory candidates were returned without a contest and two Whigs. By-elections were not usually contested, the by-election of June 1689 being an exception.[8] The prevailing Toryism of Exeter in the era of the revolution of 1688 was in marked contrast to the situation in other important cities. At Bristol, with between four thousand and five thousand electors, the corporation and the wealthier citizens were predominantly Whig. Whig mayors, sheriffs and aldermen controlled Norwich. Whig interests prevailed in Coventry, Gloucester, Liverpool and York.

For the Convention Parliament of January 1689 Exeter in fact returned without a contest the Tory magnate, Sir Edward Seymour, and a Whig, Henry Pollexfen. Devon born, Pollexfen in Tory eyes was a 'thorough-stick enemy to the Crown and Monarchy . . . a Fanatic and a frequenter of Conventicles'.[9] But the uncontested return of representatives of the two parties at Exeter, like the Convention Parliament itself, was an unstable *mariage de convenance* which quickly fell apart. Pollexfen became Lord Chief Justice and in the ensuing by-election at Exeter was replaced by the High Tory Christopher Bale, a former mayor. Bale was opposed by Henry Speke, a member of a Somerset landed family and one of the dubious and versatile adventurers who flourished in an age of plot and counter-plot. After a very tough election he was defeated on a low poll.

The freedom of the city conferred the right to vote and after about 1670, when party strife began to take the form known to the eighteenth century and later, a rise in the political temperature was usually demonstrated a by steep rise in the number of admissions to the freedom.[10] Coincidentally with the Exeter election of 1695, an affair of national significance, 312 freemen were enrolled, with over two hundred on one day. The official grounds for admission to the freedom, even in an election year, were almost invariably apprenticeship or succession by hereditary right. It was not till 1741 that the Chamber began the practice of large-scale admissions simply 'by order of the mayor and council', and to include significant numbers of country gentlemen and professional men. The new freemen in an election year represented a wide range of Exeter's artisan community, cordwainers, joiners, helliers, masons, smiths, glaziers, saddlers and the like, thus supporting the Tory claim, in the early nineteenth century, that 'interests', not 'heads', were represented in the electorate. The occupations recorded in the freemen's list, were most numerous on those occasions when there were considerable additions to the freedom, for example in 1695 and in 1734, years when the normal electoral pattern in Exeter was broken by the return to Parliament of two Whig members.

The position of freeholders on the electorate was regularised after the unusually turbulent by-election of June 1689. Henry Speke, after his defeat, claimed that 'although by ancient custom no freeholder had the right to vote, yet divers, viz. the Priest Vicars, Lay Vicars, Choristers, Court-Holders, Vergers and others belonging to St Peter's Church' had in fact been allowed to poll.[11] It was also alleged that the sheriff, Edward Seaward, had given an assurance that none made free under the city charter of the Tory reaction in 1684, and reissued in 1688 after confiscation by James II, should vote. Seaward was certainly a Whig, but he was a member of the Chamber with a large following in the city and there may well have been practical limits to the exercise of party zeal, especially on behalf of an adventurer like Speke and against a fellow alderman. But the Tories were dominant in the Commons, Speke's petition was dismissed and the Exeter freeholders were admitted to the franchise. The categories of voter cited by Speke, however, were of their nature certainly Tory.

By 1720 the electorate at Exeter numbered well over fifteen hundred and included a significant proportion of Dissenters. This was large by contemporary standards but not unique, York, Gloucester and Newcastle-upon-Tyne all having electorates of two thousand and over; at Bristol the electorate was three times that of Exeter. However, an electorate of one thousand or more was difficult and expensive to manage and there are said to have been indications that even Sir Edward Seymour was embarrassed by the cost of the election of 1695.[12] Candidates had to pay generously for the travelling expense of voters who travelled to Exeter for the election, and for unstinted food and drink for their supporters, actual or potential, during the contest. Gangs of toughs had to be recruited to intimidate rival voters, if necessary by keeping them away from the hustings.

Prospective parliamentary candidates also sought the endorsement of the Chamber. If acceptable the candidate would be informed that the Chamber would 'stand by him and assist him with all their interests', or 'with their whole weight and interest'. The weight and interest of the Twenty Four was formidable as magistrates and, for the most part as wealthy employers, backed by clients, friends and relations, by business ties, and by the hope of favours granted and the fear of favours lost. But above all Exeter at the turn of the century was a fief in the 'western empire' of the city's recorder, Sir Edward Seymour, alias 'Sir Chuffer', alias 'Tsar Semskeye', Member of Parliament for the city, with one break, from 1685 to 1708, leader of the Tory squires of England, and no courtier. Seymour nursed his constituency, advancing money to the Chamber, incurring expenses in facilitating the institution of the Corporation of the Poor and encouraging a committee of the chamber 'to lay before him the whole state of the rates of the maintenance of the poor . . . and of all things relating to the same'.[13]

Whig plans in the early 1690s included the exclusion from public office in all corporate towns of all those who had been associated with the surrender of city charters during the Tory reaction of the 1680s, a proscription which, if carried out to the letter, would have eliminated Exeter's governing class. Sir Edward Seymour and Alderman Bale had been returned unopposed in the general election of 1690, but at the next election, in 1695, a determined Whig assault was mounted on Seymour at the heart of his 'Western Empire'. The international situation was critical. The command of the Channel had been lost in 1690 and had barely been regained in 1692 in time to forestall a French landing in Tor Bay. A mainly Tory House of Commons was increasingly reluctant to vote supplies for the war. A Tory election victory could have jeopardised the future of the Grand Alliance against Louis XIV and hazarded both the permanence of the Revolution in England as well as the independence of the Netherlands. Merchants with overseas investments found them at risk; Tory errors had led to the loss of a valuable convoy in the Mediterranean.

It was in such circumstances that the contest in Exeter in November 1695 in Macaulay's words, 'fixed the attention of the whole kingdom and was watched with interest even by foreign governments'.[14] Macaulay has been faulted on points of detail, but the implications of the Exeter election justify his presentation of high drama. At Exeter, wrote the Dutch agent quoted by Macaulay,

> a large party has arisen against Seymour . . . he employs all the ordinary means not to have the shame of being rejected. His competitors, too, spend plenty of money . . . The opposite sides engage with feet and sticks.

Certainly it was a rough election. The subsequent Tory election petition claimed that the Whigs, 'by Menaces and Bribes, and by Combination with the Sheriff . . . obtained a Return to the Prejudice of the Petitioners' Rights'. The means of electoral persuasion are likely to have been much the same on both sides; but it was the Tories who were defeated.

Seymour's colleague in 1695 was Alderman John Snell, grocer, the mayor of 1687 who had been ousted by the Crown in favour of Thomas Jefford. The Whigs were Edward Seaward and Joseph Tily, the latter an attorney with a local practice and property near London. In the circumstances there could be no question of the Chamber giving unanimous support to either side. A member of the Chamber since 1688 and active in local affairs, Seaward will have had the full support of Exeter's permanent opposition, the Dissenters and their sympathisers, and also of merchants whose cargoes afloat could be hazarded by Tory naval incompetence. For the first of only two occasions in seventy years two Whig candidates were returned for the city. Seymour, for the moment defeated, had to find a seat at Totnes.

King William's war with France ended, for the time being, in 1697. In

August 1698 there was a general election. At Exeter Seymour again contested the seat, seeking to avenge the rebuff of 1695. His Tory colleague was Sir Bartholomew Shower who had been recommended as a suppporter of the Crown by James II's agents in 1688. He was the son of an Exeter merchant, the younger brother of a prominent Dissenting minister, and had been Recorder of London. Said to have been a tedious orator, Shower had also been one of the prosecuting counsel for the trial of the Seven Bishops, one of whom had been Exeter's Sir Jonathan Trelawny. He claimed to have received the bishop's support. 'I came in', he said after his election,

> by the interest of the Church of England, and by the Chamber of this City, as well as by the hearty endeavour of the good Trading People here; and, I may add, with the general Approbation of the Gentry of Devon, as well as with the good will . . . of the Lord Bishop.[15]

The two Tory candidates were returned with 751 and 743 votes respectively in a respectable poll of some 1,300. Sir John Elwill, one of the defeated Whig candidates, received 559 votes, these no doubt representing the hard core of Dissenters in Exeter's Whig party.

Henceforward for thirty years the Tories controlled the parliamentary representation of the city. In January 1701 Seymour and Shower retained their seats without difficulty, the former receiving as many as 1,200 votes. The Whig candidate, John Cholwich of Farringdon, a member of the local landed gentry, received the support given to Elwill, 570 votes. The ensuing Parliament was short-lived. War with France resumed and the King required parliamentary backing. Parliament was therefore dissolved and the general election was fought by a determined and well-organised Whig party. But at Exeter Seymour and Shower were returned unopposed. Shower's death in 1702 was followed by a by-election at which Alderman Snell, thrice mayor and a convinced Tory, was returned without a contest. Both men were returned without opposition in the first general election of Anne's reign in August 1702, and again in 1705. Both voted at Westminster with the extreme Tories in the attempt to eliminate Whig Dissenters from local office by ending the practice of a perfunctory appearance in an Anglican church to satisfy the letter of the law.

The eviction of Seymour from his stronghold was long a matter of hopeful speculation, not only among Whigs but among the numerous sub-species of Tory. Thus Lord Poulett, Lord Lieutenant of Devon and a moderate Tory, optimistically advanced the interest of Sir Francis Gwyn, reporting in May 1705 that

> many gentlemen of Dorset, Somerset and Devonshire count him as . . . Sir Edward Seymour's successor in his Western Empire . . . There almost wants nothing but Sir Chuffer's death for the management of Mr Gwyn's to take effect at Exeter.[16]

And in the terms reminiscent of those of the Earl of Bath in 1688, Poulett went on to explain that 'the spirit of the city [Exeter] does not only in great degree influence Devonshire, but Cornwall also.' Daniel Defoe was another optimist who encouraged hopes for Seymour's overthrow. Writing from Tiverton in August 1705, in the intervals of dodging hostile magistrates, Defoe reported to his paymaster, Robert Harley, Secretary of State: 'The success I have had in this part will fully satisfy you as it has encouraged me to say that Semskeye's Western Empire may with so much ease be overthrown.' At Exeter Defoe confidently devised a plan 'how Sir Edward Seymour may be thrown out without any difficulty'.[17] Sir Chuffer, however, held an impregnable stronghold and his influence locally had not been weakened by his dismissal from the Privy Council in 1704. Old age rather than political contrivance removed him at last. In October 1707 the Chamber accepted his resignation from his recordership. That winter he died, leaving no political successor, the last of the great political magnates of the old South West.

The year 1707 was also marked by the departure of the second of Exeter's two political mentors, Bishop Jonathan Trelawny. Lacking sadly in High Church zeal, to the fury of many of his clergy, Trelawny, a moderate Tory, used his considerable influence to keep the West quiet in the dangerous year of 1692. For his fellow Cornishman, Lord Treasurer Godolphin, the Bishop provided eleven reliable members for Cornish boroughs and he responded to Godolphin's appeal 'to muster up his squadron' in good time for Queen Anne's first Parliament.[18] Trelawny, 'a positive prelate', was regarded by some as over-dictatorial in his management of Exeter, 'too great a city', according to Lord Poulett, 'to be treated at the vile rate of Cornish boroughs, which our friend the bishop . . . through his warmth of temper does not distinguish'.[19] In 1705 he was at odds with his High Church clergy over elections to Convocation and exerted himself to prevent the election of their representatives. The Bishop emerged from the contest with increased authority. 'In Exeter', reported Defoe, 'the conquest the Bishop made over his clergy, and the further improvement his lordship makes of his victory, render him formidable, and exceedingly chagrins the party.'[20] His leading opponent, Exeter's Prebendary Fisher, was rusticated, and several members of the High Church clergy felt 'the effect of his lordship's displeasure'.

The Bishop's politics inclined towards those Whigs and moderate Tories who, under fire from the zealots of both parties, were working uneasily together in the Queen's service. His two leading supporters in Exeter both received high preferment, the dean, William Wake, becoming Bishop of Lincoln and later Archbishop of York, and Lancelot Blackburne, sub-dean and later dean, becoming Bishop of Exeter in 1716 and eventually Archbishop of Canterbury. Trelawny himself was translated to Winchester, a wealthier diocese on which he had long set his heart. He was succeeded at Exeter by the more congenial Offspring Blackall, a High Tory and an eloquent preacher, who had expounded the full doctrine of non-resistance to the Lord's Anointed in the approving presence of the Queen herself, to whose personal initiative he owed his preferment to Exeter.

Effective political opposition in Tsar Semskey's Exeter reflected the views of the country squires grumbling over high taxation, the cost of the war and the involvement of Britain in the problems of the Dutch. It was the era of the Tantivy parsons preaching in sermon and pamphlet the doctrine of non-resistance, harrying Whig bishops and, with Tory backbenchers, urging the extirpation of Dissent. Marlborough's victories in no way mitigated dislike of the Whigs among ardent Tories; and so William Chamberlain, collector of customs at Exeter, was removed by a Whig administation for refusing to drink the Duke's health and swearing that he should be hanged.[21]

With Seymour's removal from the scene by death in 1707, and Trelawny's translation to Winchester in the same year, the Tory control of Exeter momentarily relaxed. Seymour was replaced in the by-election of April 1708 by the shadowy figure of John Harris, a Whig, who was returned unopposed and must have been a compromise candidate acceptable to both parties. Harris was not a member of the Chamber: it has been suggested that he may have been a Topsham shipowner.[22] His election was an indication that even during the high tide of the city's Toryism there was still a Whig interest in Exeter powerful enough to exact a share of the representation of the city in favourable circumstances. That Harris was a good Whig was demonstrated by his vote in 1710 for the impeachment of the Tory parson, Dr Sacheverell, the hero of Exeter and other cathedral cities.

Exeter had now reached its zenith as a commercial and industrial city. Her merchants, self-confident and prosperous, were not yet ready to defer to the convention that the landed gentry were best fitted to represent their interests in parliament. No commanding figure had replaced Sir Edward Seymour. John Harris had been elected to a parliament on the brink of dissolution. The general election that followed, in May 1708, was designed to consolidate the political manoeuvres that had given the Whigs control of the government. The city's political managers arranged for the return, without a contest, of two businessmen. Harris again represented the Whigs. His colleague was Alderman Nicholas Wood. Neither made any impression on the wider political world beyond the city; but the fact that both the parliamentary seats could be filled by local businessmen was an endorsement of Exeter's status in Augustan England.

Alderman Nicholas Wood, a cutler by occupation, whose shop under the sign of the Sword and Glove, in the vicinity of Gandy's Lane, supplied muskets, bayonets, swords and halberds a well as gloves for funerals and other occasions, had been elected to the Chamber in 1699 and became mayor in 1706. A High Tory, he had had a brush with Bishop Trelawny and, therefore, fearing 'the prejudices of that positive prelate', applied for support in 1707 to Lord Poulett, then in office as First Lord of the Treasury. Poulett wrote to Harley, Secretary of State but at the time busily intriguing against his Whig colleagues. The letter gives a rare glimpse of Exeter's personalities as seen by their contemporaries, and of the city's practical politics in the reign of Queen Anne. Wood, wrote Poulett, 'has an absolute interest in the Chamber of Exeter and by his great trade and generous living has a mighty sway in that city'. He could be relied upon 'in acting what is right as to the choice of a Recorder in Exeter whenever Sir Edward Seymour dies' and had 'an interest to be chosen himself' at the next parliamentary election. He would be 'entirely at my Lord Treasurer's [Godolphin's] devotion; but his city pride won't submit through the Bishop.' In putting the case of a man who could be 'most useful to the Government', Poulett anxiously asked that his intervention should not come to the ears of the Bishop of Winchester.[23]

A month later Poulett returned to the charge:

> I wrote in general in Mr Wood's favour that you might know his character to be very well disposed and capable of being very useful to the public service in this part of the kingdom, and in that respect only I desired that he should not be discouraged, which he has some reason to apprehend, being turned out of half the receiver's [of taxes] place in the county and all the little officers of the Customs in that city recommended by his utter enemy. I desire particularly to know if I might encourage him to stand for Parliament man at Exeter where he has an interest to be chosen on his own credit, and I dare answer I could prevail with him as shall be judged most fit. How his character as a Churchman may agree with the present dispositions is a mystery to me and I shall with patience wait at home till the unriddling of the Juntissimo.

Wood, thus involved in the political schemes of the great — 'Juntissimo' referred to the inner ring of the Whig leaders — evidently obtained the necessary backing. His character as a churchman was demonstrated to Tories by his vote against the impeachment of Dr Sacheverell.

Sacheverell, for reasons which had little to do with religion, but with a gift for publicity, had attacked on religious grounds the very basis of the Revolution of 1688. His ill-advised impeachment — a Whig error of judgment — aroused a maelstrom of mob violence, religious zeal and political manipulation. The storm secured a virtual acquittal. Exeter joined with gusto in the bonfires and ringing of church bells, the drinking and tumult which expressed the jubilation of the High Tories of cathedral cities, though not necessarily that of their bishops.[24] The Sacheverell affair and increasing war-weariness brought down the Whigs and in the summer of 1710 the Tories wielded the government influence which contributed to their electoral victory. Exeter returned its neighbour, the Tory squire Sir Copplestone Bampfylde of Poltimore, a hard-drinking member of the October Club who dabbled in Jacobitism, the first of the succession of landed gentry who represented the city for the rest of the eighteenth century. The junior member was once more the veteran High Tory, Alderman John Snell, by then over seventy years of age.

In 1713, the last general election of Anne's reign, two Tories, John Bampfylde of Poltimore, brother of Sir Copplestone and like him a Jacobite, and Francis Drewe of Broadhembury, grandson of Bishop Sparrow of Exeter, were elected. In the following election, that of 1715, the Whigs were returned with a huge majority in the House of Commons, but at Exeter the sitting Tory members were returned, again without a contest. Both voted, ineffectually, against Whig measures to reduce the legal barriers to the participation of Dissenters in public life. It was not till 1722 that the Whigs again contested the two Exeter seats, the first time since 1698. The election, as usual, was rough and rowdy. The city's bells rang to welcome the entry of the Tory candidates, John Rolle of Stevenstone and Francis Drewe, but Whig sentiment was reviving. The Tory candidates were returned with 887 and 806 votes respectively, but the Whigs received 665 and 664. It was an encouraging outcome for the Whigs, their votes, in a poll of some 1500, demonstrating the continuing existence of a hard core in Exeter. They made the most of their revival and in the general election of 1728 Whig and Tory shared the representation of Exeter without a contest.

In the ensuing general election, that of May 1734, the Whigs took both the Exeter seats, for the first time since 1695. Of the two Whig candidates one was John King, the son of Lord Chief Justice King, who therefore had local and Dissenting connections. His colleague, Thomas Balle of Mamhead, was an undistinguished country gentleman. The Tory candidates were the city's recorder, John Belfield of Paignton, serjeant-at-law, and another country gentleman, William Upcott. According to Andrew Brice the election of 1734 was the first at which the parties appeared under distinctive colours, blue for the Tories and yellow for the Whigs, and the rival mobs bawled for one or the other colour instead of the names of the candidates.[25] In a total poll of about 1,200 the Whig candidates secured 746 and 703 votes respectively. The Tories, with 561 and 511 votes, received less than half the votes cast for the defeated Whigs in the previous general election of March 1722.

After 1715 Exeter's share of the national cloth trade declined, though the city as a whole was prosperous and Walpole's policy, in which the development of industry and commerce was prominent, was not such as to antagonise the merchant class in the city. The minister himself faced a well organised attack throughout the country supported by brilliant, if meretricious, propaganda. This campaign forced the withdrawal of sensible plans to extend the excise system to wine and tobacco and to abolish the land tax. The old bogey of French Roman Catholic despotism was revived and mobs chanted 'Excise, Wooden Shoes and No Jury'. Walpole fought back, supported by the Crown and using the wide-ranging methods of influencing elections open to an eighteenth-century administration in office. The general election of 1734 in fact returned his administration to power. Exeter had petitioned against the Excise Bill and when Walpole at last fell the Chamber would express its pleasure at the overthrow of the administration whose supporters the city returned to Parliament in 1734. In that year, however, there was no strong effective Tory organisation in the city. The Chamber itself was in disarray with the freemen creating a precedent by vigorously challenging the selection of the Mayor.

As in 1695 the Whig triumph in Exeter in 1734 was transitory. John King succeeded to his father's peerage. In March 1735 he was replaced at Exeter, without a contest, by a Tory country gentleman, Sir Henry Northcote of Hayne in Newton St Cyres. Northcote, unlike his later colleague, Humphrey Sydenham, made no demur over accepting the instruction of the Chamber to promote Tory policies, such as the restoration of triennial parliaments and the reduction of placemen in the Commons. The Tory revival was consolidated by the election of May 1741. Thomas Balle was firmly discouraged by the Chamber from standing. The King's government, he was informed, 'as the succession in his illustrious house', had to be supported 'by a similar attachment to the Church of England as by Law established and a vigorous support of the Liberties of Great Britain'. Balle, in the opinion of the Chamber, had shown himself to be a 'zealous promoter of the Destruction of either [sic]'.[26] Balle, in short, was a Whig, sympathetic towards Dissent and, at the time he received this admonition, a partisan of Walpole. The Chamber's Toryism was becoming that of Dr Johnson, conservative, reverential towards bishops and, as Johnson put it, unwilling to bandy civilities with the sovereign. The politics of the city's later respectability were taking shape.

With the unopposed election of Northcote and Sydenham in 1741 the representation of Exeter passed into the hands of the 'gentlemen of England', a robust, assured class with an individuality which at times bordered on eccentricity. Humphrey Sydenham, from remote Stogumber under the Quantocks, was returned for Exeter a second time, again without a contest, in 1744. A Tory and High Churchman, he was touchy in maintaining his independence. He expressed himself 'extremely nettled' by the Chamber's instructions, issued in the form of recommendations, that he should promote with his utmost vigour the restoration of triennial parliaments and an effective Place Bill, measures long supported by the squires of the Country Party as a means of controlling a Whig administration. Sydenham threatened to refer his instructions to the House as a breach of privilege. Worse still, he supported the Jewish Naturalisation Bill of 1753 which, though limited in scope, provoked fears on the score of business competition and aroused the prejudices of bible-reading Protestants. The Town Clerk was instructed to inform both the city members that, in the opinion of the Chamber, the Bill 'may be dishonourable and detrimental to our Holy Religion, highly prejudicial to our Constitution, and injurious to our Trade and other Rights as Englishmen'.[27] In consequence, according to a contemporary, the Chamber was hostile towards Sydenham and declined to support his candidature for the general election of 1754.

Exeter's ancient tradition of supporting order in Church and State had been re-affirmed in 1715 when the Jacobite magnifico, the Duke of Ormonde, Lord High Steward of Exeter, had been impeached and had fled to France. The Prince of Wales, the future George II, accepted the honour and received the patent from the hands of the Exeter Dissenter's son, Lord Chief Justice King. During the Forty-Five, like other property holders and investors throughout the kingdom, the Chamber blenched at the prospect of a successful raid by Highland caterans under a Catholic prince. Men were raised and armed at the city's expense. Leaseholders of the Chamber were promised concessions to their heirs if they died in battle or died later from their wounds.[28] William of Orange was now 'our great deliverer'. From the mid-eighteenth century there would be no stauncher defenders of the 'Glorious Revolution' than the Chamber and Cathedral Chapter of Exeter. Exeter's Toryism had become the conservative traditionalism of a provincial capital, a habit and an attitude of mind rather than an effective political creed.

NOTES

1. HMC 29 *Portland* iv, p. 446: J. D. Colt to Robert Harley, 22.3.1690.
2. P.S. Fritz, *The English Ministers and Jacobites between the Rebellions of 1715 and 1745*, App. iv.
3. *Western Times*, 20.11.1868.
4. A.A. Brockett, 'The Political and Social Influence of the Exeter Dissenters', *DAT*, 1961, p. 184.
5. DRO, ECA, Act Books, 4.1.1698.
6. *CSPD William III*, 1696, p. 41, Elwill to Sir George Treby, 21.2.1696.
7. *Calendar of Treasury Books*, xxiii, part 2, 1709, p. 348.
8. J.J. Alexander, 'Exeter Members of Parliament, part iv, 1688-1832', *DAT* 1930 and R. Sedgwick, *The House of Commons 1715-1754*, vol. 1.
9. R. North, *Life of the Rt Hon. Francis North*, p. 216.
10. M.M. Rowe and A.M. Jackson, *Exeter Freemen*, passim.
11. *Journals of the House of Commons 1688-93*, pp. 188, 224.
12. H. Horwitz, *Parliament, Policy and Politics in the reign of William III*, p. 150, footnote 96.
13. DRO, ECA, Act Books, 4.1.1698, 20.11.1699; Corporation of the Poor, Court Book 1698-1702,16.9.1701.
14. J.J. Alexander, 'The Exeter Election of 1695', *DCNQ*, 1930-31. The contest at Exeter was between the war party, primarily Whig, and the anti-war party, primarily Tory. The outcome would therefore have been of great interest to foreign diplomats.
15. *The Substance of what Sir Bartholomew Shower spoke at the Guildhall Exon, August 19 1698*, Exeter 1698.
16. HMC 29 *Portland* iv, p. 177: Poulett to Harley, 2.5.1705.
17. *ibid.*, p. 222: Defoe to Harley, 14.8.1705 and p. 270, 'An Abstract of my Journey', 25.7.1705.

NOTES *continued*

18. *ibid.,* p. 28: Godolphin to Harley, 4.12.1701.
19. *ibid.,* p. 426: Poulett to Harley, 16.7.1707.
20. HMC 29 *Portland* iv, pp. 213-4: Defoe to Harley from Crediton, 30.7.1705. For Trelawney's battle with his clergy see N. Sykes, 'The Cathedral Chapter of Exeter and the General Election of 1705', *English Historical Review,* 1930.
21. *Cal. Home Office Papers,* 1714-19, CCxxiii(5), p. 380.
22. J.J. Alexander, 'Exeter Members of Parliament', *DAT* 1930, p. 211.
23. HMC 29 *Portland* iv, p. 420: Poulett to Harley, 16.6.1707.
24. G. Holmes, *The Trial of Dr Sacheverell,* passim.
25. Andrew Brice, *The Mobiad,* p. xi.
26. DRO, ECA, Act Books, 31.3.1741.
27. HMC 73 *City of Exeter,* pp. 245-6; DRO, ECA, Act Books, 16.10.1763; Cobbett, *Parliamentary History,* xiv, 1813, p. 1431.
28. DRO, ECA, 15.10.1745, 178.10.1745.

Chapter Five

Georgian High Noon 1760-1793

Defoe's formula for the vitality and prosperity of the early eighteenth-century city had been a blend of gentry and good company with trade and manufacture. In the last decades of the century the value of the latter components fluctuated and declined. By the 1790s the ancient cloth industry was moribund beyond hope of recovery and banking and ancillary activities rather than investment in industry became the favoured road to wealth. That of the first increased until in the days of the Regency the key to Exeter's prosperity was to be found in the city's social amenities and attractions for the polite world of Jane Austen's novels. The representation of the city in Parliament, once the climax of the *cursus honorum* for a city merchant, had become the undisputed monopoly of the landed gentry, whether Whig or Tory.

True, there were occasions when in monetary terms the cloth trade in the evening of its life recalled the great days of the Augustan city. In terms of money the peak year of 1710 was surpassed in 1775, and again in 1780, years when the value of exports was reckoned to be £773,000 and £476,000 respectively, compared with £473,000 in 1710. The trade had shown remarkable ability to survive dislocation caused by war, especially the War of American Independence (1776-1783). Exeter's main markets by then were in Spain and Italy across seas exposed to the Bourbon fleets and privateers. There was still an outlet in France, but the Dutch market, though still substantial, was dwindling. The German market had declined sharply. The city still retained an extensive coastal trade, especially in Sunderland coal, at a time when coal was rapidly replacing the dwindling supply of wood. Wines were imported in ever-increasing quantity from Portugal and there were vestiges of the old triangular trade with North America, particularly Newfoundland, and the Mediterranean.[1] Tea was an important import and the Exeter tea-merchants complained bitterly in 1783 when it was enacted that tea seized by the customs should be sold in London instead of in local customs houses, thus adding to the cost of carriage of the cheaper teas sold in Exeter.[2] Despite the efforts of the Chamber Exeter could no longer claim to be a port of national significance.

By 1788 Dartmouth had outstripped Exeter as the largest port of registration in Devon. Ships were increasing in size and by 1760, in spite of the Canal, few vessels except coasters could reach Exeter's quay. Larger vessels usually anchored off Starcross after experiencing the difficulties of wind and tide in entering the Exe estuary and the consequent delays. A vessel missing the highest spring tide had to wait for two weeks.[3]

On the other hand in 1778 a correspondent in the *Exeter Flying Post* expressed the view that the five guinea bounty offered for enlistment in the army would not have much effect because 'the present state of Trade affords full employment'.[4] There were, indeed, grounds for optimism, as the figures for 1775 and 1780 indicate. But the crucial figure was Exeter's share in the national trade and this was declining; by the 1790s Yorkshire woollens dominated the market. Devon cloth had become a pensioner dependent for survival on the goodwill of the East India Company which could afford to sell cloth at a loss and recoup from the handsome profits from tea. It was some recompense, perhaps, that so many of the officers of the Company would retire to Exeter and foster a demand for houses and consumer goods.

As an industrial city, by eighteenth-century standards, Exeter was being left in a backwater by the changing tides and currents of national economic life. With bad inland communications, an unsuitable terrain for canals and no expansion of mass purchasing power such as was stimulated by mining and other growing industries in the North, entrepreneurial risk-taking was discouraged. Banking rather than merchandising now offered the surest road to wealth and power, and able businessmen with fortunes based on the cloth industry, John Baring, John Duntze, the Kennaways and Samuel Milford, were foremost in sensing the wind of change. Clothiers and merchants engaged both in the financing of the various stages of the cloth industry and in overseas trade had long been accustomed to handling credit. Attorneys and others with spare cash, their own or their clients', advertised on the lines of David Phillips, builder and auctioneer, who announced that he was ready to offer on freehold security 'several sums of money from £4,000 to £330'.[5] In the second half of the eighteenth century banking spread through the small clothing towns of Devon, Ashburton, Totnes and Newton Abbot, as well as in Exeter itself. Hitherto, apart from the employment of capital in trade, investment had been virtually limited to real estate.

At Exeter the new banks were founded almost wholly on capital derived from the cloth industry. The first to open, in 1769, was the Exeter Bank, under the partnership of William Mackworth Praed, Sir John Duntze and Joseph Sanders. Praed had a political interest in the city and had already invested in real estate. The Duntze fortune came from cloth. Sanders, a prosperous woollen draper, like so many bankers, was a member of the Society of Friends, though his son, Charles Rogers Sanders, was to marry an archdeacon's daughter in the Cathedral itself.[6] The City Bank opened at Exeter in 1786 with the Unitarian Samuel Milford, son and son-in-law of sergemakers, as senior partner. In 1770 John Baring and Charles Collyns launched the Devonshire Bank in partnership with Alderman Gregory Jackson, ironmonger,[7] who had already made many loans to the Chamber. Jackson, who was mayor in 1772–3, dealt in naval stores such as hemp, pitch and tar. The Devonshire Bank provided the Chamber's first bank loan, a small advance to buy corn for resale at cost, in 1790. Charles Collyns himself became a member of the Chamber in 1799, and in 1802 was the first banker to become mayor of Exeter. The partners of the General Bank, opened in 1792, were all members of the Society of Friends, at their head the much repected Joshua Williams. The following year Richard and William Kennaway launched the Western Bank with Sir Henry Stafford Northcote of Pynes as one of the proprietors, although he retired from the partnership in 1803. Thus by 1793 six banks were operating in Exeter and competing briskly. In that year the Western Bank announced that interest on deposits would be raised from two-and-a-half to three per cent. The General Bank followed suit 'in consequence of unquestionable information that a Bank lately opened in this city' would pay the higher rate.[8]

Exeter's greatest asset was still its position as the nodal point of land communications in the West Country, as an Act of Parliament put it, on 'the public High Road leading from London and the Eastern Parts of this Kingdom to the Western Parts of the County of Devon, and to the County of Devon and the County of Cornwall'. It was the road that led to the western ports, to the fleet anchorage in Torbay in an age when, beyond the Western Approaches, naval and commercial war was fought across the seas and oceans of the world. Roads offered a safer means of transport than the sea could provide, especially in wartime. An American privateer was reported within two miles of Bude in 1779, and the cannonades of the combined fleet of France and Spain were heard at Plymouth, bringing all business to a standstill. Two years later bystanders in the developing coastal resort of Exmouth watched a French armed lugger take a Scarborough coaster.[9] The ports of the Exe estuary, as they had done two centuries earlier, shared in the hazards and profits of privateering. Topsham sent out ships like the 400-ton *King George,* well armed and needing a crew of 150 men, and at Starcross the *Molly* called for men willing to make their fortunes.

The roads brought the wagons and coaches, the marching troops, generals and their staffs; the Olympian Chatham himself was acclaimed by Exeter when he came to receive the freedom of the city in 1771; Admiral Hood, fresh from his achievements in the Caribbean, came to stay with his brother-in-law Alderman Walker in 1773 and seamen in Exeter hauled his carriage in triumph through the streets.[10] The roads brought territorial magnates like the Duke of Richmond to inspect the Sussex Militia, royal dukes, York and Clarence, and also John Wilkes returning from a brief exile. Genteel tourism, too, was beginning. In 1788 Mrs Piozzi, formerly Dr Johnson's Mrs Thrale, asked why there was no talk of the beauties of Exmouth; she described Devon as 'the Italy of England'.[11]

By means of the turnpike trusts the roads were being developed and both the speed and comfort of travel were improving for all but the poor. In the 1760s, and in good conditions, London was brought within two long days' journey from Exeter by way of Dorchester, Blandford and Salisbury for a fare of £2. From the New Inn, in the last years of its long life, coaches set out for Plymouth on three mornings a week offering breakfast at Ashburton and dinner at Plymouth for a fare of 15 shillings. In the 1780s mail coaches between Exeter and London were scheduled to complete the journey in twenty-four hours, charging £2 12*s*. 6*d*. per passenger. They were supported by the slower Balloon coaches between The Hotel in Cathedral Yard and the Saracen's Head, London at a fare of £2 for the four inside passengers and 25 shillings for the uncomfortable outside seats.[12] By 1784 coaches were leaving the major hotels daily, and the leading innkeepers and coach proprietors were men of mark. John Land moved in 1772 from the Half Moon in High Street to the New London Inn (formerly the Oxford Inn) in a more spacious situation outside the East Gate, the point at which all major communications converged. Coach-building was becoming a major industry in Exeter; by the early years of the nineteenth century one coach-builder employed over seventy men.

In the deep lanes of rural Devon the sledge and the pack horse were still in use. In 1796 Marshall wrote that 'Twenty years ago there was not a pair of wheels in the county, at least not upon a farm; and nearly the same may be said at present.'[13] This was an exaggeration but the rector of Bridford, a few miles west of Exeter, later recorded that at the end of the eighteenth century there were still no carts in his parish. But the main roads carried a heavy wheeled traffic. In the forefront of the local transport industry was the wagoner Thomas Russell. In 1786 Russell's wagons were advertised to take four days from the Bear in South Street to the Bell and the Saracen's Head in Friday Street, London, a possibility in good summer weather. They connected at Exeter with the wagons leaving for Falmouth and Plymouth twice a week.[14] The wagons of W. Clapcott & Co. of Exeter, Plymouth and Falmouth, were scheduled to leave the Castle Inn, Cheapside, on Tuesdays and Fridays at 3 o'clock in the afternoons and to arrive at the Mermaid, Exeter, on the Friday and Tuesday following.

The transport industry in all aspects was a major source of employment and required vast quantities of fodder for the horses. Above all Exeter's leading inns were entering upon their greatest period of fame and prosperity before the Railway Age. Many who entered the trade made it their business to cater for the tastes of fashionable society, some having acquired experience in the service of neighbouring nobility and gentry, others by working in subordinate roles in the inns. William Gates, the proprietor of a flourishing hair-dressing and perfumery business in High Street, invested in the Globe in Cathedral Yard and left his sister in charge of the perfumery. Richard Lloyd, once cook to one of Exeter's Members of Parliament, John Tuckfield, acquired the White Swan in High Street, a tavern and coffee house with stalls for over sixty horses, which had already had the distinction of accommodating Lord Chatham in 1771. It was improved and enlarged by Lloyd who went on to attempt to restore the fortunes of the ancient New Inn and Hotel, as it was styled in the new fashion, while his cook, James Brewer, took over the White Swan. In 1782, however, the New Inn in High Street was sold with stabling for forty horses, three dining rooms and forty rooms for guests.[15]

The Hotel in Cathedral Yard, built in 1769, was acquired by Peter Berlon, of French origin, who first established its position as Exeter's social centre for balls, assemblies and concerts. Berlon went bankrupt in 1774, selling his horses, coaches and chaises, his furniture and equipment, and also his supporting stock and fodder on farms on the outskirts of the city.[16] The Hotel then passed to Thomas Thompson who, from 1778 to 1793, re-established its reputation and continued the coaching business. In the coffee room, Thompson informed his clients, were to be found all the London and provincial papers; turtle and pease soups were available at all hours. One of Thompson's employees prospered sufficiently to move to the Globe, Exmouth.

Assizes and quarter sessions were now more than ever social occasions when balls, assemblies and concerts were held at the leading inns. Local defence matters, the organisation of militia and volunteers and the payment of bounties for enlistment also brought to Exeter the Lord Lieutenant and the leading landowners. Military occasions, the reviews of regular troops, militia and volunteers, were watched by hosts of spectators and ended with convivial dinners. Each summer the gentry organised races on Haldon. Also rougher sports such as the main of cocks fought between the Gentlemen of Devon and the Gentlemen of Dorset, at ten guineas a battle with forty-one cocks a side, were organised at the Half Moon in July 1784. Exeter was even infected by what Mrs Piozzi described as the 'Rabies Balloonica' when, in 1766, a balloonist was airborne from Rougemont and landed in an irate Farmer Whipple's cornfield in the parish of Cadbury.[17] Whipple assessed his damages at five guineas. Down river, at Powderham, young Lord Courtenay entertained lavishly and instituted popular regattas at Starcross. Contested elections were of course notoriously popular with innkeepers, such as those who entertained the gentry and free-holders, some thousand strong, who rode into the city in 1780 to support the candidature of John Parker and John Rolle.

Gentlemen were expected to spend as such and the luxury trades flourished. But an increasing number of middle-class Exonians were enabled to compete in conspicuous consumption. Improved roads brought to Exeter new fashions and household goods, including the latest products of the Potteries brought down by the prosperous 'china-man' W. Eardley. By the end of the century even local cloth was facing the competition of new materials, cheaper, easier to clean and lighter to wear, muslins from Glasgow and cotton goods from Manchester. Sometime before 1789 Mrs Colson, a war-widow, embarked on the foundation of a business which until far into the twentieth century was well known in the South-West under her name. Describing herself as 'linen draper, haberdasher, milliner and tea-dealer' she announced that she had taken over the stock of a linen warehouse.[18] Milliners, habit-makers, hairdressers and perfumers provided the latest modes from Paris, London and Bath. Shirley Woolmer, father of a future Conservative mayor, set up in business near the Guildhall in 1783 as book-seller and stationer. He provided a circulating library and undertook that any book required would be 'instantly acquired from London, cost what it may'.[19]

Exeter's first theatre, except for inn courtyards, had been a cramped and dirty building behind the Guildhall. This was replaced in 1787, with the blessing of the Chamber, by a theatre in the new Bedford Street opened under the patronage of Lord Courtenay. In the following year the Kembles were engaged. Mrs Siddons appeared in 1789, playing in the popular historical dramas of the day, as Lady Randolph in *Douglas* and as Lady Macbeth. The theatre now depended on the encouragement provided by genteel society, on the patronage of county families, the officers of the garrison and the mayors, such as Edward Ragueneau, who chose a comedy for the Christmas season of 1790. The amenities demanded by the theatre-going public, and the provision of lavish effects, such as volcanoes, were expensive. In 1791, after the opening of the new theatre, 'decorated with scenery and ornaments superior to almost any out of London', the management was reduced to organising a special subscription to pay off debts. But it was these years, the remarkable period of economic resurgence at the end of the American war, that saw the genesis of the great days of the provincial theatre which lasted at Exeter until the First World War.

It was also a time when the dancing master became a feature of the Exeter scene, especially French refugees like Mons. Le Charriere, of Paris, who, in or before 1787, opened his academy in Southernhay to teach the minuette and gavotte, country dances, cotillons and even the hornpipe, and was followed by another compatriot from Paris entreating the patronage of the nobility and gentry.[20] Later, as the romantic movement began, a dancing master arrived from London to teach reels and 'Scotch steps'.

Respectable citizens, in a highly competitive world, were increasingly acknowledging the practical and social value of education. There was money to pay for it and by the last decade of the eighteenth century private schools were proliferating in Exeter to meet the demand. The business world was advertising for educated young men, clean, with good manners, able to write well and qualified to draw up accounts, suitable applicants being offered a good salary of £30 to £40 a year. In 1789 Mr Cronhelm's academy in Bartholomew Street offered 'young gentlemen' English grammar, French, Italian and Spanish, while 'commercial youth' were instructed in business correspondence, book-keeping and the mysteries of foreign exchange. There were courses in stenography 'as useful an art as any man of business or scholar can be master of '. Boys 'designed for the military line' could receive instruction in geometry, fortification and the preparation of plans. The Devonshire Mathematical, Naval and Commercial Academy provided education suitable for land-stewards, 'the mechanical professions', the navy and trade. Clergymen, such as the Rev. Collyns with his Classical Academy in Paris Street, provided the classical education required for the professions. For high-class private education for boys the Rev. John Stabback, rector of St Edmunds, charged as much as £40 a year for tuition in English, Greek and Latin with board and washing in his house on St David's Hill; but this was for the sons of clergy and gentry who would usually go on to a university. Thomas Turner's Exeter Academy specialised in arithmetic, book-keeping and drawing and taught the handling of the latest telescopes and mathematical instruments. Across the river in Alphington Thomas Halloran prepared his boarders for careers in commerce or at sea and also provided instruction in the classics, French and dancing, and as early as 1776 Messrs Weekes and Stokes announced from St Martins Lane that 'In order to stir up a joint Emulation among their pupils (so absolutely necessary) they will be publicly examined.'[21] Though the Grammar School was prestigious and had had some distinguished pupils its numbers were declining and by 1818 there would be only twenty-two boarders, each paying 30 guineas a year, and ten day boys.[22]

Girls' schools were severely handled by the Evangelical Hannah Moore for their cult of 'abused, misunderstood or misapplied accomplishments'.[23] Some reports of prizegivings at girls' schools in Exeter are reminiscent of Miss Pinkerton's Academy at the time of Becky Sharp. (They were, of course, esentially social occasions.) The girls' schools were expensive, but as educational establishments they were not to be despised. Mrs Chappell's boarding school near the Cathedral taught English grammar, French, reading, writing and arithmetic, music, drawing and embroidery, and also paid particular attention to morals. For this parents paid twenty-five guineas a year. Mrs Braddock's school in the same neighbourhood, and Mrs Webber's Boarding and Day School for Young Ladies, hinted at some corroboration of Hannah Moore's comments. The first taught 'every fashionable accomplishment of all kinds of useful and ornamental work'; the second taught music 'and other polite accomplishments'. Mrs Braddock's Boarding School for girls charged £14 a year for board and instruction in English, geography and needlework.[24]

The Company of Weavers, Tuckers and Shearmen still provided

education of a sort, in unsuitable premises, and paid an allowance of £5 or £10 a year to the master.[25] In general, however, the provision of education for the poor, never adequate, was at a particularly low ebb and it was not till the end of the century that attempts were made to revive it. Some education, usually rudimentary, was provided by dames' schools, and it was at such a school in Magdalen Street in the later 1790s that the young Henry Ellis learnt his ABC.[26]

Henry Ellis Sr, the son of a farmer of Newton St Cyres, had failed for lack of capital in his business as a fuller. He became a clerk in the Exeter wharfinger's office and later earned £80 a year as a trusted employee of Robert Sanders, iron merchant. In the reign of George III this was comfortably above the lower levels of middle-class income. Ellis also owned a little property and had a small sum invested in government stock.[27] He was well read, his books, in addition to the bible, including Thompson's *Seasons,* which Gilbert White so often quoted, Young's *Night Thoughts,* Bunyan's *Pilgrim's Progress,* works by Richardson, Fielding, Smollett and Goldsmith and some volumes of theology. He married the daughter of a tanner of Heavitree. Young Henry, born in 1790, was placed, when he was nine and a half years old, with Philip Grove who, in 1800, became the last headmaster of the then moribund Tuckers' School. He next attended the efficient establishment of Mr J. Mullings, a Young Gentlemen's Academy then in Waterbeer Street and according to Henry Ellis regarded as the leading commercial school in the city with over one hundred pupils. Mr Mullings was no narrow pedagogue. During the assizes he gave his boys holidays to enable them to go to the Castle 'to bring the youthful mind acquainted with the forms of our Courts of Justice'.

The family income needed to be supported — young Henry's sister Elizabeth had to earn a little money as a milliner — but the Ellises could certainly not be classed with the poor whose plight from the 1760s onward was forced with growing urgency upon the notice of the more prosperous. There had been bad times in the first half of the century but in general the period had been marked by good harvests, low prices and, on the whole, little unemployment.[28] After 1760 the prices of foodstuffs began to rise, stimulated by mediocre or disastrous harvests, and also by the dislocation caused by war. Wages remained virtually unchanged for fifty years.[29] In 1804 the woolcombers of the South West would claim, apparently with justice, that their wages had remained static for the last one hundred years. Certainly the wages of labourers in rural Devon changed little between 1700 and 1790. In Exeter labourers' wages rose from 1s. 2d. a day at the beginning of the century to 1s. 4d. at the end, craftsmen's wages from about 1s. 8d. to 2 s. But the proportion of daily earnings that a labourer would have had to spend on basic food, reckoned in terms of the price of wheat, had risen sharply. In the best of circumstances, with uninterrupted employment and good health, the labouring poor of the city could exist, but the margin between existence and starvation was precarious. At a time when Exeter was approaching its zenith as the social capital of the South West and when the 'spirit of improvement' was in the air, the balance began to tip decisively against the poor, and they comprised at least half the population of the city.

Food riots first occurred in September 1766 when a mob threatened to destroy a corn mill. A cart leaving the city with a load of peas was stopped and the driver roughly handled before being rescued by the timely intervention of city magistrates. Further attempts to send loads of corn, bacon and other foodstuffs out of the city were also thwarted and a warehouse containing provisions was broken into by a mob. Some arrests were made and constables had to repel an attack on the Guildhall intended to rescue prisoners. In St Sidwells magistrates and constables were stoned. At Topsham a vessel laden with corn was plundered and the corn itself distributed at what was regarded as a fair price.[30]

By the standards of eighteenth-century rioting the Exeter affair was of minor significance. There were similar disturbances the same year at Honiton, Ottery, Sidmouth and Crediton, but none was as serious as those in Bath, Tetbury, Malmesbury and in expanding industrial towns such as Leicester, Norwich, Derby and Nottingham. The King, opening the November session of Parliament, observed in the Speech from the Throne that 'notwithstanding My Care for My People, a spirit of the most daring insurrection has in divers Parts broke forth in violence of the most criminal Nature.'[31]

Exeter still belonged to the older England. The authorities, like those in Devon as a whole, attributed the disorder to exasperation at the 'infamous practices of Forestalling and Regrating' rather than to criminal intent. The buying of foodstuffs by dealers in anticipation of price rises, or to corner the market and thus push up prices, had offended public morality since medieval times. Respectable tradesmen were enrolled as special constables but only two individuals were subsequently presented for trial and, according to the *Exeter Evening Post,* the rioters were rather 'objects of charity than resentment'.[32] This view was widely shared. In North Devon Lord Fortescue bought large quantities of corn for resale to the poor at cost. On 7 November 1766 the Chamber, fearing that scarcity of corn and high prices would not only 'strike at the Trade and Commerce of this Nation but [also] loosen the very bonds of government', requested the city's MPs to make strenuous endeavours in Parliament to procure 'an adequate remedy'.[33] It also ventured to suggest that the profits made by middlemen should be restrained. The grand jury of Devon noted 'with the deepest concern the Distresses of the People, on account of the high price of provisions' and urged likewise, as well as recommending that laws should be made against profiteering in substitutes for corn, such as potatoes and the produce of gardens and orchards. In 1796 Joseph Bidwell, a trader of St

Thomas, announced the arrival from Baltimore of a shipment of Indian corn (maize), maize flour and some wheat flour; but subsequent attempts to remove 'ill-grounded prejudice' against maize suggests that it was not popular. Wheat in fact did fall in price that year but only momentarily and farmers were soon being accused of making fortunes out of 'the wreck of the industrious mechanic and inferior tradesman'.[34]

The winter of 1771–2 was epecially severe and in the following April there was trouble in St Sidwells where a mob stopped a wagon setting out for Taunton with flour and defied authority in the person of the mayor, the town clerk and the constables. The winter of 1775–6 was also hard. The Exe was frozen from Exeter to Topsham, the mills were deprived of power and it was estimated that more than two thousand families were in distress through unemployment and other circumstances. In 1784 a committee distributed relief to 2,318 families comprising 'at least 7,000 persons'. During the hard winter of 1788–9, when there was much frost and snow, two collections for the relief of the city's poor were reported to have provided relief for 2,418 and 2,480 families respectively.[35] Applications for relief may not always have been scrutinised very strictly; on the other hand the city parishes were small and sufficiently close-knit for clergy, parish officers and neighbours to keep a check on the distribution of the relief for which they had raised the funds. In January 1783 the Corporation of the Poor attributed its own current financial problems at the time to 'The Increase in the Poor, the Advance of Provisions, and the great decline of Commerce (particularly in the Woollen Industry)'. Exeter was faced by a problem created by growth of population coinciding with the decline of its industry and soon to be compounded by the conditions arising out of twenty years of war. In July 1789 the local papers announced the fall of the Bastille, the premonitory tremor of an earthquake that would shatter the assumptions that had dominated public and private life since 1688. For the moment, however, the old regime in the city received the accolade conferred by a royal visit, the first since 1671. In August Exeter was informed that George III would shortly arrive from Weymouth.

In 1788 the serious illness of the King had led to a political crisis caused by controversy over a regency which threatened to place the kingdom into the hands of the Prince of Wales and Charles James Fox, neither of whom appealed to serious citizens in the provinces. Public opinion in Devon, as expressed by the country gentlemen and the urban oligarchies, expressed firm support for the Prime Minister, the younger Pitt, against a Whig faction. The Whig proposals were defeated in the Commons and a meeting in Exeter's Guildhall passed resolutions thanking the Members of Parliament who had voted with the majority. At that meeting Archdeacon Moore made it clear that in a Tory city the revolution of 1688 had at length become glorious in the eyes of the Church. Also prominent among the speakers in the Guildhall in January 1789 was Samuel Milford, one of the proprietors of the City Bank, and, until his death in 1800, a member of the Committee of Thirteen which administered the affairs of the Unitarian church, George's Meeting.[36]

The political crisis passed with the recovery of the King, an event celebrated at Exeter with gunfire and illuminations. The Chamber, supported by the incorporated trades and militia bands, marched in solemn procession to the Cathedral. The officers of the Inniskilling Dragoons entertained the mayor and leading citizens. The old Toryism of the city, its veneration of Stuart monarchs as the Lord's anointed and its unwilling acceptance of the Hanoverians, had long since been transmuted into a devotion to the throne in the person of George III, who himself successfully contested the pretentions of the great Whig families. One hundred years after the revolution of 1688 the city's loyalty was an expression of a determination to hold fast to stability, property and privilege in a dangerous world. Indeed the royal visit conferred a reassuring prestige on a city becoming uncertain of its traditional status.

The royal party was received at the site of the former East Gate (demolished five years previously) by the mayor, Jonathan Burnett, and members of the Chamber.[37] Two hundred respectable tradesmen had been marshalled as special constables and crush barriers were erected in the High Street. There was a procession through crowded streets to the Deanery, and a service in the Cathedral attended not only by the Chamber but also by the incorporated trades of the city in all their traditional finery, each headed by its beadle in lace-trimmed cloak and hat and bearing his staff of office. Thereafter the King held a levée in the bishop's palace, the first to be held since his recovery from illness.

Fanny Burney, the novelist, who held a position in the royal household, accompanied 'the Royals' as she termed them. She was impressed by the enthusiastic welcome of the crowds, by 'the rejoicing, the hallooing, and singing', though she thought that 'the excessive and intemperate eagerness of the people' discouraged the royal party from venturing into the streets. Her fastidious taste was not impressed by the city which she found 'close and ugly',[38] and indeed Exeter was still essentially a medieval city, compact, intimate and unplanned. There was as yet little of the classical symmetry, the vistas, terraces and crescents, approved by Georgian taste.

The royal visit provoked the disputes and recriminations that are not unusual on such occasions. The Chamber had spent lavishly. In the Receiver's accounts 'The Expences of their Majesties honouring this City with a Visit' amount to £437, including £130 for transparencies and illuminations.[39] Alderman Dennis was paid £24 to re-equip the city band with lace-trimmed cloaks. Preparations were made for the royal party to be entertained in the Guildhall and it was therefore galling to find that the King preferred a quiet tour of the Cathedral in the company of the Bishop and the Dean. The irascible Alderman Dennis swept into the Cathedral with the intention of expostulating to the King himself, but Dean Buller, whom Miss Burney described as 'very civil and in high glee', was the grandson of the masterful Sir Jonathan Trelawny. He firmly intercepted the irate alderman and the King was left in peace. The explanation of Exeter's historian Alexander Jenkins, that the King wished to avoid a precedent exposing him to endless similar entertainment, is likely to be correct.[40]

The King's visit to the Cathedral in that fateful year 1789 underlined the role of the Church and its bishops in contemporary society. Since 1688 religion had become essentially a matter of civilised behaviour. In 1732 a contributor to the *Gentleman's Magazine* had expressed the view that the business of the priesthood was to 'instruct the People in such a Method of Life as tends to render them happy here, and on the Principles of Freethinking, pleasing to the Divine Being.' The vicar of St Lawrence in the High Street preached that religion, whatever some might say of it, was a 'good natur'd institution' tending to soothe the passions and to harmonise with Newtonian physics.[41] But religion as a form of good manners was becoming meagre fare for the hungry sheep of the Christian flock, and more than good manners were required to answer the questions posed by revolutionary France. With the notable exception of Lancelot Blackburne (1717–24) Exeter's bishops were conscientious and well-educated men. As members of the House of Lords they were also politicians and, with governments sometimes dependent on their votes, long absences from the diocese were necessary. Yet Bishop Frederick Keppel (1762–77), son of the second Earl of Albemarle, contrived to hold systematic visitations despite the difficulties of travel. Keppel's example was followed by Bishop John Ross (1778–92), a member of the Royal Society, who personally examined all candidates for deacons' orders and in a sermon to the House of Lords advocated toleration for Dissenters. Keppel confirmed over 3,600 persons at Exeter in 1764, Bishop Ross over 5,000 between 1782 and 1794.[42]

Dissent was no longer persecuted but, subject to the insidious pressure of social disapproval, dwindled and fell apart. In 1715 adult Dissenters in Exeter, excluding the Society of Friends, were estimated at 3,070, including 2,250 Presbyterians. With the small community of Quakers, and children, the Dissenters must have numbered some 4,500, perhaps between one quarter and one third of the total population of the city. By 1744, according to the returns of the Anglican clergy, the Dissenting community had fallen to 1610.[43] The Presbyterians had split over the nature of the Trinity, a complex matter of religion and philosophy which, in the fourth century AD had fully exercised Greek intellectual sublety. The dispute was followed by conferences, ejections and secession. In 1719 the Mint Chapel was founded by an unorthodox minister and his supporters, seceding from James's Meeting. In 1753 the Exeter Presbyterian Assembly abandoned its attempt to impose orthodoxy on candidates for the ministry. Individual congregations were left to reach a decision on the views required of their ministers, marking, writes Allan Brockett, 'the end of Presbyterianism in Devonshire and Cornwall'.[44] Henceforward many of the ablest and most successful heirs of the old Dissent went over to Unitarianism.

Others, many of them humble folk such as artisans and small shopkeepers, and especially the underemployed, looked elsewhere for the comfort which the formal, and sometimes perfunctory, Anglican services failed to provide. Whatever the devotion and charity of individual priests, the parish churches did not encourage active participation by the poor. Vestries were composed of prosperous tradesmen whose main concern was the menace of Jacobinism and the influence of Tom Paine. Eighteenth-century rationalism, and the agnosticism of many of the upper classes, concealed the yearning of many ordinary people for support amid the hardships of the temporal world and for the compensating assurance of salvation in the eternal. John and Charles Wesley first visited Exeter in 1739, and in 1743 Charles Wesley preached, it was said, to one thousand persons. This was an innovation, and Exeter was not disposed towards religious innovations. The Victorian city would 'rabble' clergy who re-introduced the surplice for the sermon, burn effigies of the Tractarians and later assault the Salvation Army. In 1745, a small congregation of Methodists meeting in a building in Waterbeer Street, behind the Guildhall, were attacked by a mob watched, and encouraged, by spectators in the Three Tuns. The mayor, John Hawker, was reluctant to intervene; as a Methodist eye-witness put it, 'The Men in Power were in no hurry to repress the Tumult'.[45] For ten days the small Methodist community was exposed to the practised brutality of an eighteenth-century mob with some encouragement from their 'betters' and with little interference by the aldermen-magistrates. Forty years on there were still only twenty-six Methodists in the city.

But while Exeter in general accepted St Paul's teaching that lawful temporal authority was ordained by God, there was no disposition to regard the ministers of the Crown as men enjoying divine protection. John Wilkes, a gifted and cynical libertine, contrived to become a standard bearer of constitutional liberty and the hero not only of the London mob but also of a cathedral city such as Exeter. Exeter's own recorder, Serjeant Glynn, was one of Wilkes's most effective supporters and was elected with Wilkes as Member of Parliament for the great constituency of Middlesex. The Wilkes affair, which plagued King and government from 1763 to 1774, was a brouhaha of rioting, party politics and stately definitions of high constitutional principles. When, in 1763, Lord Chief Justice Pratt held that Wilkes, as a Member of Parliament, could not be arrested for libel, the Chamber at Exeter hastened to bestow on Pratt the freedom of the city, for 'maintaining and vindicating the Liberty and Property of the Subject which makes so essential a part of the Legal and Constitutional Rights of a free People'. Pratt himself returned thanks to the 'capital of that county where his father and ancestors had been born'.[46] The Mayor presided over a meeting in the Guildhall which was addressed by Serjeant Glynn on the 'violated right of election in the person of Mr Wilkes'. The city's Members of Parliament, both Tory, went to some pains to demonstrate that they had voted with the minority and against the government on the issue of Wilkes's seat in the House.[47] In 1774, when Wilkes was finally released from comfortable confinement, Exeter celebrated with illuminations and peals on the church bells.

Even dukes, reigning in splendour at the peak of the social pyramid, were apt in those days to be reminded by local popular opinion that they were but human, as the Duke of Bedford found when he visited Exeter in 1769, during the Wilkes affair, to inspect Bedford House and to receive the freedom of the city. John Russell, fourth Duke of Bedford, had held high offices of state since 1745. He had been associated with the unpopular cider tax. He had also been accused, unjustly, of accepting bribes for the return to France and Spain of territories captured during the Seven Years War. Since he had also been an opponent of Wilkes his arrival at Exeter provided a suitable excuse for demonstrations with banners proclaiming 'Wilkes and Liberty' and 'No Cider Tax'. On arrival at the Guildhall the Duke found the mob, in his own words, 'very outrageous'. It became 'extremely outrageous' when, after dining with the judges, he went to the Cathedral for a reception by Bishop Keppel and the Chapter. The mob forced an entry into the Cathedral itself and the Duke had some difficulty in escaping to the Bishop's palace. On his departure from Devon he experienced further rough treatment at Honiton where dogs were set upon his horse and he himself was pelted with stones.[48] He was not unaccustomed to such treatment, having been handled even more roughly in London in 1765 for his opposition to reducing the tariff on Italian silks at a time when there was serious unemployment in Spitalfields.

Riotous demonstrations of this nature in the eighteenth century often had no great significance other than the exercise of the 'Rights of a free People' to express disapproval of a government at a time when few had a vote. Even Bishop Keppel himself, with unimpeachable credentials as the son of a Whig earl, had been mobbed on account of his association with an unpopular administration when he made his ceremonial entry into Exeter in 1765. William Pitt, Earl of Chatham since 1766 and the organiser of victory during the Seven Years War, had became the hero of the city, for Exeter's trade had managed to prosper during the war. In the country generally too the public appetite for territorial aggrandizement and victory had increased with success and was by no means favourable to concessions to the Bourbon powers, even for the sake of peace.

By the 1760s the party labels Whig and Tory had lost their original significance. The country gentlemen usually proclaimed their independence of all parties. Elections were becoming contests for family prestige and were often ruinously expensive. In Exeter at this time there were some twelve hundred voters to be cajoled, entertained and, if they were out-voters, transported to the poll and maintained while in the city. Between March 1761 and June 1790, Exeter experienced six general elections and two by-elections; three of the general and one by-election were contested.[49] The general election of 1761, as witnessed by a contemporary, Alexander Jenkins, was particularly violent and was the last election at Exeter recalling the divisions of the past, the era of 1688. It was fought, said Jenkins, between 'the Merchants in general, the Dissenters and the Low Church' against the candidates backed by the Chamber and the High Church.[50] The supporters of the former seized the hustings to prevent their opponents from polling. The latter, reinforced by their employees and tenants from the country, stormed the Guildhall, and were in their turn ousted with the help of sailors from Topsham aided by the city mob. The candidates supported by the Chamber were, however, decisively returned after order had been restored. The opposition remained in being and in due course would support parliamentary and municipal reform.

By 1760 Exeter's older merchant class ceased to expect the honour of representing the city in parliament. William Spicer, a retired glover, was the last of the city merchants to be elected. He received the honour without a contest in 1761 to fill the vacancy created by the death of one of the two Tory members. He declined to stand for the general election of 1768 because, it was said, 'he soon found that . . . his money which was his only qualification had not weight enough to command respect from the other members.'[51] Monied arrivistes were not absent from the eighteenth-century House of Commons and Spicer was connected with county society through his wife, but it seems that he drifted into an honour which he had neither the qualities nor, perhaps, the inclination, to support. Possibly he had been supported by the Chamber in 1761 as a convenient stop-gap and he did not manage to convince his backers that he was worth retaining. In December 1767, well before the dissolution of parliament in March 1768, John Rolle Walter and John Buller had already offered themselves as candidates and the thirteen members of the Chamber present had unanimously resolved to support them 'with their votes and interest'.[52] Henceforward, with the exception of John Baring, who was not representative of the old merchant class, the city's MPs would all be members of Devon's political families.

Men such as these proudly proclaimed both their independence of party and their freedom from the fetters of office. 'I am not conscious, Gentlemen, since I have had the honour of representing you in Parliament, that an Attachment to any particular Person or Party has ever influenced me to give a single Vote but what I imagined to be the real interest of my Country', John Walter wrote to an approving mayor and Chamber in 1764.[53] John Cholwich, another country gentleman, declared in 1776 that, if elected, he would never 'either under the present, or any future administration, accept of any Pension, Contract or Emolument whatsoever'. He would support the government when convinced that it was right to do so, otherwise he would oppose. The Chamber, fully endorsing these principles, ordered that Cholwich's letter should be printed in the newspapers of the South West together with the text of the resolution endorsing his candidacy.[54]

In 1776 John Baring decided to stand for the vacancy created by the retirement of John Walter. A merchant of great wealth, grandson of a German Lutheran immigrant, Baring was on his way to admission to the ruling classes. He had acquired that essential status symbol, landed property, by the purchase of the Mount Radford estate close to the southern boundary of Exeter. But in 1776 he stood as an independent businessman. 'I cannot suppose', he declared, 'that a great commercial city would be unwilling to have a Man of Business for one of its Representatives.'[55] The Chamber thought otherwise and preferred a more traditional candidate though allied by marriage to successful trade and commerce in the South West. It supported John Cholwich of Farringdon, near Exeter, son-in-law of Sir John Duntze, the latter like Baring a man of great wealth derived from the cloth trade and also the grandson of a German immigrant. The Duntze and Baring families had long been business rivals and the by-election of 1776 involved family prestige. Baring was supported by those who were usually unwilling to accept the Chamber's choice, and his wealth, business interests and family background won him further support. He was elected by 659 votes to 588 and the inevitable petition against his election occasioned a significant demonstration of support by workers in the cloth industry. Baring later made his peace with the Chamber and represented the city for twenty-six years at, he complained, 'monstrous expense and trouble'.

The general election of 1780 was conducted at a time of deep division throughout the country over the issue of the American War of Independence (1776–83) in which France and Spain had become belligerents on the American side. In 1779 the Chamber had affirmed its 'steady and most zealous support in the Prosecution of the present War'. Rodney's victory off Cape St Vincent in January 1780 was celebrated by the usual illuminations; the rougher patriots smashed unlighted windows and molested Quakers who were unwilling to indulge in drunken rowdyness. Nevertheless there were signs of war-weariness and questions of national policy were now intruding on local and personal issues at elections. In January 1780 a meeting of the gentry, clergy and freeholders of Devon, on Exeter's Rougemont, expressed concern over 'the declining situation of the British Empire', the growth of the National Debt, the increase of taxes and the decline of trade, the traditional objections of the country squires in the days of William III and Queen Anne. Baring was moving towards the opposition. He had married the daughter of his fellow Devonian John

Dunning who had moved, and carried, the famous motion that 'the influence of the Crown has increased, is increasing and ought to be diminished.' Baring himself took no part in that division but he later voted for his brother-in-law's motion, this time unsuccessful, that Parliament should not be prorogued until steps had been taken to reduce the powers of the Crown. In September 1780 the Chamber supported Baring and John Cholwich of Farringdon, but the latter, after assessing the situation, prudently declined the poll and there was no contest. Baring was returned, and with him the Foxite Whig, Sir Charles Bampfylde of Poltimore.

Bampfylde was a neighbouring landowner of long descent. For generations his family had been associated with Exeter. He was prepared to go to the brink of bankruptcy to secure the prestige of a seat in Parliament. By the time he was murdered, by a former employee, in 1823, he was reported to have spent over £80,000 on elections, and in 1780 he was already financially embarrassed as well as being a member of the 'fast set' of London's political clubland.

In 1784 the Chamber gave its *placet* to Baring and John Buller, the latter a more sedate member of a West Country political family. But Bampfylde, though his reputation was not of the highest in respectable circles, had an inherent electoral appeal in a traditionalist society and, as a Whig, could attract the anti-establishment opposition of the city. Despite the Chamber's support of Buller, Bampfylde headed the poll with Baring second. John Buller ceased to contest Exeter. The influence of the Chamber on parliamentary elections was becoming uncertain and ineffective, perhaps because it included no member of stature capable of exercising a decisive political influence. As a body, however, it invariably came to terms with candidates elected without its support.

The election of 1790 at Exeter was a contest over prestige fought to the limits of each candidate's financial resources. The Chamber again gave its support to Baring, and also to James Buller, of Downes in Crediton, nephew of John who had represented Exeter in 1768–74, noting in a resolution of the 10 September 1789 that he had met with 'very general approbation and great success in his Canvass'. Since the election was not held till June 1790 Buller had eight months to prepare the ground. His electoral cash book still breathes the excitement of the gambler doggedly raising his stakes as the pace quickened throughout the game. It provides a vivid and detailed picture of a hard-fought election reported to have cost Bamfylde £8,000, Baring £10,000 and Buller £16,000, in soliciting the support of the 'free and independent' electors of the city.[56]

Buller's cash book accounts for an expenditure of some £12,000, most of this being distributed through the landlord of the Three Cranes in Milk Lane, in the angle between Fore Street and South Street, and long used by the Chamber for doing business over a drink. Other innkeepers and victuallers distributed about £4,000, including £1,313 by Robert Howell of the Swan Tavern and £300 by the licensee of the Valiant Soldier. The landlord of the Bull Inn, Goldsmith Street, received £258; John Land, of the London Inn £206; Thomas Pratt, of the Bristol Inn £158. Various victuallers in the West Quarter received £300 between them. Illiterates, both men and women, acknowledged with their crosses generous payments for undisclosed services, William Buslett on a receipt for £131 and Jane Haddon for £56.[57]

The usual insults and allegations were exchanged in pamphlets and broadsheets. Bampfylde, inevitably, was attacked for his association with Fox, the 'English Catiline'; 'No Foxites, Spendthrifts, nor no Gamblers' was the cry. Baring was accused of neglecting his constituency, of making a fortune out of tea at a time when the East India Company was selling cloth to China at a loss and making a handsome compensating profit out of China tea. He was also accused of dealing in Yorkshire cloth, to the detriment of local industry, and of exporting butter and oats at a time of local scarcity.

Buller headed the poll, receiving twice the votes given to Baring in second place, 1,106 to 588. Bampfylde, with 550 votes, lost his seat. According to such figures as are available Baring had paid about £17 a vote, Buller and Bampfylde £14. Baring had never been a popular Member and he himself attributed his seat to his generous expenditure. His support had in fact declined (from 659 in 1776) in this, his last and most expensive, election.

By 1790 there were indications, even in the South West, that the sanctity of the settlement of 1688 and the parliamentary representative system were under scrutiny. In 1782 the inhabitants of Tiverton, 'that almost ruined town', according to the *Flying Post*,[58] had petitioned for reform of the method of choosing their representatives. The declining clothing towns of Devon, such as Crediton, South Molton and Cullompton, were evincing political restlessness. At Exeter, in 1782, the founding of the Constitutional Society for the Redress of Grievances, though lacking influential members, presaged the campaign over the Improvement Act of 1810. One of its first demands was that, in order to eradicate 'the lamentable effects of the power and influence of the Chamber of Exon', no member of the Chamber should become a member of the Corporation of the Poor. There was also a call for a right of appeal from the city magistrates to the justices of the county of Devon because, it was argued, the latter were more likely to resolve disputes impartially. The Chamber, it was said, should publish the accounts of the charities it administered for the benefit of the poor. There were also purely humanitarian proposals, such as that children, pregnant women and infirm persons should not be removed or enticed away by parish officers anxious to avoid expenditure by their own parishes, and that 'labouring men and men of mean circumstances' should not be allowed to exploit apprentices for the sake of the premium.[59] There followed a letter to the press from 'Many Citizens' urging that members of the Chamber should be elected by the citizens.

The members of the Exeter Constitutional Society carried little weight, but they voiced the sentiments of many respectable and prosperous citizens. The society's activities were the first local ripples that marked the turn of a tide, they questioned the principles on which local authority was based and gave expression to rising concern over moral and humanitarian problems. They heralded the activities that followed the rise of Evangelicalism and the revived power of Dissent; prison reform, the reconstruction and building of churches and eventually the agitation for parliamentary reform. On the slave trade the city's views were forthright. A Guildhall meeting in 1788 petitioned for its abolition in the name of the mayor, gentlemen, clergy and other inhabitants of the city. By 1790 meetings were being held calling for the repeal, in respect of Protestant Dissenters, of the Test and Corporation Acts.

But Reform had to wait, for in 1792 Exonians were reading of the deposition of Louis XVI and the annihilation of his Swiss Guard. The fleet was mobilised and sailed past the Devon coast, Admiral Lord Hood taking the opportunity to send a fine turtle to Alderman Walker. A royal proclamation required magistrates to suppress seditious writings and to preserve order, and at Exeter a large public meeting, said to have been unprecedented for size and respectability, drew up an address expressing thanks to the Crown. The Chamber's own loyal address was inspired by:

> a just sense of the invaluable advantages which the country hath derived from its excellent form of Government, a System which wonderfully invites the Blessings of Liberty and Order . . . affords a perfect Security to the Persons and Property of the Individual, holds out every Inducement to Emulation and Industry amongst all the Orders and Ranks of the Community, and is therefore the foundation of that Wealth, Strength and Prosperity which the Country at present enjoys.[60]

The Protestant Dissenters of Devon also hastened to express their loyalty to the throne and to the 'Constitution established by the Glorious Revolution of 1688'. In 1791 Robert Trewman's bookshop in the High Street had been selling Tom Paine's *The Rights of Man*. In the winter of 1792–3 Paine was burnt in effigy in small country towns and in Devon hamlets whose people, though unlikely to have read the inflammatory text, were stimulated with beer and cider. At Exeter the effigy was carried appropriately along the processional route of death from the gaol to the gallows off the Magdalen Road. Under the pressure of war and the fear of revolution men of property closed ranks and carried the greater part of the population with them.

NOTES

1. W.G. Hoskins, *Industry, Trade and People*, especially pp. 78-86.
2. *Journals of the House of Commons*, xxxix, pp. 372-3, 15.4.1783.
3. E.A.G. Clark, *Ports of the Exe Estuary*, pp. 36, 39.
4. *Flying Post*, 13-20.2.1778.

NOTES *continued*

5. *ibid.*, 14.10.1787.
6. *Notes and Gleanings*, 1880, i, pp. 113-5.
7. *FP*, 14-21.10.1774, 13-20.2.1778.
8. *ibid.*, 24.1.1793.
9. *ibid.*, 29.6.1781.
10. *ibid.*, 21.8.1773.
11. K. Balderston, *Thraliana*, ii, p. 718.
12. G. Sheldon, *From Trackway to Turnpike*, and *FP* passim.
13. W. Marshall, *The Rural Economy of the West of England*, ii, pp. 113-4.
14. *FP*, 10.8.1786.
15. *ibid.*, 2.12.1790; *Exeter Evening Post*, 4-11.1.1771; *FP*, 2-10.5.1776, 28.7.1780; *FP*, 5.12.1777, 11.1.1782.
16. *Exeter Evening Post*, 2-9.12.1774.
17. *FP*, 13.8.1785; Balderston, *op. cit.*, ii, p. 626.
18. *FP*, 13.8.1789.
19. *ibid.*, 24.1.1783, 12.5.1785.
20. *ibid.*, 11.1.1787.
21. *ibid.*, 20.8.1789; 16.7.1795; 18-25.10.1776; 16.1.1791; 30.6.1791; 3.1.1786.
22. N. Carlisle, *Concise Description of the Endowed Grammar Schools*, i, p. 316.
23. Hannah Moore, *Strictures on the Modern System of Female Education*, 1811 edn, i, p. 75.
24. *FP*, 12.5.1785; 16.6.1791; 9.6.1791.
25. Joyce Youings, *Tuckers Hall Exeter*, pp. 157-8.
26. DRO, 76/20, Memoirs of Henry Ellis, p. 14.
27. *ibid.*, pp. 14-19.
28. W.G. Hoskins, *Industry, Trade and People*, passim and E.W. Gilboy, *Wages in Eighteenth Century England*, especially pp. 82-121.
29. Gilboy, pp. 120-21.
30. *Exeter Evening Post*, 29.8-5.9.1766; 17-24.4.1767.
31. *Annual Register*, 1766, p. 220.
32. *Exeter Evening Post*, 12-19.9.1766.
33. DRO, ECA, Act Books, 7.11.1766.
34. *FP*, 21.4.1796, 5.5.1796.
35. *ibid.*, 8-15.3.1776; 5.1.1786(sic); 15.1.1789.
36. *ibid.*, 22.1.1789.
37. J. Gidley, *History of Royal Visits*, 1863.
38. C. Barrett (ed.), *Diary and Letters of Madame D'Arblay*, ii, p. 203.
39. DRO, ECA, Receivers' Accounts, Book 148, 1788-9.
40. A. Jenkins, *History of Exeter*, p. 221.
41. John Fisher, *Sermons on several Subjects*, Sherborne, 1741, p. 232.
42. N. Sykes, *Church and State in England in the Eighteenth Century*, pp. 100, 126, 433-5.
43. A. Brockett, *Nonconformity in Exeter*, pp. 71-2, 115.
44. *ibid.*, p. 108.
45. John Cernick, *An Account of the late Riot in Exeter*, 1745.
46. DRO, ECA, Act Books, 17.3.1764.
47. *Exeter Evening Post*, 20-27.10.1769.
48. 'The Private Journal of John, fourth Duke of Bedford', in J. Wright, *Sir Henry Cavendish's Debates of the House of Commons 1768-71*, 1841, pp. 620-21.
49. J.J. Alexander, 'Exeter Members of Parliament, part iv, 1688-1832', *DAT*, 1930, pp. 195-223 and L. Namier and J. Brooke, *The House of Commons 1754-90*, i, p. 253.
50. A. Jenkins, *op. cit.*, pp. 108-9.
51. Sir William Drake (ed.), *Heathiana*, p. 15.
52. DRO, ECA, Act Books, 26.12.1767.
53. *Exeter Mercury*, 21.9.1764.
54. DRO, ECA, Act Books, 5.8.1776.
55. *FP*, 20-27.9.1776.
56. Devon and Exeter Institution, 'John Baring's Autobiography', in G. Oliver, Biographies of Eminent Exonians, a scrapbook.
57. DRO, 2065M/SS2/16-18, Buller Election Account Book.
58. *FP*, 11.10.1782.
59. *ibid.*, 18.11.1784, 28.11.1784.
60. DRO, ECA, Act Books, 12.12.1792.

Chapter Six

The Chamber at work

It has been said of the eighteenth-century corporations that they 'might be controlled by some very queer people but at least they had a certain status for expressing feelings which everybody held'.[1] Hogarth at one end of the century, Rowlandson and Gillray at the other, present a picture of high-living and unabashed corruption. Neither can be denied. Standards of public life and private behaviour in the England of Walpole were not those of middle-class Victorian England and folk-memories of a more uninhibited age were revived as propaganda in the 1830s at the expense of the then highly respectable members of the Chamber of Exeter. The Chamber in the first half of the eighteenth century may well have been controlled by some 'queer people'; if so they have left little trace of their existence though occasionally there emerges from the reticent records the voice of an independent-minded alderman and, more frequently, of generous expenditure on hospitality. Andrew Brice in *The Mobiad,* especially in his footnotes, certainly supports the impression of coarseness, drunkenness and dirt in Exeter in the 1730s. But the Chamber of this period undoubtedly took pains to keep in touch with prevailing public opinion and, though procedures were leisurely and financial controls negligent, it endeavoured to carry out its duties to the city according to the unexacting standards of the time.

Because there was no professional local administration in the modern sense, duties which later would be carried out by permanent technical officers were assigned to members of the Chamber who of course also had their own business affairs to attend to. It was not till March 1737 that the Chamber, on the motion of Thomas Heath, appointed a committee to select a suitable person to act as 'Accomptant General'. On 30 May 1739 it was resolved that a surveyor be appointed to manage the properties of the Chamber and to supervise public works. Such appointments were not of full-time technical officers but the fact that the appointments were deemed necessary indicates that the Chamber was not without an awareness of the need to improve administration. Most of the work of the Chamber nevertheless depended on the capacity and diligence of the members, working through committees.

The Chamber's activities were restricted by a carapace of law and custom. The Chamber was a trustee administering corporate property, the Chamber's property. It was accepted that the property was administered in the interests of the city as a whole, but the Chamber was the final judge of what those interests might be. Its financial resources depended on the income from that property and activities were accordingly restricted. It was not till the second half of the century that effective public opinion in the city seriously looked to the Chamber for improved amenities and, since there was little the Chamber could do to provide such amenities out of its traditional resources, the citizens had to accept the necessity of contributing by means of rates; rates, however, inevitably inspired a demand for a share of the administration which previously had been accepted as the business of the Chamber.

Not till the passage of the Municipal Corporations Act of 1834 would it become possible to impose a rate on modern lines, a possibility faced with horror by the early Reformers. The principle had been established when the Corporation of the Poor was formed in 1699, for this body not only levied a rate but its members, the forty Guardians, were elected by the ratepayers. The Chamber's own responsibility for the poor was confined to the administration of the city's ancient charities, in which task it would tolerate no outside interference. In 1784 it was put to considerable trouble and expense when the Corporation of the Poor, with the Chamber's support, was seeking parliamentary sanction to increase the poor rates. The Chamber had to be represented by counsel to rebut arguments by Exeter ratepayers that the funds of the charities were legally available for the relief of the poor in general and thus rendered unnecessary an increase in the rates.[2] Improvements in street lighting, drainage and security, which required expenditure beyond the traditional financial resources, similarly could not be carried out by the Chamber but required the creation of an Improvement Commission, with members elected by the ratepayers. One prominent Reformer in the 1830s held local taxation to be 'a great curse', and a mayor of the new regime declared that he would 'sell every stick of property . . . before he would inflict that most dangerous thing, a borough rate'.[3] Selling property indeed is precisely what the Chamber had to do in a crisis; by this means funds had been raised for the reconstruction of the canal in 1699 and would be again in 1811 to pay off the more pressing debts.

The Chamber undoubtedly wined and dined well, as did most people when they had an opportunity. Wine and ale were safer drinks than water and the Chamber would have lost face if it had neglected the customary hospitality. Wine for the Guildhall on the occasion of the coronation of George I cost £2 4s., and for the same King's birthday £3, in addition to a hogshead of ale at £2, all this at a time when a craftsman, such as a carpenter or a mason, was earning about 10s. a week and a master craftsman 12s. According to the accounts of John Newcombe for 1727–8, audited in 1749, two hogsheads of ale bought for the celebration of George II's coronation cost £6 10s. and ten sturgeon and pickles 16s.[4] The same accounts contain two items of £4 5s. and £4 8s., being the cost of wine for the judges. The accounts for 1779–80 record an expenditure of over £145 on entertainment in the Guildhall, including half a hogshead of port at £11 15s. and a further pipe of port for £45 5s., both of which were purchased from Councillor James Grant. In the financial year 1790–1 £46 11s. 7½d. were spent on a turtle feast, the only occasion on which this traditional symbol of aldermanic good cheer appears in the Exeter accounts; in the year 1800–1, however, a pipe of wine supplied by Alderman Chamberlain cost £80, and no less than £178 7s. 6d. was paid for an unspecified quantity of wine supplied by Alderman Bale.[5] These were substantial items of expenditure at a time when the Chamber was becoming increasingly concerned over its financial position, when repeated efforts were being made to make economies, and when economic distress was causing disturbances in the city.

The mayor himself received generous assistance towards maintaining the dignity of his position. His salary in the early eighteenth century had been £100 a year. By 1760 it had been raised to £250; and in 1812 it stood at £300 a year. A sixty per cent increase between 1760 and 1812 barely reflected the increase in the cost of living, but labourers' wages had remained unchanged. Apart from his salary the mayor also received substantial assistance from the Chamber's funds to meet the cost of miscellaneous personal expenditure during his year of office, including the wages of a butler and a cook.

By the end of the century most mayors required assistance to maintain their dignity, though in 1789 the wealthy plumber, Jonathan Burnett, refused assistance for entertainments not classified as official mayoral dinners and declined an offer of fifteen guineas towards the cost of an entertainment on the occasion of the Gaol Delivery. The Chamber graciously recorded that the mayor's gesture 'met with the approbation of this Body', but it was agreed that entertainments of this nature should henceforward be regarded as official mayoral dinners, the cost of which would be taken into consideration in future in determining the mayor's salary.[6] It was evidently assumed that in general mayors would no longer be able to afford prestigious hospitality as they had done in the past. Nicholas Brooke, merchant, had the mortification to appear in the *London Gazette* as a bankrupt in the middle of his mayoralty of 1781–2 and was expeditiously removed from the Chamber after the termination of his office as chief citizen.

The Receiver's accounts for 1760–1 are a representative example of the Chamber's activities and expenditure at mid-century.[7] Like all these accounts, however, they have their limitations. The full value of the emoluments and perquisites of the permanent staff cannot be ascertained as they included a good deal of food and drink on special occasions. According to the accounts in this year the Chamber spent £575 on personal emoluments, the greater part consisting of the salary and expenses of the mayor:

The Mayor:	
Salary	£250
Allowances	£18 11s. 8d.
Butler	£15 15s.
Cook	£15
Mayor's band of music (the city waits)	£26
Permanent staff	
Recorder	£20
Town Clerk	£3 12s.
Chamberlain	£5
Swordbearer	£40
Surveyor	£35
Accountant	£25
Keeper of Southgate Prison	£25
4 sergeants-at-mace, including duties as cryer of the courts and attendance on committees	£69 10s.
4 staffbearers, including duties as Bridewell Keeper and 'lookers after the conduit and pipes'	£25
Verger of St Peter's 'for the Chamber's sitting at the cathedral'	£1
Keeper at West Gate	£1 1s.
Porters at five city gates	£3 7s. 8d.

The Keeper of the South Gate prison in addition to wages exacted official charges from prisoners and expected to make a profit on their maintenance. The existence of illicit perquisites is indicated by the Chamber's order that when the city gates were closed they should not be opened on any pretext.

In 1760 the canal accounts were not yet the responsibility of the Receiver. He was responsible, however, for the presentation of the accounts of the Blue Boys Hospital of St John and of the Blue Maids Hospital, for both of which, during his year of office, he was steward. The payments to the staff of the Blue Boys in 1760–1 amounted to £371, including two years' maintenance of twenty-two boys at £7 a head and £30 4s. 4d. for 'necessaries for the boys'. It would have been contrary to the accepted practice of the time if these outgoings had not included a profit for the master of the establishment, a clergyman who also received a salary of £40 a year. His subordinate, the master of the writing school, received £26 a year, and £10 a year was also paid to the master of the writing school at Moreton-hampstead. There were other payments which, with so much else, contributed to the value of appointments by the Chamber. The town clerk was paid £3 a year in his capacity as deputy steward of St John's Hospital, the senior sergeant-at-mace £1 for his attendance on committees. At a time when a half-penny appeared from time to time in the Chamber's accounts these amounts were not derisory. However the total expenditure of the Blue Maids Hospital amounted to only £61 8s. 2d., of which £40 was accounted for by the salary of the matron.

The basic revenue of the Blue Boys and Blue Maids Hospitals derived from endowments, but the Chamber made up deficits and, in return, received surpluses which were credited to its account. It was a system that required scrupulous accounting, and its traditional easy-going relationship with the charities for which it was responsible led to serious financial embarrassment for the Chamber when the finances of charitable institutions were subject to more rigorous examination in the 1820s.

The financial year 1760–61 had its share of ceremonial and celebrations. It saw the death of one king and the proclamation, marriage and coronation of another. The closing years of the Seven Years War were still producing their victories, which also required official celebration. There was therefore relatively heavy expenditure on ceremonial trimmings. Alderman Trosse was paid £10 17s. 6d. for new cloaks for the members of the mayor's 'band of music', who also received new hats and silver lace at a cost of £14 14s. 9d. The sergeants-at-mace received new hats and gold lace trimmings at a cost of £6 15s. and Alderman Elliott was paid £2 2s. 2d. to provide new gloves for sergeants and staffbearers. Ale, 'given away at the Guildhall', cost £12 18s. 6d. Nevertheless the cost of ceremony and festivities under the head of 'Regalia' came to only £94 15s. 8d. out of a total expenditure in that year of £2787, and this included expenditure on the traditional ceremonies which helped to enliven city life, the mural walk, the anniversary of the Gunpowder Plot on 5 November and of the restoration of Charles II on 29 May. In this year at least the Chamber was not noticeably wasting money on conspicuous consumption.

Reformers of the 1830s were inclined to arraign their predecessors for their failure to live up to what were then the new ideals of Utilitarianism, and a later age permitted itself a superior smile at the details of administrative practice or the story told by the wine-bills of the Chamber. Yet during the last decades of the century the Chamber of Exeter showed a remarkable ability to initiate or facilitate what now would be described as development schemes. These formed a major break with traditional policy and made a decisive contribution to the future development of the city. In 1771 a committee met to consider plans drawn up by Robert Stribling, the builder-architect primarily responsible for the construction of the first part of Bedford Circus.[8] In 1774 the Chamber resolved to take the initial steps which led to the development of Southernhay, and in 1775 a committee was formed to take measures to improve the flow of traffic, in particular by the demolition of the city gates.[9] The Chamber gave full cooperation to the County of Devon in the construction of the new Exe Bridge, completed in 1778, and took the initiative in the consequential action, the breaching of the West Wall, the construction of New Bridge Street and the removal of the pig market from the bottom of Fore Street Hill.[10] These were major policy decisions, taken at a time when the Chamber was repeatedly undertaking investigations into the state of its finances and the city's economy was necessarily adjusting to the perturbations caused by the American war which the Chamber warmly supported and the entry of France and Spain into the conflict. Among those often tetchy aldermen of considerable age and experience in their powdered wigs and three-cornered hats there were clearly men of ability and vision capable of decisions as far-sighted as any taken by subsequent city councils after 1835. At the same time they strove to protect the visual amenities of the city, as in February 1775 when Nicholas Brooke, a future mayor, was refused permission to remove trees on the Bonhay.

By 1760, when the Chamber banned bull-baiting, there was a marked growth of more refined taste among those whom financial resources freed from a harsh struggle for survival. The Chamber, however, still contained men whose characters had been formed in the more robust world of Walpole and the first two Georges. Alderman William Newcombe died in 1776 after forty-one years of membership. Men such as he retained office and authority to the last even though, like Newcombe and also Alderman Crossing, they had to be carried to the Guildhall in sedan chairs at the Chamber's expense. The aldermen who died between 1760 and 1790 accumulated 250 years' experience between them as councillor, alderman, magistrate and mayor. They had prospered as businessmen when the cloth industry was paramount and, in an age when custom and precedent were strong, they carried into a new era formidable experience of the past. Yet there is no indication that they imposed brakes on the Chamber in its efforts to improve the amenities of the city.

The successors of such men tended to be less prominent as businessmen and to have more restricted commercial interests than had the previous generation. They were more representative of the emerging professions. Of the thirty-five councillors elected between 1760 and 1790 eleven were apothecaries, druggists and surgeons; the first bookseller to be elected was Richard Thorn in 1786. Grocers still contributed five members to the intake of 1760–90; four of that intake ended their careers in bankruptcy. However, both the older generation and the new moved with the times, exercising common sense in avoiding conflict with the propertied classes and in handling the mob with restraint.

The only permanent executive officers of the Chamber, the supporters of its dignity and enforcers of its authority in the streets, were eight men, the four sergeants-at-mace and the four staffbearers. The latter's duties ranged from cleaning the candlesticks in the Guildhall to preventing the illicit slaughtering of animals within the city.[11] They also operated the fire-engine, a portable pump kept behind the Guildhall. By 1790 the senior sergeant-at-mace was paid £24 a year and his juniors £20 and in 1791 the staffbearers' salaries were raised from £5 a year to £7.[12] All were still provided wih free accommodation, uniforms with gold and silver lace, and a share of the food and drink available on ceremonial occasions, though in 1796 they were deprived of the perquisite of wine on 'guildhall nights'. As personalities they must have been well-known and subject to flattering attention. They retained their offices until death or senility intervened and while their original occupations were such as fuller, landwaiter or hairdresser, they acquired a certain expertise in civic duties through practical experience. As freemen they all had votes which they used in accordance with the Chamber's policy, in the by-election of 1776, for example, they followed the example of the aldermen by voting for John Cholwich.[13]

For the prevention of crime and the arrest of offenders Exeter depended on the uncertain efficiency of the 'corps of constables', twenty-eight in number, who were appointed annually at the meeting of the Chamber immediately following the election of the new mayor.[14] They had to be householders. In 1766 the Chamber resolved that William Floyd, elected constable for the East Ward, not being a householder was therefore 'according to the custom of this city, not obliged to do that office'. Dissenters were also ineligible and were required to provide substitutes. The constables held an ancient office, medieval in origin, and were empowered under Common Law to arrest felons and other persons threatening a breach of the peace. They were responsible to the aldermen-magistrates and their status as a corps was recognised by an annual dinner. By no means wholly inefficient the Exeter constables were not necessarily of the type satirised by Dickens in his account of the arrest of the Pickwickians at Ipswich in the reign of William IV. There were active men among them, such as two who rode apace to Taunton in 1814 and arrested two soldiers of the Light Dragoons wanted in Exeter for robbery. The mainstay of the corps were those constables appointed *ex officio,* such as the sergeants-at-mace, or William Westlake, Keeper of the Southgate Prison, whom the Chamber paid an extra £10 a year for his duties as constable and who was described admiringly on his death in 1811 as a terror to evil-doers. But the constables in general were part-time amateurs, shopkeepers and tradesmen pressed into assuming sometimes arduous, and always unpopular, duties and often only too glad to pay a fine of £10 or £15 to avoid them. In 1788 the Chamber raised the fine to the very substantial sum of thirty guineas, a sum which was paid in 1809 by Thomas Horrell, later the builder of the second stage of Bedford Circus.[15] Joseph Pinkard was fined by the Chamber in 1791 for failing to carry his staff of office while in attendance on the Mayor.

In quiet times the traditional organisation of constables was adequate since it was supported by the discipline of a small, close-knit society, tolerant of disorder and violence up to a point (provided it did not affront respectable citizens) but keeping suspicious characters and strangers under the close observation of parish officers, beadles and neighbours. In an emergency, such as a fire, the regular troops of the garrison were available, not only to assist in controlling the fire but also to prevent looting. This assistance, which was always forthcoming, was gratefully acknowledged by the local press. In 1788 the Chamber paid ten guineas to the dragoons for dealing with a fire.[16]

When the social fabric itself seemed threatened even citizens normally reluctant came forward to accept office and were enrolled as special constables, backed if necessary by the troops of a garrison city and the militia or yeomanry. But it was not till the long war with revolutionary and Napoleonic France, with its accompaniment of serious privation, high prices and profiteering, that Exeter experienced more serious riots than the customary rabbling of bishops and noblemen. Crises of this kind were strictly the concern of the aldermen as magistrates rather than of the Chamber itself, a distinction which the Reformers of the next generation would regard, with some justification, as an indefensible concentration of executive and judicial power. Serious trouble required the personal intervention of the mayor rather than a chief constable, and it was useful to have the ability to confront with local dialect and intimate knowledge a bewildered, but hungry, crowd.

But the main day-to-day tasks of the Chamber in the last four decades of the eighteenth century were the maintenance of its property, the administration of its finances and the improvement of the city. Changes and innovations required much expenditure of time and effort in order to cajole or placate citizens who fancied themselves inconvenienced, and despite the resolutions and admonitions of the Chamber, little progress was made in enforcing cleanliness in the streets or the removal of obstacles such as the paraphernalia of hucksters and stallholders. Eighteenth-century Exonians did not take kindly to regulation. From time to time energetic mayors, such as Thomas Floud in 1802, deserved praise for their efforts to enforce regulations but not all mayors were conscientious. Nor were they always well served. A Whitestone yeoman, to whom the Chamber gave the soil of the streets for a year, on condition that he carried away the dung and swept the streets at least three times a week, saw no pressing reason to work to schedule and in fact did not do so.

Nevertheless the Chamber persevered. In 1771 it was decided, at the request of 'many Gentlemen of this City', to remove the water-spouts and shop signs which made High Street picturesque but hazardous to both pedestrians and traffic. In 1769 a committee of the whole Chamber considered the construction of a market and thereby to remove 'Nuisance and Annoyance' from the streets. There were the usual delays over the acquisition of property and the need to meet objections but by 1783 properties had been purchased in the neighbourhood of the Swan Inn in Goldsmith Street, and market stalls had been erected. The fish market was then moved there from its site in the High Street near the junction with Martins Lane. The market for greens, peas, potatoes and other vegetables was likewise transferred the following year from its site near St Olave's church on Fore Street. The new market was then leased for thirty guineas a year and a fine of £30.[17] All this involved little more than the transfer of markets from one street to another. It was not till the very end of the Chamber's existence, in the 1830s, that handsome market buildings were erected after the controversy usual over such matters.

A more offensive nuisance than street marketing was the crudities of Butchers' Row and the appalling conditions in which animals were slaughtered throughout the city. By 1771 the situation had become intolerable to polite society; a powerful committee including the mayor, justices, deputy recorder and the town clerk, was accordingly appointed to review the situation. This committee acted swiftly. Within three weeks it was recommended that all slaughtering should be prohibited within the walls of the city and that informers should be paid 10s. a time for reporting any such activities.[18]

Nevertheless, despite the good intentions of the Chamber the city remained far from salubrious. Pigs roaming as omnivorous scavengers were said to include in their diet the corpses of rabid dogs left in the streets. Under by-laws made in 1772 fines could be imposed for keeping cattle within the city walls, including a fine of £5 for keeping pigs, and for 'filth, garbage or other annoyance'.[19] Rules were not necessarily obeyed or adequately enforced, and the butchers were traditionally unruly. The staffbearers were ordered to enforce the new rules, but in 1783 there were still complaints of cattle being illegally slaughtered at night and of piles of offal and dung being allowed to accumulate until they could be removed surreptitiously. In 1791 the Chamber appointed another formidable committee — mayor, justices, receiver, and town clerk — which was directed to maintain the 'Powers, Control and Authority of the Body'.[20] Nevertheless Dr Maton, physican to Queen Charlotte and the Princess Victoria, found the streets in 1794 'extremely incommodious' by foot or horseback, being rough, filthy and only partially paved.[21] In 1817, during the spring cattle fair, most of High Street, Fore Street and Bartholomew Street was blocked by cattle and in that same year S.F. Milford complained that the congregation in the church of Holy Trinity was exposed to the 'noisome and noxious effluvia of corrupting mortality'. The Chamber found it difficult to eradicate the personal habits of Old England; fines still had to be imposed for 'emptying a necessary into the street' or for 'committing a nuisance against the public conduit'.

The personal performance by members of the Chamber of duties which would in later times devolve on technical officers took up much time. A committee appointed in September 1782 to examine trees on Northernhay, which an occupier, Captain Bellew, wished to have felled, consisted of no less than two aldermen, the receiver and the surveyor. Even the collection of rents usually involved personal contact between members of the Chamber and lessees, this being lubricated by means of the traditional hospitality, as in 1789 when the landlord of the Swan was paid over £30 for entertainment in connection with the collection of rents for fish and vegetable stalls, mills and other properties.[22] Members of the Chamber were required to advise on the terms of the building leases for the new properties along the approaches to the new Exe Bridge, for the repair and improvement of water cisterns and lead piping, and on the negotiations with the Duke of Bedford's agents over the terms of an agreement on the connection between a sewer in the preparatory work for Bedford Circus and the reconstructed public sewer in Southernhay.[23] A committee was appointed in 1768 to examine the profitability of the Chamber's New Inn in the High Street, and this led in 1771 to the commencement of negotiations with the Chapter for the termination of the Chamber's longstanding connection with that ancient inn.[24]

The multifarious business of local administration included the issue of permits for rod and line fishing in the Exe, the control of the removal of sand and gravel from the river, and a study of damage to the river banks caused by the effect of the new bridge on the current of the river.[25] The development of Southernhay for select residential houses gave rise to an order to prohibit the exercise of horses in that neighbourhood.[26] Street congestion caused by heavy wagons required frequent admonitions and the imposition of fines, the well-known carrier Thomas Russell being fined for blocking South Street. The money was later refunded on the grounds that Russell had gone to the expense of providing himself with a wagon park, but he was again in trouble for the same reason some years later.

In 1777 the Chamber gave a grant to encourage, in the days before vaccination, innoculation against smallpox, and another in 1786 to support a private school to teach the poor to read. In 1778, thinking that it was 'Highly proper in the Present Situation of affairs between Great Britain and her Colonies in America to strengthen the Hands of Government by every Constitutional Method', it paid a bounty of five guineas a head to supplement the government bounty for enlisted soldiers.[27] Bounties of three guineas for able seamen, one-and-a-half guineas for ordinary seamen and one guinea for able-bodied landsmen enlisting in the Navy were also contributed from the Chamber's funds, and forty guineas were contributed towards the cost of manning a sloop of war operating between the Exe and London for the protection of coastal trade.[28]

But resources remained limited. According to the receivers' accounts, the scale of financial operations remained virtually unchanged for sixty years, as the following figures indicate:[29]

Financial Years	Average Revenue p.a.	Average Expenditure p.a.
1698/99 – 1703/04	£3,262	£3,334
1704/05 – 1708/09	2,546	2,449
1715/16 – 1719/20	2,053	2,071
1725/26 – 1729/30	2,216	2,129
1732/33 – 1736/37	3,084	3,009
1738/39 – 1742/43	2,975	2,945
1744/45 – 1748/49	2,416	2,380
1749/50 – 1753/54	2,619	2,563
1756/57 – 1760/61	3,059	3,012
1761/62 – 1765/66	2,985	2,979
1766/67 – 1770/71	4,919	4,871
1771/72 – 1775/76	5,440	5,249
1776/77 – 1780/81	5,654	5,484
1781/82 – 1785/86	6,333	6,250
1786/87 – 1790/91	6,389	6,290

The relatively high average figure for the years 1698–9 to 1703–4, as compared with the following period, is due to inclusion on the expenditure side of extraordinary expenses on the canal and on water supplies, and on the revenue side of the proceeds of loans and the sale of the Duryard property required to meet this expenditure. There was no capital budget or loan account. Extraordinary receipts were brought into the accounts under 'Other Sums Received' and were promptly spent.

The receivers' accounts were statements of cash transactions. They were audited and approved by members of the Chamber itself and for their own use. They were not intended to provide information for ratepayers. They do not provide a comprehensive statement of the Chamber's financial position and they conceal many liabilities. Paper credit balances seem to have been achieved by the postponement of the payment of tradesmen's bills or by making part payments, these being cleared when opportunity arose. Thus in 1787 when the sheriff happened to have funds in hand he was requested to use them to pay off the longest-standing bills and to pay £150 to the town clerk 'in part of his Bill of Costs for work done'.[30] The often long-delayed payment of the outstanding credit balances of the receivers contributed to the fluctuations of the revenue side of the accounts. Nevertheless the accounts present in general a comprehensive picture of the Chamber's activities and demonstrate the limitations under which those activities were conducted.

Ordinary recurrent revenue depended on the Chamber's ownership of real estate, that is, house property, the canal and the markets. Real property was leased for terms of lives and it was only when a lease fell in, or its terms were varied, that the Chamber could, and did, profit by means of entry fines based on the condition of the market. In 1763 £270 was paid as a fine for a lease of Chamber property out at Awliscombe, near Honiton. Joseph Gattey paid as much as £330 for a lease of property in Exeter in 1788. The accounts of Joseph Rowe, receiver in 1760–61, illustrate the normal financial transactions of the Chamber at this time, and its dependence on earnings from property. Revenue amounted to £3,045 19s. 8d. and expenditure to £2,787 12s. 10d.[31] These figures do not indicate substantial wealth for a corporate body. A contemporary private individual such as Mrs Piozzi, the widow of the millionaire brewer, Henry Thrale, reckoned on a clear £2,500 a year after the settlement of her deceased husband's estate.[32] In the financial year 1760–1 the Chamber's revenue from its property amounted to just over half the total revenue. The following table sets out, to the nearest £, the Chamber's income from property in a year when there was no windfall arising out of very large fines on the renewal or grant of leases:

Income from property 1760–61	
Rent of mills	£249
Rent of drying racks (for cloth)	78
Rent of butchers' stalls	147
Rent of markets	124
Fines for leases	541
High and conventionary rents	303
Miscellaneous rents, including	
Rack Rents	318
	£1,760
Canal profits	800
Quay dues	111
	£2,671
Other credits	832
Total revenue	£3,503

In 1760–61 the total under 'Other Sums Received' was only £413. It was under this head that the receiver entered miscellaneous credits of all kinds, loans from aldermen, the belated payment of balances from previous receivers and the capital payments for annuities. In some years, therefore, this became the dominant revenue head in the accounts, as in 1781–2 when it contributed £2,266 out of total revenue of £5,709. An exceptional year was 1788–9 when fines for leases amounted to £1,694, including £525 from the haberdasher Charles Upham and £250 from Smith & Hore, bankers.

Quay Profits for the financial years 1760–61 to 1792–3 averaged, to the nearest pound, £1,875. In a good year, such as 1769–70, £2,170 was credited to revenue, 41 per cent of the total. It was augmented by £220 in Town Dues and £133 from Topsham Quay. The highest figure during the period was £2,385, forming 46 per cent of the total revenue of that year and it was augmented by £261 in Town Dues and £123 from Topsham Quay. In a bad year such as 1790–91 Quay Profits fell to £860. In general, however, the yield was high. Five-year averages were:

	£
1760/61 – 1764/65	1,208
1765/66 – 1769/70	1,858
1770/71 – 1774/75	2,506
1775/76 – 1779/80	1,889
1780/81 – 1784/85	1,960
1785/86 – 1889/90	1,704

The financial situation caused continual anxiety and necessitated frequent reviews of the situation. In June 1761 a committee was appointed to survey revenue and expenditure and to report thereon. In 1764 the accountant was instructed to include with the receiver's accounts a statement showing rents in arrear.[33] At the end of 1768 the Chamber determined to take the financial situation firmly in hand and to reduce debt. Since a survey had revealed that annual interest of £540 was being paid on debts totalling £11,550 and since, after allowing for all contingencies there was a revenue surplus, it was resolved that it was the Chamber's duty 'by all Lawfull Means to Discharge the Body Corporate from the Load of Heavy Debt'.[34] It was resolved accordingly to raise up to £4,100 by 'annuities' and to apply this sum to the reduction of the principal debt, and the Chamber forthwith approved the formal sealing of bonds guaranteeing annuities in the amount of £341 for a capital sum of £3,610. These varied from sums of £7 per annum for payments of £100 by George Andrew, gentleman, of London and by Elizabeth Parr, widow, aged 42, of Ashcombe, Devon, to £50 per annum on payment of £500 by Samuel Simmons of Exeter, druggist, aged 60 and the same to Alice Pierce, of Topsham, widow, aged '60 years and upwards'.

The surplus of £540 in 1768, substantial by the standards of the day, was no guarantee of financial reserves in future. Sufficient cash was rarely available when required and the practice of deferring payment of tradesmen's accounts, or giving bonds in lieu of prompt payment, continued. The Chamber also, it seems, was still diverting to its own use charitable funds for which it was responsible and thus was accumulating an embarrassing liability for the future. In the meantime there remained the customary support from the wealthier members of the Chamber at five to four-and-a-half per cent: £600 from the town clerk, Henry Lee; £200 from Jonathan Burnett, the plumber, on the eve of his election as councillor; £500 from Alderman Elliott; £900 from Alderman Dennis and £250 from Alderman Coffin.[35] In the financial year 1790-91 the first bank loan was received, from the Devonshire Bank of which Alderman Jackson had been a founding member.

From time to time steps were taken to tighten financial control. In 1769 the wharfinger of the Canal, who hitherto had merely handed over to the Receiver the net sum remaining in his hands after the deduction of expenses, was instructed to 'pay to the Receiver the gross sum which he has received for the use of the Chamber', the Receiver being authorised to pay and discharge all sums for which the wharfinger had been responsible.[36] In 1780 it was resolved that the Receiver himself should meet no expenditure in excess of £40 without an order of the Chamber. It was also prudently decided to insure, with the Sun Fire Office, all real estate belonging to the Chamber including the property of the charities.

Zeal and industry on the part of the Chamber's financial officers were generously, though, in the light of later events, ill-advisedly, rewarded. Thomas Hayman was appointed as part-time accountant in 1760, at a salary of £25 a year, raised by a satisfied Chamber in 1772 by an extra £14 10s. a year 'in consideration of his large family and his industry and diligence'. But by 1780 the work was beyond him and Hayman was dismissed, but with a pension of £40 a year. In 1797 the Rev. John Ridd, curate of Coldridge for the last twenty years, was attempting to support seven young daughters and two sons in apprenticeship, on a stipend of the same amount.[37] Hayman, however, had to make up all outstanding accounts before he received his pension and since he failed to do so it was withheld.

The Chamber had an even more unfortunate experience with the wharfinger, William Walker, whose salary was increased in 1760 from £50 to £70 a year, 'in reward for his extraordinary zeal and diligence in the execution of his office' and in particular for the collection of the debts outstanding for 'so many years'. Yet two years later Walker had to be ordered to present his accounts more regularly. The order was ignored and the Chamber issued an ultimatum, that it would 'understand a Refusal or Neglect punctually to comply with their Order as a Declaration that he is no longer inclined to continue in their service'! Nevertheless by the end of 1771 there had evidently been no audit of his accounts for several years and by 1793 he was in deep trouble. Walker was found to owe over £5,887 which, he declared, he was incapable of discharging.[38] He was therefore dismissed and the Chamber lost its money, an incident which would have evoked thunderous criticism in the Victorian press.

In spite of the resolution of 1768 to apply the capital derived from annuities to the reduction of debt it was spent forthwith on the acquisition of Topsham Quay at a cost of £3,740.[39] The annuities scheme merely resulted in a steep rise in both revenue and expenditure, to £8,065 and £7,716 respectively in the year 1768–9, as compared with £3,416 and £3,189 in the previous financial year. Henceforward the annual accounts record revenue and expenditure on a markedly higher level than that prevailing during the previous seventy years, but on the whole they remained at the level of 1778–86 until the financial difficulties and unprecedented capital expenditure of the Chamber's final years when, between 1826 and 1831, average expenditure rose to £18,744 and revenue to £18,621.

In 1789 the Chamber took advantage of the general decline in interest rates which marked the successful policies of the younger Pitt, but the acknowledged capital debt still stood at £21,425, twice the total accepted by the Chamber's survey of the situation in 1768.[40] There was no sinking fund and if the city as a whole profited from the Chamber's capital expenditure, as it undoubtedly had done after the canal improvements at the end of seventeenth century, the Chamber's share of the benefit, in the form of quay profits or town dues, merely enabled a modest surplus on the year's operations to appear in the accounts. In an exceptional year, such as 1776–7, revenue from the quays at Exeter and Topsham, and town dues, amounted to £3,064 out of a total revenue of £5,371 and helped to provide a substantial surplus, but still no attempt was made to build up a reserve fund and as the payment of tradesmen's bills were often overdue, or only paid when cash was available against promissory notes issued by the Chamber, it is not at all clear whether in most years a true surplus really existed. There was no lack of good intentions to improve the finances of the Chamber as demonstrated by the repeated financial inquests. The real problem was that, at a time of growing middle-class prosperity, especially for those who catered for the requirements of Exeter's social world, there was no means by which the Chamber could speedily and effectively tap the new wealth and thus obtain a contribution to the cost of improved amenities. The late-Georgian Chamber, in effect, gambled on the restoration and maintenance of Exeter's role as a major port such as it had been in the days of Queen Anne.

In minor matters of procedure and administration the Chamber effected some improvements. In 1764 it was resolved that differences of opinion at meetings should be decided by a formal vote.[41] Attempts to enforce prompt attendance at the Guildhall evidently had little success since they were made repeatedly throughout the century – a fine of one shilling had been imposed in 1707 – and in 1770 it was resolved that a fine of five shillings should be imposed on members who, after due summons, failed to appear within one hour of the appointed time. In the event of failure to pay the Chamber ordered that the fine should be levied by distress warrant on the goods and chattels of the offender.[42] This decision aroused strong feelings on the part of senior members of the Chamber. 'The Twenty Four', as the Chamber still liked to call itself, was rarely complete, the average attendance at 160 meetings between 1770 and 1790 being 13-14 members. In the 1790s men paid as much as £150 to be excused election. Committees as a general rule were reduced in size so as to consist of not more than seven members including the receiver, three former mayors and three councillors 'below the Chair' selected by ballot, but in important or controversial affairs it was always prudent to commit the whole Chamber to major decisions; committees dealing with such matters were therefore declared open to any member of the Chamber who wished to attend. The town clerk was also instructed to provide a book of record 'in order to make entries of Committees and other material Business ordered to be done' and this book was to be made available for inspection by members. In 1775 an attempt was made to discourage the practice of regarding public documents as private property, the Chamber resolving that no member 'do take away any of the original Books or Papers belonging to this Body out of the Council Chamber'. Nevertheless in 1782 the town clerk had to apply to the executors of the deceased Alderman Jackson for the return of the title deeds and other papers relating to Topsham Quay.[43]

The members of the late eighteenth-century Chamber had their idiosyncracies and prejudices but they reflected the character of the city. Sturdy upholders of the rights of free citizens, who did not include the pauper, the vagrant or the criminal, firm supporters of the Church and the Throne, they acclaimed the elder Pitt in 1757 and his son in 1789, and in 1768 they authorised the payment of £2 12*s.* 6 *d.* for peals on the city church bells when Wilkes's colleague, Serjeant Glynn, was elected, despite the government, for the Middlesex constituency. They protested vehemently 'from the middle of their Great Cyder Country' against the unpopular cider duty of 1763, and in 1779 in an address to the King proclaimed their 'steady and most zealous support in the Prosecution of the Present War' against the American colonies.[44]

Public opinion, in the closing years of the century, was expressed ever more frequently at well-attended meetings of what the newspapers called 'respectable citizens', which meant property owners, businessmen and shop owners, held in the Guildhall under the chairmanship of the mayor. Such meetings were summoned following a requisition to the mayor signed by leading citizens. Only on one occasion did the mayor refuse the request; this was in April 1797 when Charles Upham, supported by the Chamber, rejected a requisition despite the weighty backing of prominent businessmen such as three Kennaways, William Nation, Samuel Frederick Milford and George Hirtzel, and even John Land, proprietor of the New London Inn. The object was to consider a petition to the King calling for the dismissal of the ministry and the conclusion of peace with France.[45] In fact tentative peace negotiations had begun, and this was also the year in which the celebration of the birthday of Charles James Fox had provided an opportunity to toast 'the Sovereign majesty of the People', but for the Chamber the proposed public meeting at Exeter savoured too much of Whig faction at a time when what was happening in France seemed to threaten Church, property and king. That the Church might be in danger was indicated by a strong element of Dissent among the signatories of the requisition, one of whom, S.F. Milford, had presided in 1790 at a meeting in the Globe Tavern which called for the repeal of the Test and Corporation Acts. A similar petition had however been discussed at a Devon county meeting where the proposal had been opposed by influential landowners such as Lord Fortescue. Only one public meeting duly authorised by the mayor failed for lack of support and this was during the rabies epidemic of 1791 to consider a petition to Parliament in favour of a tax on dogs.[46] The proposal involved too much interference with the traditional rights of free-born Englishmen, and rural England, including Exeter, had not yet become submissive to urban opinion.

In the final decades of the eighteenth century, however, the conscientious performance of their duties by members of the Chamber and their reflection of the views and prejudices of the city was no longer enough. 'The lamentable effects of the power and influence of the Chamber' and the dual role of its senior members as both aldermen and justices, had featured in proposals for reform in 1782. The members of Exeter's ephemeral Constitutional Society for the Redress of Grievances carried no weight; but by the end of the century pressure by more substantial citizens for improved public amenities led to more widespread questioning of the Chamber's powers and organisation. The proposed improvements would be expensive. Funds could be provided only by means of rates and wealthy citizens were not prepared to stand aside and leave the rates to be determined and levied by the Chamber subject only to the control of magistrates who were also aldermen. It was an important question of principle which, in the 1830s, would become a factor in the agitation for municipal reform.

Reform was delayed by its association with French Jacobinism but even during the long war of 1793–1815 there were indications that traditional authority was being questioned. In 1795 a public meeting was held in the Guildhall to consider the establishment of a night watch. At that time there was no regular organisation for the prevention of crime at night unless a city constable happened to be on hand or could be persuaded to put in an appearance. The proposal was dismissed, inevitably, by a majority of those present on the grounds that it would impose 'a burdensome and unnecessary tax on the public'. It was agreed, however, that street lighting could be improved and the streets better paved. A citizens' committee was appointed which estimated that the whole of the city could be paved, within six years, at a cost of not more than £6,000 and that the programme could be financed by a rate of 6*d.* in the pound. Inevitably the proposals were shelved on the grounds that it was 'an improper time to lay any additional tax on the inhabitants'.[47]

The Chamber itself was not unsympathetic to the need for lighting in a city that was laying itself out to attract polite society. Already, by an Act of 1760, street lights were to be kept burning from sunset to sunrise between 20 August and 20 April. A rate, not to exceed £200 in any one year, was therefore determined by the Chamber and levied on the parishes through the churchwardens and overseers of the poor. The mayor and justices were also given the necessary executive powers to enforce contracts, remove obstructions, impose fines for damage to lights and to determine what other offences were punishable by fine. An attempt to improve security was made by an act of 1806 which empowered the justices to enlist able-bodied men to keep watch and ward, to prescribe the conditions and hours of their work, to make regulations and to direct payment of expenses by the taxpayers.[48] But by then to give such powers to members of a select club, as the magistrates were, and, in particular to submit to directions for claims on their pockets, was intolerable to citizens who had applauded 'Wilkes and Liberty' and contained an important element sympathetic to Fox and his Whigs. The Chamber soldiered on, increasingly an anachronism in the face of the new demands on local authorities at the close of the eighteenth century. The campaign over the Improvement Act of 1810 would demonstrate that a select club was no longer an effective, or acceptable, instrument for the administration of Exeter.

NOTES

1. R. Pares, *King George III and the Politicians,* pp. 198-9.
2. DRO, ECA, Act Books, 19.7.1784.
3. *Luminary,* 13.11.1837, *Western Times,* 26.10.1839.
4. DRO, ECA, Receivers' Accounts, Book 30, 1713/14; Book 54, 1727/8.
5. *ibid.,* Book 137, 1779/80; Book 152, 1790/91; Book 161, 1800/01.
6. DRO, ECA, Act Books, 13.1.1789.
7. DRO, ECA, Receivers' Accounts, Book 108, 1760/61.
8. DRO, ECA, Act Books, 29.1.1771.
9. *ibid.,* 8.11.1774; 24.3.1775.
10. *ibid.,* 9.3.1769 and 9 George III, cap. xCiii, a local act 'to continue and render more effective the acts for amending several roads from the city of Exeter'.
11. e.g. DRO, ECA, Act Books, 28.11.1780. See also Receivers' Accounts, passim.
12. DRO, ECA, Act Books, 7.4.1790, 19.7.1791.
13. West Country Studies Library, *List of Freemen and Freeholders . . .* 1776.
14. e.g. DRO, ECA, Act Books, 20.9.1763, recording a long list of appointments from aldermen to scavengers.
15. *Flying Post,* 21.7.1814; DRO, ECA, Act Books, 20.2.1809.
16. DRO, ECA, Act Books, 11.11.1788.
17. *ibid.,* 31.10.1769, 29.1.1771, 12.11.1782, 19.12.1784.
18. *ibid.,* 8.10.1771, 29.10.1771.
19. *ibid.,* 14.1.1772.
20. *ibid.,* 18.10.1791.
21. R. Pearse Chope, *Early Tours,* p. 235 and C. Barrett, *Diary of Madame D'Arblay,* iii, p. 203.
22. DRO, ECA, Receivers' Accounts, Book 148, 1788/9.
23. DRO, ECA, Act Books, 23.4.1771; 18.9.1771; 16.7.1762; 12.6.1787; 31.8.1763; 29.10.1771, 16.11.1779; 12.9.1775; 14.4.1773.

NOTES *continued*

24.   *ibid.*, 15.9.1768.
25.   *ibid.*, 10.8.1765.
26.   *ibid.*, 10.1.1792.
27.   *ibid.*, 25.10.1777; 22.8.1786; 10.2.1778.
28.   *ibid.*, 13.7.1779; 15.6.1779.
29.   DRO, ECA, Receivers' Accounts and Vouchers.
30.   DRO, ECA, Act Books, 17.4.1787.
31.   DRO, ECA, Receivers' Accounts, Book 108, 1760/61.
32.   Balderston, *Thraliana*, i, p. 562.
33.   DRO, ECA, Act Books, 2.6.1761; 15.10.1764.
34.   *ibid.*, 28.12.1768.
35.   *ibid.*, 15.2.1779, 25.1.1782, 29.9.1783, 14.2.1786, 1.1.1793.
36.   *ibid.*, 25.9.1769.
37.   *ibid.*, 29.9.1760, 3.11.1772, 11.3.1780; *FP*, 25.5.1797.
38.   DRO, ECA, Act Books, 29.9.1760, 6.7.1762, 6.11.1771, 9.4.1793.
39.   DRO, ECA, Receivers' Accounts, Book 119, 1768/9.
40.   DRO, ECA, Act Books, 23.9.1789, Receivers' Accounts, Book 144, 1784/5.
41.   DRO, ECA, Act Books, 24.9.1764.
42.   *ibid.*, 21.1.1707, 9.1.1770.
43.   *ibid.*, 15.8.1775; 21.11.1780; 25.7.1782.
44.   *ibid.*, 6.5.1763; 13.7.1779.
45.   *ibid.*, 10.4.1797 and *FP*, 13.4.1797.
46.   *FP*, 24.2.1791.
47.   *ibid.*, 5.1.1795, 22.1.1795, 12.3.1795.
48.   1 George III, cap. 28, 46 George III, cap. 39.

Chapter Seven

The Years of War 1793-1815

The declaration of war by the French Republic arrived in London in February 1793. Apart from two brief lulls, in 1802–3 and 1814–5, Britain was continuously at war for twenty-two years. When the end came at last, at Waterloo, steam had been applied to industrial use, particularly for the haulage of coal, and Britain's burgeoning industrial power was the wonder of the Western World. Exeter endured the war years with sturdy patriotism which gave no encouragment to peace movements. At the theatre in 1793 audiences cheered chauvinistic plays such as *Richard I* and *The surrender of Calais*, the latter referring to its capture by Edward III in 1346 and not to its surrender in 1558.[1] Citizens raised funds for the war effort, and at reviews on Woodbury Common and Broadclyst Heath the volunteers prepared to face the veterans of Bonaparte wherever they might land, not, however, without an uneasy feeling that they might also have to face their hungry fellow countrymen, the peasantry, who 'know no harm of Bonaparte but plenty of the squire'. Meanwhile, amid military ceremonies and a lively social life, the industrial and trading city admired by Celia Fiennes and Defoe was disappearing. Exeter was slipping back into the embrace of rural England.

For a time the war and the boom in agriculture, and consequently in rents, masked the decline of local trade and industry. Exeter was a garrison city close to a critical naval zone, especially to Torbay whence the fleet blockaded Brest and watched the Western Approaches. The war brought inflation and hunger, but also opportunities for profit and even pleasure. There was military expenditure on a vast scale, on victualling and uniforms, transport and accommodation. Officers of the garrison required appropriate goods and services. Military stores, canon and ammunition were stored within Rougemont Castle. The city stirred to the colour and ceremony of military occasions. Military bands entertained the city. The officers of smart cavalry regiments entertained Exeter's society, supported benefit nights at the theatre and applauded fashionable stars of the London stage. Dancing masters perfected themselves in the 'different Scotch dances' in time for the arrival of the Scots Greys for the winter. Innkeepers and others did well out of the conviviality that was an accompaniment of the war effort, as when Colonel Stribling of the volunteers gave a handsome entertainment to the mayor and Chamber in 1794. On Sundays the employees of Russell & Co. the carriers exercised as artillerymen in the Friars. In 1798 young Henry Ellis was taken to watch parades at Aylesbeare Common; his father, in red coat with white facings, white duck trousers, black gaiters, black cross belt and slouched hat which he provided at his own expense, prepared to meet the French, who were themselves mustered, it was rumoured, on Haldon Hill.[2]

The excitement and patriotic fervour of the war years were offset by rising prices, hunger and business difficulties. Trade was dislocated: Exeter's last markets in the Mediterranean were closed. In January 1793 Exeter's businessmen assembled to oppose the renewal of the charter of the East India Company and to urge the establishment of free trade to the Far East in substitution for vanishing markets in Europe.[3] For the city's overseas trade the final blow came in 1796 when the French armies occupied Leghorn and city merchants were reported to have lost £100,000. No attempt was made by the merchants of Exeter, unlike those elsewhere, to penetrate the French blockade.

Naval victories provided welcome opportunities for celebrations. The city's houses were decorated with laurel, wine was supplied in abundance at the Guildhall, and the volunteers paraded to fire their muskets in celebration of Lord Howe's victory off Ushant on 1 June 1794. Nelson's victory of the Nile, on 1 August 1798, became known in Exeter on 3 October and the city shared with gusto in the national celebrations. Exeter's pride in its association with the victory was suitably marked in the following year by the grant of the freedom to Captain Thomas Louis of the *Minotaur*, a native of Exeter, whom Nelson had thanked for his support at a crucial stage in the battle. After both victories funds were raised towards the support of widows and orphans of casualties in the fleets. But there were also years of gloom, particularly 1797. At Christmas 1796 the French had taken an invasion force to Bantry Bay in Ireland, and had returned to Brest in January, defeated by the weather but facing little inconvenience from the British Navy. In the following summer it was an Exonian, Richard Parker, son of a baker of St Mary Major, who led the naval mutiny at the Nore and became 'president' of the Floating Republic. Parker was hanged, having achieved an uncharacteristic notoriety for a son of the 'Ever Faithful City', and received no mention by Alexander Jenkins in his record of these years. Meanwhile the coasts of Devon were rarely free from the depredations of privateers and the people of Exmouth anxiously debated precautions to be taken against enemy raids. The naval situation was restored by the victories of St Vincent and Camperdown but Exonians of an antiquarian cast of mind canvassed the exhumation of the Saxon fyrd and the organisation of all able-bodied citizens in defence.[4]

Citizens in arms under local commanders reflecting the social structure were traditionally popular, except with the professional soldiers who had to put up with the consequent diversion of recruits from the regular army. Exeter provided men for the militia, Fencibles and Volunteers, both raised for the duration of the war for home service. The latter, providing their own horses and uniforms, were the friends, relations and clients of leading businessmen and, in the countryside, the tenants and dependents of the landed gentry. Exeter's first company of Volunteers, fifty or sixty strong, was raised and commanded by Alderman Kitson. Alderman Walker raised a second company in 1796 and after a successful field-day on Broadclyst Heath had the satisfaction of hearing his men declare with cheers that they would follow their officers to any part of the kingdom at an hour's notice. A third company, formed, according to Alexander Jenkins, of 'gentlemen of the first distinction in this city', was raised in that bleak year 1797 for interior defence, their duties significantly including the security of the property of the citizens 'in case of intestine troubles'.[5] A fourth company was raised the following year by John Short, one of the founders of the Devonshire Bank, at a time when the citizens anxiously assembled at the Guildhall to discuss measures for the security of the realm as Exeter was emptied of regular troops.

By 1802 Exeter had raised, and to a great extent financed, eight companies of Volunteers who, it was claimed, were 'of the greatest utility in preserving the peace of the county and intimidating our enemies from the project of invasion'. Local forces certainly contributed to the peace of the county but their reliability was at times uncertain. In 1793 men of the Cornwall Militia assembled in a disorderly manner on Southernhay Green and then proceeded to break into the Guildhall in an attempt to rescue a comrade under arrest for assault. Two years later the rank and file of the Exeter Fencibles showed a disconcerting tendency to sympathise with the inhabitants of Barnstaple when the latter demonstrated over food prices.[6] Local forces, however, did take over static duties from the regulars. They provided guards for Rougemont, escorted prisoners and stores and assisted in the grim ceremonial that attended the execution of rioters. Volunteers willing to provide their own uniforms and horses under the command of their employers or landlords could be relied upon to protect property and to overawe agricultural labourers.

Events in France convinced many that the Christian basis of society was endangered. Fugitive Catholic priests, like their Huguenot predecessors, were given a kindly welcome by a city which usually drew a distinction between the Rome portrayed by Protestant polemics and the handful of local Catholics with whom the average citizen was acquainted. Mons. Dutrieul, who arrived at Exeter at this time, was for many years a teacher of French. When he died at his house in Bedford Circus in January 1829 he was praised for his 'urbanity of manners, gentle disposition and goodness of heart'.[7] The Catholic priests brought with them grim tales of persecution and terror and it was in support of the Christian foundations of society that the inhabitants of the Cathedral Close pledged themselves in 1793 to resist 'that Monster of Infatuation and Inhumanity, the Anarchy of France'.[8] Timothy Kendrick, the conscientious minister of George's Meeting, had considerable trouble with his congregation when he suggested that the French under their revolutionary regime should be supported by prayers in their struggle for liberty.

Despite naval victories and patriotic volunteering Alexander Jenkins regarded the first phases of the war as a period of calamities, privation and distress. During the winter of 1799–1800 the condition of the poor was especially harsh. Heavy snow and severe frost disrupted transport and stopped outdoor work. The price of poor quality potatoes rose to 2*s*. a peck while labourers' wages remained at 1*s*. to 1*s*. 2*d*. a day. Flour went under the counter and Henry Ellis Sr walked in vain to Newton St Cyres and back to buy flour from country relations.[9] In 1800 farmers sending produce to Exeter had to be reassured with the news that respectable inhabitants of the parishes in the poor and disturbed areas had been enrolled as special constables with the duty of apprehending all who assembled in a riotous or disorderly manner in order to obstruct the free sale of corn. A disturbance at Crediton was quelled by the appearance of dragoons from Exeter and by Sir Stafford Northcote's volunteers. Serious distress was experienced in particular by the workers in the declining cloth industry, both in Exeter and in its rural hinterland. In contrast to the prosperity of landlords and farmers, agricultural labourers deprived of secondary occupations were driven to express their grievances by means of the disturbances and minor riots which broke out between 1795 and 1801. The governing classes in the city and countryside handled the situation with humanity and restraint and landlords and businessmen contributed to the provision of relief, but it was not within their philosophy to consider an increase in wages. The county magistrates, meeting at Rougemont Castle in April 1798, firmly rejected applications for an increase in rural wages on the grounds that any such increase would prejudice rather than benefit the labourers,[10] and in Exeter, now fast declining as an industrial city, the mass of wage earners, devoid of the opportunities opening in the emerging industrial Midlands and the North, were left to survive as best they could under the tight social controls of rural England. At a public meeting held in April 1801 under the auspices of the Chamber over £2,000 was subscribed on the spot to be used for the purchase of food, including herrings from Scotland, and its sale at reasonable prices. James Buller MP contributed £200 and the Chamber and the Cathedral Chapter one hundred guineas each.

The first stage of the war ended in 1801 with the ratification of the preliminaries of peace, news of which arrived at Exeter by the London mail on 11 October, ten days after it had been signed. The news was greeted with

with much rejoicing, parades and *feux de joie*. The formal proclamation of peace was celebrated in May 1802 with all the traditional ceremony. The incorporated bodies of tradesmen marched in procession with their banners and insignia and were followed by the band of the Inniskilling Dragoons. Mr Jaffe the ironmonger, on a borrowed charger, 'conducted himself very respectably' as herald; the sergeants-at-mace and the swordbearer paced before the right worshipful the mayor, Thomas Floud, and the aldermen and councillors walking two by two. At the Guildhall Archdeacon Moore moved an address to the king on the blessings of peace.[11] The militia and volunteers were promptly disbanded and golden snuff boxes presented to commanding officers.

Among the most obvious blessings of peace was a fall in the price of bread. The price of the quartern loaf stood at 9¼*d*. in December 1801 and at 10*d*. in January and February 1802. It fell to 8½*d*. in July 1802 and to 8*d*. in September on the first anniversary of the tumults of the previous year. Stocks of corn were released. Wheat was on offer in Exeter at 6*s*. a bushel compared with 16*s*. 6*d*. in the previous December. Devon innkeepers announced a reduction in the hire of postchaises owing to the fall in the cost of oats and hay. According to the price-tables published in the *Gentleman's Magazine* Devon wheat in mid-August 1801 had been 146*s*. 1*d*. per quarter, barley 75*s*. 11*s*. and oats 32*s*. 10*d*. By the end of October the prices had fallen to 56*s*. 1*d*., 22*s*. 3*d*. and 22*s*. This proved to be a temporary respite. Though prices never returned to the level of 1801 the average price of wheat in July would be over 123*s*. a quarter and the quartern loaf in Exeter would cost 1*s*. 8*d*.[12]

The return of peace and stability appeared to be confirmed by the low key of the general election of July 1802. John Baring had retired, disillusioned by the cost of Exeter's politics. The candidates were the Whigs, James Buller and Sir Charles Bampfylde, and the Tory wine merchant Edmund Granger. The Chamber resolved unanimously that Buller, a conservative-minded gentleman of impeccable local connections would be supported by 'their Votes and Interest' and recommended that their candidate should give their support full publicity. Buller and Bampfylde were returned after a quiet election. The electors were congratulated by the local press on supporting their chosen candidates 'without being swayed by those Electioneering Entertainments which so often influence and frequently subdue weak minds'.[13] Weak minds were to be spared such temptation until after Waterloo.

When in March 1803 the local newspapers carried reports of Napoleon's menacing and ill-tempered conversation with the British ambassador, the ruling classes of the city and the county of Devon again rallied to defend the established order. At a meeting of the nobility, gentry, clergy and freeholders of Devon, at Rougemont Castle, the philanthropist banker S.F. Milford declared that the constitution, next to Christianity, was the greatest blessing that could be conceived.[14] In May plans were made to raise a corps of volunteer infantry and a county meeting was held at the Castle to plan local defence and security in the event of invasion. In August Edmund Granger, the unsuccessful parliamentary candidate of July 1802, produced his plans for raising six companies of Exeter City Volunteers: six companies of sixty men, each with a lieutenant colonel, six captains, twelve lieutenants and an adjutant. Six hundred men were raised and volunteered to serve in any part of the Western Military District, that is Devon, Cornwall and Somerset. While across the Channel an army of one hundred and fifty thousand men, Napoleon's Army of England, was assembled at Boulogne and Europe, from Holland round to Genoa, was pressed into the French war effort, Exeter agreed that 'the peculiar Situation of Men of Property, Tradesmen and other Respectable Persons, tenders it expedient that a volunteer corps, of limited service, should be raised in the city',[15] to play their part against the 'haughty tyrant, the modern Attila'.

By November 1803 the regiment of foot volunteers, armed, clothed and paid by the government was undertaking guard duties at military stores, magazines and the Castle.[16] Two companies of artillery were formed under Alderman Thomas Floud as colonel, and officered by men such as Samuel Kingdon the ironmonger and future mayor. The militia was again brought up to strength, its officers directed to turn their minds to the potentiality of West Country topography for 'ambuscading French invaders'.[17] The camp on Woodbury Common was enlarged and General Simcoe, commander of the western military district, wrestled with the task of turning the militia into a force capable of resisting invasion; he also spent much time on the scarcely less intractable problem caused by Lord Rolle's anxiety over damage to his new plantations by military exercises.

During these years, when France dominated Europe and allied coalitions repeatedly fell to pieces, only naval successes, as in the first phase of the war, provided opportunities for the city's church bells to ring good tidings. There was a heartening reminder of Sir Francis Drake in November 1804 when Russell's wagons passed through the city from Plymouth carrying under armed escort treasure from a Spanish frigate taken off Cadiz.[18] After Trafalgar, French prisoners became a familiar sight in Devon parole towns; young Henry Ellis, enduring his apprenticeship at Tiverton, saw Admiral Dumanois in full uniform and watched Sir Sidney Smith, the hero of Acre, call on that distinguished survivor of Trafalgar.[19]

In March 1804 the *Flying Post* complimented Exeter on its position as 'the metropolis of the West of England', despite its being very dirty.[20] There was little apparent concern for the loss of its industry. The assize ball in August 1804 at the assembly room in The Hotel was attended by an imposing gathering of the county's, and indeed of the nation's, ruling class: Lord Fortescue, Lord Lieutenant; the millionaire landowner Lord Rolle; John Parker, later Earl Morley, friend of Pitt and Canning; Edward Law, Baron Ellenborough, leading counsel for Warren Hastings, Chief Justice and father of a governor-general of India; Sir Robert Wilson, governor of Gibraltar, baron of the Holy Roman Empire, author, soldier and politician; General Simcoe, the military area commander, first governor of Upper Canada and soon to be appointed commander-in-chief in India; and local magnates, Sir John Duntze, Sir Stafford Northcote, Lord Clifford and Lord Graves.[21] These men, by hereditary descent or adoption, were members of that powerful brotherhood, the gentlemen of England, who made, and enforced, the law. They ruled the countryside and now, less directly, the city. In the general elections of 1806 and 1807 James Buller and Sir Charles Bampfylde were returned without a contest and in 1812 Buller, by then a Tory and another Tory, William Courtenay, were returned, again without a contest and with the full backing of the Chamber.

The social activities that accompanied the assizes were again unusually well-attended in 1806 after the freeholders of Devon had assembled at the Castle to return the knights of the shire, without a contest, and to hear S.F. Milford's peroration, 'May the British Constitution last for ever'. In 1807, at a time when Napoleon and the Russian tsar were arranging the affairs of Europe, there was again a large number of visitors to Exeter for the summer assizes and the major event of the season, the sheriff's ball, was well attended by county families. Spectators thronged in good weather to watch Haldon races. The streets were blocked by race traffic, gigs, carriages and wagons, and by the cattle driven in from the country for the Lammas Fair. It was a self-confident society, free from moral doubts as to the justice of the war and with an indomitable confidence in ultimate victory. In the dark days of 1797 the organisers of a petition urging on the King a change of government and peace with France had received no effective support. During the serious banking crisis of 1810 men of property assembled at the Guildhall to declare their confidence 'in the strict honour and undeniable credit and respectability' of the local banks. There were minor failures, such as the small Western Bank which involved the Exonian John Wilcocks, brother of the prosperous draper James Wilcocks, and although the larger bankers weathered the storm a long list of lesser bankruptcies reflected the strain imposed on the local business community by the hazards of wartime conditions. Members of the Chamber itself achieved a wholly unprecedented prominence among the business casualties of the period. John Balle, silversmith, and Joseph Greenway, cotton manufacturer, both former mayors, were removed from the Chamber in 1809 after a face-saving formula had been substituted for the original 'circumstances due to poverty'.[22] William Bate, who had been mayor in 1789–90, was allowed to retire from the Chamber in 1808 on account of ill-health and reduced circumstances, and Councillor Jackson was removed that same year on account of poverty.[23] John Bennett, dyer, who had attempted to modernise the Exeter woollen industry, went bankrupt and so also, in 1813, did James Phillips, proprietor of The Hotel since 1799.

While speculators of genius like the Barings moved their operations elsewhere and the heirs of city merchants turned to country banking, on the surface, in Exeter, there was vigour and confidence. The brief high noon of horse travel had set in. By 1800 the crack stage coaches were a daily wonder in Exeter, painted and emblazoned, swaying, creaking and jingling between The Hotel, the Half Moon or the New London Inn and the Bath or London roads. During the final decades of the war, when despatches from Falmouth carried the news of Wellington's Peninsular victories, Exeter evoked the world of *Lavengro*. In 1802 an officer of the garrison and a Chichester of Arlington demonstrated their skill with the ribbons by racing the London Mail and the Plymouth Mail from the East Gate to Honiton for five hundred guineas, driving picked teams of horses provided by Phillips of The Hotel and John Land of the New London Inn.[24] Cricket was becoming popular and in 1808 an elegant entertainment with dancing to the band of the Light Dragoons accompanied a match near St Davids church. But the lesser orders were also in evidence. At the Haldon races the nobility and gentry were incommoded by roughs whose activities made it necessary for Sir Henry Stafford Northcote to swear in a posse of mounted special constables. Wrestling attracted large crowds to Ide and to the fields at the outskirts of the city, at Hills Court and off Blackboy Road. The proceedings were rough and in 1816 it was reported that an innkeeper died of injuries received at a match. It was at Exeter, in 1812, that the celebrated pugilist Molyneaux, then turned wrestler, was thrown by the Moretonhampstead champion.

The surface of life in Regency Exeter was rippling with the premonitory breeze that heralded the controversies of the future, religious and political, but the long war was ending at last. In 1812 Lord Clinton passed through the city with despatches from Wellington and the eagles captured at Salamanca. The news was celebrated by John Land with a lavish display of illuminations at the New London Inn and Exeter crowded the theatre to applaud that talented actress Mrs Jordan, the mother of the Duke of Clarence's ten children. In the following year fireworks and the peal of bells acclaimed Wellington's victory at Vittoria and ladies were invited to wear the 'Wellington' or 'Vittoria' style in evening dress with the hair carefully arranged in dishevelled curls and held in place with a laurel bandeau.[25] Peace in 1814, confirmed the following year at Waterloo, was hailed as the 'permanent return of Peace and Plenty'. In sunny June weather Exeter organised pageantry that in fact was a memorial service for a vanished world. There was the usual procession of city dignitaries, the Chamber, the trade incorporations, the guardians of the poor, the militia and the volunteers. The theme of the pageant was the story of the woollen industry 'from the wool on the sheep's back to the finisher and the shipping of the bales': shepherds and shepherdesses with their crooks and a lamb; children under a banner proclaiming, 'We are the children of industry'; Jason on horseback with the Golden Fleece; a horseman representing the foreign merchant; a full-rigged ship laden with bales marked Hamburg, Cadiz and Oporto, sailing out of a vanished past. Sheepshearers, woolsorters, shearers, fullers, dyers, hotpressers marched in a procession which began at nine in the morning and did not end till seven in the evening.[26] It was an expression of pride in the past and of hope, destined to be unfulfilled, in the future.

By September 1815 the wine merchants were again offering for sale French wines of good quality. A crowd assembled on the Quay to watch a French ship unload fowls, turkeys and ducks, butter, fruit and onions, and public debate became acrimonious once again over a petition to Parliament against the renewal of income tax, 'born in corruption, fostered in iniquity'. Napoleon's Hundred Days interrupted the euphoria, but the Waterloo despatch appeared in the local press on 29 June. The Chamber promptly bestowed the freedom of the city on the Duke, to be presented in a gold box worth one hundred guineas. In the August race-week Eastlake's celebrated portrait of the fallen emperor was being exhibited at Exeter, and the Chamber, 'being always desirous of cooperating with any plans tending to the improvement of the city' gave its benevolent support to a meeting of citizens assembled at The Hotel to form the Exeter Gas Company.

According to the census of 1801 Exeter at that time had a population of approximately 17,400,[27] growth having been negligible since the entry of the Prince of Orange. The great naval base and arsenal of Plymouth had a population of over 43,000 and Bristol, which Exeter had once rivalled as a port, had over 63,000. Exeter however was still significant in terms of population at a time when only thirteen towns and cities outside London exceeded 20,000 and, with the exception of Plymouth, Exeter dwarfed the other towns of Devon. Crediton, the largest of these, had a population of 4,929 and Barnstaple only 3,743. On the national scale, however, the population figures indicate decline, Exeter, having been fourth or fifth in terms of population at the end of the seventeenth century, was fourteenth by 1801.

The mass of Exeter's population still lived below the line of North Street and South Street. St Mary Major, with 299 inhabited houses and a population of 2,135, was by far the largest of the intra-mural parishes and was exceeded only by St Sidwells and St Davids. St Sidwells had a population of 2,707 and 403 inhabited houses concentrated between the East Gate and the Blackboy Road and along Paris Street as far as Cheeke Street. The built-up area of St Davids, a parish with 313 inhabited houses and a population of 1854 inhabitants, was concentrated along the road between the North Gate and the Packhorse Inn and also along the line of Longbrook Street to Hills Court. Within the walls the tiny adjacent parishes of St George and St John were too poor to support more than one parish church between them, but they contained about 155 and 213 persons per acre compared with less than four in St Sidwells. Apart from Southern-hay there was no significant building development outside the walls until the end of the war. The new County Gaol, where thousands gathered to watch unfortunate wretches expire on the 'new drop' stood alone in the fields beyond the Longbrook. It had been completed by William Hooper in 1794. Behind the gaol were the fine new cavalry barracks completed in 1792. Both were evidence of the concern of the government and the property owning classes generally for the preservation of a social structure threatened by Jacobinism.

Over 70 per cent of the population, 12,692 persons, were said in 1811 to derive their living from manufactures, but Exeter was far from being a manufacturing city of the new pattern such as Birmingham or Leeds. A few, ninety-two families out of 2,898, were employed in agriculture. 1,411 families, 31.42 per cent, were classified under 'others', which included professional occupations and retired people. In contrast, contemporary Bradford, which with other Yorkshire towns had wrested pre-eminence in the woollen industry from the South West, had only 14.2 per cent of families in this category.

Without access to raw materials, such as coal and iron, and with no easy access to mass markets, Exeter's economic prospects were discouraging. Industrial activity included brewing, soap making, tanning, boot and shoe making, cabinet and furniture making, building and all the manifold activities of the transport industry, but all was small-scale and directed at local markets. There was employment for inn servants, male and female, for ostlers, grooms, wagoners, coachmen and post-boys, for wheelwrights, coachmakers, saddlers and blacksmiths, the smiths making an impressive contribution to the procession celebrating peace in 1814, but the 'mills' which had once employed Exeter's workforce were closing one by one. The property of John Bennett, dyer, sold in 1804 after his bankruptcy, included not only his dye-houses in Exe Island but also a factory containing machinery for worsted yarn, carding engines, devils and jennies, furnaces, beams and weights, labourers' cottages and a spinning factory and workshops near Lions's Holt in St Sidwells.[28] In 1800 a witness informed a select committee of the House of Commons that, despite the cost of transport, Devon wool was being sent to Yorkshire.[29]

Attempts to develop new industrial techniques failed through lack of a base in local markets, bad communications and inadequate financial resources. Paper-making had emerged as a modest local industry early in the eighteenth century, the raw materials being available in the form of cordage and similar materials, and rags imported by sea. But Edward Pimm's paper mill, which opened with a flourish in the Bonhay in 1798, was bankrupt by 1814.[30] A more ambitious venture was the Wear Field Cotton Manufactory of Joseph Greenway and Partners situated downstream of the quay. This enterprise claimed to be the only cotton mill in the west of

England. When sold on liquidation in 1807 the property comprised an imposing edifice of brick and stone with four floors containing water-twist spinning frames, each with eighty-four spindles, two mules with 204 spindles, thirty-one carding engines, stocking frames and 141 looms for the manufacture of calicoes. Adjoining were workmen's cottages, each with a small garden.[31]

Some attempts were made locally to introduce new techniques to agriculture. William Beal, of Pancras Lane, was experimenting in 1804 with threshing machines capable of threshing 200 bushels of barley in under eight hours,[32] in contrast to the flail which threshed sixteen bushels in a long day's work. In 1805 James Beal announced that he was constructing threshing machines on a 'new principle' at his 'manufactory' behind the Dolphin Inn. In 1811 the American, Charles Vancouver, who reported on Devon for the Board of Agriculture in 1808, was encouraging the use of threshing machines costing forty guineas each.[33] But rural labour was cheap. Farmers were doing well enough out of the war and in the post-war slump were more inclined to reduce wages than to experiment in improved techniques.

Elsewhere in England river transport was being supplemented by canals to bring together raw materials, manufactured goods and markets. There were plans in 1796 for the construction of a canal from Topsham to Cullompton, and ultimately to Taunton, to provide an alternative to the perilous sea-route from south Wales round Hartland Point and Land's End. The Chamber was not favourable, fearing that the project would be detrimental to the trade and interests of the city and likely to affect the rights and revenues of the Chamber.[34] The Chamber did however endorse plans for the construction of a canal from Exeter to Crediton; in 1811 the engineer James Green called for one hundred canal cutters to begin work but the project got no further than a short length of excavations. In Exeter and the small towns of Devon the prosperous gentry and middle classes in general supported a demand for luxuries and services but their spending power alone could not reinvigorate the declining industrial economy of the county.

Although for a whole generation after 1800 there were no serious disorders in Exeter a large proportion of the population remained permanently on the edge of starvation. During the peace celebrations of 1814 it was estimated that 8,000 'poor persons' were entertained to a meal,[35] and although the figure must have included many who were not strictly 'deserving poor', on the face of it about one-third of the population of the city qualified for a free meal. Throughout the war there was pressure in Exeter for an increase in wages. The journeymen bricklayers extracted some increase in 1793 and the master bricklayers raised their prices accordingly. In the same year the journeymen tailors were warned against precipitate action because many were already out of work.[36] The master tailors that year offered 2s. a day to good workmen, which was about the rate earned by carpenters and plumbers in Walpole's England of fifty years before. During the war labourers on the Exeter canal were paid 1s. 6d. a day and this was raised to 1s. 10d. in 1813, when the price of the quartern loaf was 1s. 4½d.[37] For a labourer earning 1s. 10d. a day the loaf would have cost over ninety per cent of his daily earnings. Much, of course, depended on a man's capacity and the nature of the job. In 1810 a man employed by the builders William Hicks & Sons received 1s. 9d. for four days 'half work' filling in ground and loading carts.[38] On the other hand a labourer clearing up after sawyers was paid at the rate of 2s. 6d. a day. Men were not paid if they did not work and winters were cold, especially the winter of 1813–4 when the city experienced the worst snowfall within memory and the streets were deserted for three weeks. In that chill winter, coal, by then the predominant fuel, used even by bakers, pastry cooks and confectioners, was on sale for 24s. a quarter for ready cash, a price well beyond the reach of the poor. The distribution of small quantities below cost by the Society for the Assistance of the Sobre and Industrious Poor, established during the war, continued to provide for some an opportunity for a hot meal and some heat.[39] The desperate need explains the wall constructed round the coal quay in 1802 to prevent pilfering.

Skilled artisans were better off than labourers and the earnings of some of them rose substantially over pre-war levels. Carpenters employed by a builder working for the Chamber were paid at the rate of 3s. 4d. a day in 1809 and at the same rate for similar work in 1811.[40] In 1813 and 1814 the same builder was charging at the rate of 3s. 10d. a day for work on Chamber property. Plumbers repairing water closets and pipes in St John's Hospital in 1814 were paid 3s. 6d. a day and smiths at work in the Southgate Prison that same year received 4s.[41] Some sawyers in 1810 received 4s. each for what was entered as 'one day four hours at trees', but in 1811 for what may have been lighter work they were paid 3s. 6d.[42] In 1796, according to a statement by the master sawyers, a sawyer could have earned 30s. to 40s. a week; if this statement is correct it probably referred to a special rate for what was always gruelling labour. The evidence suggests that while in the 1790s craftsmen might have earned 2s. 6d. per day, in the latter stages of the war their rate of pay had increased by 53 per cent. For labourers, if the usual wage in Exeter was 1s. 4d. a day before the war, there was an increase of barely 35 per cent by 1813, at least for labourers employed on the canal.

The employment of women and girls gave some assistance to family budgets. Mrs Henry Ellis Sr made some money for a time by knitting mittens, and both her daughter and future daughter-in-law were employed in millinery. Domestic service was the largest source of employment for women though pay was low and conditions often harsh. Young Ellis, soon after his marriage, paid £5 a year to 'a strong girl' from Dolton, in North Devon.[43]

By this time the Chamber too could no longer live within its means as prescribed by law and tradition. Repeated attempts were made to reduce expenditure. A jovial custom, long reflected in the receivers' accounts, went into limbo in August 1809 when the Chamber ordered 'that in future there shall be no Meetings previous to Chambers at the Swan as hath been customary'. In 1811 the Chamber made a despairing gesture of self-denial by a resolution that 'all Dinners and other Entertainments usually given by this Body be discontinued.' Second thoughts revoked this decision a month later. In 1812 the surgeon, Benjamin Johnson, was allowed a salary of £400 for his mayoralty, from which he was to defray the cost of sixteen official dinners, the Chamber supplying furniture, china and cutlery. Mayors continued to be reimbursed on this scale.[44] The wine bill continued to worry the Chamber: an item of £245 for wine provided by Messrs Kennaway appears in the accounts of 1807–8 and in 1812 a committee was requested to review expenditure on wine at meetings of the Chamber. In 1813 the Chamber, as usual short of ready cash, had to give a bond for £170 to meet the unpaid balance of another wine account.[45]

The essential financial problem, however, transcended bills for wine. The Chamber was facing retribution for the casual handling of charities over the past century. In 1814 it was decided that the accounts of the curators of charities should be inspected, if necessary twice a year, 'for the purpose of ascertaining the funds of such charities and to carry into effect the intentions of the original founders'. It was too late. The Chamber was already expensively involved in a law suit over Spicer's Charity and in June the receiver had to report that he had remitted £2,000 to London in accordance with an order of the Court of Chancery. Since no funds were available 'the Right Worshipful the Mayor had most kindly assisted him with the Loan of a considerable sum.'[46] The mayor in question was Burnet Patch, hop and spirit merchant, who was also buying property put on the market by the Chamber at that time. The cost of rebuilding Cowley Bridge, severely damaged by flood in January 1809, was a further liability. The total cost, £9,000, was shared by Exeter and the county of Devon, and £800 had to be borrowed to meet initial expenses.[47] Even the repayment of advances from members of the Chamber itself were in arrears. The Chamber had to approve a bond of £300, instead of £200, in favour of Mayor Benjamin Johnson 'he having received but one hundred instead of two hundred' previously authorised.

Canal administration, as usual, was also causing difficulties. Coal merchants, whose barges contributed a major part of canal traffic, were not paying their dues. In 1810 the canal was therefore closed to their barges until the dues were paid and the possibilities of landing coal elsewhere than via the canal had to be investigated. The accounts of the wharfinger were in their traditional disarray, despite the Chamber's good intentions to keep them under review. In 1814 it was noted that Thomas Balle's accounts had not been examined for several years notwithstanding the appointment of a special committee for that purpose. Balle resigned in August. Later he prudently declined 'to state the profits accruing to him for collecting the freight charges' and merely acknowledged that in addition to his annual salary of 100 guineas he had received an average of £45 for collecting the town dues.[48] By the end of 1816 investigation revealed that there appeared to have been 'a very large balance in Mr Balle's hands for many years past'.

Wharfingers must always have been tempted to keep on good terms with traders by refraining from too much zeal in the collection of dues. In 1814 the firm of Joseph Sanders and Partners finally compounded with a payment of £490 for dues unpaid for 'many years', and this at a time when the Chamber, short of cash, was borrowing £500 at interest from Charles Collyns the banker.[49] The problem, however, was not solved by the errant Balle's departure. Thomas Upham, brother of Edward Upham, mayor in 1809–10, was appointed wharfinger in September 1815. In 1821 investigations of Upham's accounts revealed a debt to the Chamber of £2,705. He was continued in office 'notwithstanding the enormous Deficiency in his accounts . . . from a feeling of respect to his brother' and the hope, unfulfilled, was expressed that he would give some explanation of the deficiency.[50] Incidents of this nature inspired the rhetorical denunciations of reformers in the 1830s.

Alarmed by the financial situation the Chamber, as it had done so often throughout the eighteenth century, in 1811 appointed a committee to

> consider of some plan for arranging the affairs of this Body and to point out some measures for the discharge of existing Debts and for providing for the future regular payment of the Annuities either by the Sale of a sufficient part of the Property of this Body which they may have the power to dispose of or by such means as may appear to them most eligible.[51]

The outcome was the disposal of property on a scale unprecedented since the sale of the Duryard estate in 1700. Property for sale was valued at £10,176 and most of it was sold forthwith for £7,405. Further sales in 1815 included the Bonhay fulling mills to Edmund Gattey, the town clerk, and of Duryard Mill to Thomas Gray, attorney.[52] Like many an embarrassed landowner the Chamber felled trees wholesale; 118 trees in the Bonhay and on the slope above Exe Lane were sold in 1812. Customary perquisites such as loppings were no longer to be disposed of by the Chamber's officers.

Efforts were also made to improve the easy-going eighteenth-century administration. In November 1814 the sheriff, Robert Trewman, printer and proprietor of the *Flying Post,* successfully moved that a committee should be appointed to 'consider a Plan for better regulating committees for the purpose of arranging and accelerating the concerns of this Body'.[53] The outcome was the appointment of three committees, navigation, general purposes and finance, the embryo of the committee system of the reformed corporation after 1835. Fines of 2*s.* 6*d.* were imposed for the non-attendance of committee-members without legitimate excuse and a committee clerk was appointed and sworn to secrecy. At the end of the year it was resolved that 'all officers in attendance on this Body in Chamber be sworn to secrecy'. It was the emergence of a new professionalism. Attempts were made yet again to improve lackadaisical attendance and discipline at meetings of the Chamber. In April 1801 eight members of the Chamber had been absent at 11 a.m., one hour after the meeting was due to begin, despite the Chamber's decision in 1770 to impose a fine of five shillings for such absences. At the ensuing meeting there were still absentees and three aldermen were asked for an explanation. It was this which provoked Alderman Dennis to inform the Mayor that 'having been near forty years as a member of the Chamber he was very desirous of resigning that honour'. A compromise enabled Dennis to remain in office till his death in 1816 when he was honoured as 'Father of the City . . . A true patriot of the old school, a staunch friend to Church and King'.[54] He was of an enduring type in local government, but in the emerging new England it was not only factory hands who were required to submit to the discipline of the clock. The Mayor was requested to authorise no leave of absence unless fourteen of the Twenty-Four were in attendance and even then should use his discretion if the business required the attention of the whole Chamber. In 1815 two aldermen were fined one guinea each for failing to attend without excuse.[55]

NOTES

1. *Flying Post*, 4.4.1793.
2. DRO, 76/20, Memoirs of Henry Ellis, i, pp. 7-8.
3. *FP*, 17.1.1793.
4. A. Jenkins, *History of Exeter*, p. 226.
5. *ibid.*, p. 225.
6. *FP*, 19.9.1793, 9.4.1795.
7. *ibid.*, 29.1.1829.
8. *ibid.*, 17.1.1793.
9. DRO, 76/20, i, p. 12.
10. *FP*, 18.4.1798.
11. *ibid.*, 6.5.1802.
12. *ibid.*, passim and monthly tables in *Gentleman's Magazine*.
13. DRO, ECA, Act Books, 22.5.1802, *FP*, 15.7.1802.
14. *FP*, 24.3.1803.
15. *ibid.*, 11.8.1803.
16. *ibid.*, 1.9.1803, 6.10.1803 and Jenkins, *op. cit.*, pp. 253-5.
17. H. Walrond, *Historical Records of the First Devon Militia*, pp. 211-30 and A. Temple Patterson, *The Other Armada*, pp. 141, 226.
18. *FP*, 22.11.1804.
19. DRO, 76/20, i, p. 26.
20. *FP*, 8.3.1804.
21. *ibid.*, 2.8.1804.
22. DRO, ECA, Act Books, 7.2.1809, 3.5.1809.
23. *ibid.*, 29.9.1808.
24. *Annual Register* 1802.
25. *FP*, 5.8.1813.

NOTES *continued*

27. PP *Abstract of the Answers and Returns made pursuant to an Act passed in the forty-third year of his Majesty George III.*
28. *FP,* 26.1.1804, 2.2.1804, 7.6.1804.
29. *Sessional Papers of the Eighteenth Century: Minutes of Evidence relating to Wool,* 24.4.1800.
30. D.C. Coleman, *The British Paper Industry 1495-1860,* pp. 37, 58, 222; *FP,* 9.3.1799, 19.5.1814.
31. *FP,* 27.11.1806, 28.5.1807.
32. *ibid.,* 2.2.1804.
33. Charles Vancouver, *General View of the Agriculture of Devon,* p. 121.
34. DRO, ECA, Act Books, 11.2.1796, 19.5.1801.
35. *FP,* 12.5.1814.
36. *ibid.,* 4.4.1793, 30.5.1793.
37. DRO, ECA, Act Books, 18.5.1813.
38. DRO, ECA, Receivers' Vouchers, Box 190, Hicks and Sons, Builders, 1817-18.
39. *FP,* 21.1.1814 and W.G. Hoskins, *Industry, Trade and People,* pp. 133, 136.
40. DRO, ECA, Receivers' Vouchers, 1809, 1811.
41. *ibid.,* 1815-16 (sic), and Tradesmen's Bills, 1815-16.
42. *ibid.,* 1810-11.
43. DRO, 76/20, iii, p. 78.
44. DRO, ECA, Act Books, 22.11.1811, 5.12.1812.
45. *ibid.,* 15.12.1812, 10.4.1813.
46. *ibid.,* 1.12.1814 (report of a Committee on Procedures); 23.6.1814.
47. *ibid.,* 17.6.1813, 7.9.1813.
48. *ibid.,* 22.2.1810, 1.6.1810; 8.11.1814, 8.8.1815, 21.8.1815, 11.12.1816.
49. *ibid.,* 17.4.1814.
50. *ibid.,* 12.9.1815, 27.3.1821.
51. *ibid.,* 27.4.1811.
52. DRO, ECA, Receivers' Vouchers, Box 1816, 1815-16; Act Books, 13.6.1815, 10.10.1815.
53. DRO, ECA, Act Books, 13.11.1814.
54. *ibid.,* 7.4.1801, 19.5.1801, 15.9.1801, *FP,* 11.4.1816.
55. Act Books, 31.1.1815.

Chapter Eight

The Spirit of Improvement 1769-1834

According to Alexander Jenkins it was in 1769 that the 'spirit of improvement began to manifest itself' in Exeter.[1] The occasion was the construction of The Hotel, the future Royal Clarence in Cathedral Close, an establishment which rapidly became the rendezvous of influential society from the city and the county of Devon. The term 'improvement' signified moral as well as technical progress and covered the active involvement of respectable citizens in humanitarian and religious activities, the reform of prisons, the construction and repair of churches, the distribution of bibles, the education of the poor and the relief of the destitute. Architecturally the spirit of improvement inspired the brief flowering of Georgian and Regency building which in Exeter began towards the end of the eighteenth century, acquired full vigour about the time of Trafalgar and dwindled in the 1830s. Buildings from the age of improvement in Exeter are still to be found scattered throughout the city from St Thomas to Heavitree, from the heights of Pennsylvania to the Topsham road. Most of them are terraces by means of which the Georgian builders sought to impart to comfortable domesticity the unity and dignity of classical taste. They include a provincial, almost rustic, interpretation of the classical such as Sydney Place in Alphington Road and Devonshire Place off Union Road below Pennsylvania. Above all the builders and architects of late-Georgian Exeter gave to relatively small houses the dignity and unity of crescents and terraces. They built to scale, conserving and not dominating, maintaining the intimacy of a medieval city.

The end of the eighteenth century which ushered in the age of improvement was also the golden age of the amateur historians, naturalists and scientists, men of education and intellectual curiosity with sufficient means to indulge their tastes. Though their conclusions and theories were sometimes erroneous or far-fetched in the light of modern scholarship they provided material which formed essential bricks in the expansion of the edifice of knowledge. It is true that Robert Southey, wrting in 1802 under the name of Dom Manuel Espriella, was critical of the citizens of Exeter, dismissing them as 'behindhand with their countrymen in information and refinement'.[2] In the course of his brief visit he presumably did not meet those Exonians most closely associated with the age of improvement. He may not have been aware that in 1796 Robert Trewman, bookseller and newspaper proprietor, had published *Essays by a Society of Gentlemen at Exeter* on topics such as 'British Monuments in Devon', light and the contraction of the iris of the eye, a historical survey of falconry and, inevitably, classical themes, including studies of Pindar, Hesiod and Homer. John Bowring, born in Exeter in 1799, began his polyglot achievements in the library of Robert Kennaway, a library purchased from the profits of trade.[3] His less-privileged contemporaries were likewise not starved of good reading. The Public Select Library, founded in 1807 with Alderman White in the chair, contained between eight and nine thousand volumes, 'to interest, to inform and to instruct the mind', though books on controversial politics and religious issues were banned as well as books regarded as unfit for the perusal of the young. In the same spirit Samuel Kingdon, the Unitarian ironmonger, presided at a public meeting in 1825 at which it was agreed to establish a Mechanics' and Tradesmen's Institute, with the important proviso that the library should not contain books on controversial theology or politics. But with such responsible members of county society as a Buller, a Northcote, an Acland and a Kekewich among its members the Devon and Exeter Institution, founded in 1813 for the promotion of science, literature and the arts, could risk temptations from which it was thought necessary to preserve artisans. For a subscription of one guinea members were able to hear Robert Bakewell, a distinguished geologist and mineralogical surveyor, lecture on the natural history of the earth. To a wider public in the Theatre lecturers on astronomy were careful to explain that science demonstrated that 'the intelligence of nature agrees with the divine revelation'.[4]

Robert Trewman, bookseller, stationer and publisher and for nearly forty years editor and proprietor of the *Flying Post,* had purchased the goodwill of two of Exeter's more evanescent newspapers, Brice's *Old Journal* and the *New Exeter Journal* which he acquired in 1791 from the bankrupt Edward Grigg. Trewman's shop in the High Street offered Exeter's reading public a wide range of choice: science, history, theology, poetry and *belles-lettres.* In January 1797 his stock included the popular novelists Fielding, Smollet and Goldsmith, sermons by local clergy, and for those anxious to cut a dash in local society, *The Complete Art of Carving.* Among other books suitable for the respectable were *Trials for Adultery, Crim. Con. etc.*, published in sixpenny numbers with illustrations 'Humerous, Ridiculous, Whimsical or Amorous' and for a time, before it accompanied effigies of its author to the flames, Trewman stocked Paine's *Rights of Man.* He died in February 1802, mourned by his friends as 'a zealous supporter of our present happy Constitution in Church and State'.[5] Under his son the *Flying Post,* unlike Woolmer's *Gazette,* would support the cause of Reform.

Even Southey conceded that Exeter had a bookseller of learning and ability. Indeed Shirley Woolmer was a respected member of the society of scholars and dilettanti whose articles filled the pages of the *Gentleman's Magazine*. Since he had first set up shop in Exeter in 1785 as bookseller and stationer he had established his reputation as bibliophile and antiquarian, student of mineralogy and geology, editor and newspaper proprietor, philanthropist and one of the Guardians of the Poor. In 1796 he bought the old county gaol which he handed over to the Dissenters for use as a chapel. Like other devout Christians Woolmer would agonise over a reconciliation of geological knowledge with Genesis: shortly before his death in 1831 he wrote to the *Gentleman's Magazine* on 'The Geological Effects of the Deluge', an attempt to check the 'torrent of infidelity and atheism'. Both Trewman and Woolmer reflected the rise in the status of newspaper editors, carrying on from where Andrew Brice, in more difficult circumstances, had left off. They founded newspapers which the *Athenaeum* would later describe as a credit to literature.[6]

In Exeter the primary task of improvement was to adapt the city to meet the demands of increasing traffic and, in particular, to improve the road link between London and the western ports. Hitherto the city had been adapted to conform with the natural environment. In the late-eighteenth century the transport system could no longer tolerate a street pattern that had evolved when wheeled vehicles were rare. An act of 1769 empowered trustees appointed by the city and the county to rebuild or repair the medieval Exe Bridge and to make 'the avenues thereto more commodious'. After a disaster in 1772 when the new structure was carried away by a flood the New Bridge was opened to the public in 1778. Because of the 'Inconvenience and Damage complained of by the Public on account of the Narrowness of the Avenue leading to this City on the West side', the West Wall had been breached at the bottom of Fore Street hill, affording a more direct and wider approach from High Street to the bridge.[7] This was named New Bridge Street. In 1772 it was resolved to remove the Great Conduit from the Carfax and thus to continue the programme to improve the flow of traffic across the city. The Chamber also encouraged development along the new route from the river by means of building leases.

The removal of the city gates as major obstacles to the flow of traffic originated with a resolution by the Chamber in 1775 to the effect that a committee should be appointed comprised of 'every member who shall think proper to attend' to undertake the demolition of the city gates and the walls.[8] The East Gate was pulled down in 1784. The demolition of the North Gate, probably the worst impediment to traffic, followed in 1789. The South Gate, the most imposing of all, was destroyed in 1819. The destruction of these gates removed impressive memorials of Exeter's historic past but although the vogue for 'gothic' ruins and 'ivy-mantled towers' had already set in, the more practical minds of the late-eighteenth century regarded such things as the vestiges of barbarism. Alexander Jenkins applauded the removal of the East Gate and welcomed the opening of a 'beautiful vista' into the High Street. To S.F. Milford the South Gate was nothing more than 'a nest of dungeons'; while young Henry Ellis contemplating the Guildhall from his neat new shop at 199 High Street, mused on the bad taste of his forebears.[9]

The streets, despite the repeated efforts of the Chamber, were cramped, crowded and dirty, blocked by coaches and wagons, builders' debris and the baskets of vendors of country produce. Horse-drawn vehicles striving to pass each other became further entangled amid the herds of bullocks passing through the city to satisfy the demands of naval victuallers in wartime Plymouth. Magistrates repeatedly fined carters for riding casually on the shafts of their vehicles leaving the initiative to their horses in the urban hurly-burly. The mayor's court imposed fines on the owners of loose cattle and of stallions out of control in the streets, for leaving refuse and other obstacles in the streets and for exuberant behaviour such as 'violently driving a dray without proper control'. In September 1800 the Chamber made yet another attempt to improve the cleanliness of the streets by ordering occupiers to sweep the pavement in front of their houses three times a week before 9 a.m. in winter and 8 a.m. in summer; the punishment for failure was severe, a fine of 20s., more than a week's good wages for an artisan. At times parish vestry meetings took the initiative. When Joseph Greenway became mayor in 1804 he not only announced his intention of imposing severe fines on those who left rubbish in the streets but explained that his own parish of Holy Trinity had already made arrangements to clean the streets, number houses and to mark the streets for the benefit of strangers.

Improved communications and Exeter's growing attractions for residents, coupled with the rising standards of living of professional men and county families, created the demand for comfortable modern houses, and in 1774 the Chamber took the unprecedented step of meeting this demand by means of what was virtually a municipal housing scheme. It was resolved, in November of that year, that 'Mr Receiver do employ Mr Stowey and Mr Jones of this City, Builders, to draw a proper plan for Buildings on Southernhay as soon as possible and to lay the same before this Body'.[10] Until 1774 Southernhay was mostly an open space outside the walls, used for grazing and rope-walks, useful ground for exercising horses under the elms and with a view over the fields and gardens of rural St Leonards. The site was ideal for providing that *Rus in Urbe*, that ordered city life against a conventional rural backcloth that was so attractive to educated society and the over-quoted tag from Martial became a popular advertisement for suburban property. Many Exeter builders shared in the development of Southernhay but the first of the new residences were not completed until the 1790s. The *Flying Post* of April 1797 advertised an unspecified number of new buildings for sale at 1,000 guineas each and in 1798 the builder William Hicks had certainy completed two houses. The pace of building seems to have quickened in the era of Trafalgar. John Brown, the builder of Baring Crescent and one who was prominent in the construction of houses in the New Bridge Street area, had completed at least one house in Southernhay by 1804. In 1810 the Southernhay Committee of the Chamber examined plans by William Hicks for six houses. Joseph Rowe, who built Pennsylvania Terrace, worked there and built six houses. Thomas Cole, later the builder of Northernhay Terrace and the Devon and Exeter Subscription Rooms also made his contribution. Though much altered and marred by a multiplicity of traffic signs Southernhay today remains a study in the development of provincial classical taste over some thirty years. It contains the houses of the unassertive Georgian terrace with their roundheaded doorways and lower windows. Then there is the more assertive Southernhay House, with its Tuscan portico, where General Kirkpatrick of the Hon. East India Company sold his mahogany bedsteads, wardrobes and chairs, his bookcase and Grecian sofa shortly before his death in 1812.[11] The series ends with the Doric columns of William Hooper's Chichester Place, completed in 1825.

The Chamber throughout exercised a meticulous control over building operations. No trees were to be cut down without express permission. Ground was levelled and laid out at the expense of the occupiers and under the Chamber's supervision. Alterations and additions were scrutinised; a proposal by a householder as important as the rector of St Martins and St Pancras, who wished to make additions of larger dimensions than were originally approved, was rejected. But in the area within the walls there was no room for crescents and circuses such as were coming to adorn Bath, nor indeed any landlords in Exeter owning the contiguous property, and the financial resources, necessary for the greatest architectural achievements. Of all Exeter's private landlords only the Duke of Bedford owned land suitable for an emulation of Cheltenham.

Plans for the construction of Bedford Circus, subsequently described as 'one of the best examples of unified urban architecture in England',[12] were drawn up in 1773, thus preceding the Chamber's decision to develop Southernhay. In May the Exeter builders Robert Stribling and Giles Painter contracted with the Duchess of Bedford to purchase the buildings and materials of Bedford House, the ancient Exeter town house of the Russells, and to construct within five years 'seven brick houses with vaults, areas, stables, coach houses and garden walls'. The original plans had provided for the construction of twenty-five houses but the circus was not completed until, in March 1825, Thomas Wills Horrell contracted to build thirteen 'full-sized, first rate houses'.[13] The Chamber and the Bedford agents had shared equally in improving the sewerage system in the area in the 1770s and, in 1777, the Chamber appointed a committee to 'superintend the opening of Bedford to Southernhay' in the neighbourhood of the modern post office. (Bedford Circus itself was demolished by the orders of the then City Council after damage by enemy action in 1942.)

Bedford Circus was the first of the select precincts in which the prosperous middle classes, principally bankers, lawyers and medical men sought to maintain a genteel detachment from 'trade' and the noise and smells of city life. The social standing and conservative respectability of their occupants was demonstrated in 1820 when they maintained a disapproving darkness while Whigs illuminated their windows for the acquittal of Queen Caroline.[14] Mathew Nosworthy (1750–1831), the most gifted of Exeter's builder-architects, constructed Barnfield Crescent, off Southernhay, in 1792 and Alexander Jenkins claimed that it would 'scarcely be excelled by any pile of brick buildings in the kingdom, even at the capital itself'.[15] Barnfield Crescent was never completed though Dr Thomas Shapter added a house in 1840. Nosworthy's outstanding work was situated on the magnificent bluff overlooking the river, land owned by the Colleton family. Here in 1805 he completed Colleton Crescent amid general rejoicing over this new manifestation of improvement. On a site once occupied by the drying racks of the cloth industry arose a gently curved terrace, discreetly but plainly indicating opulence and becoming forthwith the home of bankers such as Joshua Williams and Charles and Joseph Barnes Saunders, and of Samuel White, brewer, militia colonel and twice mayor. The crescent, together with the whole of the extensive Exeter estate of the Colletons, was sold by auction in 1827,[16] a sale followed by the construction of the second-rate Regency buildings of Melbourne Street, Melbourne Place and the Friars. Nosworthy himself went on to design and construct Dix's Field, a project which had first been broached in 1796[17] though no work was carried out till 1808.

On Nosworthy's death in 1831 at the age of 81 it was remarked that he had done more than any other individual to develop Exeter 'by constructing mansions to invite the opulent to reside' in the city. Solid though limited wealth, a demand for comfort and sound workmanship, and the willingness to pay for it, certainly inspired the housing boom of the decades after 1800. Not all buildings can have reached the highest standards but the assured prosperity and the standards of taste that prevailed are demonstrated by the specifications for John Brown's Baring Crescent. This development on Baring property was begun on the 1 October 1818 when the first stone was laid for what were described as 'superior cottages'. The specifications insisted that the exterior walls were to be plastered in a 'handsome and durable manner', the painting was to be not less than three coats thick and 'deviations' were not to reduce the value of each house below £1,000. These 'cottages' were to be provided with stables and a coach house and to comprise basement, kitchen and housekeeper's room, pantry, beer and wine cellar, dining room, drawing room and butler's pantry, a second drawing room on an upper floor and eight bedrooms.[18]

Nosworthy's great rival was William Hooper (1751–1831), of whom it was said that Exeter's 'public buildings would long form a monument to his public usefulness.'[19] William Hooper had already built the much admired new county gaol and the great house, now demolished, of Lord Egremont near Silverton. His work in Exeter in the era of Trafalgar consisted of modest terraces designed for retired people of unimpeachable respectability but of modest wealth. For these clients Hooper constructed Higher and Lower Summerlands between 1804 and 1812, the former on the site of the present police station and magistrates court. Known at first as Hooper's Buildings, Higher Summerlands was badly damaged in the Second World War and was demolished. Lower Summerlands remains, though not in its original integrity, a terrace designed for retired officers, clergy and widows with somewhat more modest resources than those enjoyed by the inhabitants of Higher Summerlands. In 1812 Hooper changed his style and turned to the stucco which he used for Baring Place on Magdalen Road, on land acquired from the Barings, houses with doric porticoes and graceful fanlights, the iron balconies and delicate glazing bars of Regency taste. About the same time he built the similarly modest houses forming Midway Terrace on the Heavitree Road, one of which he used as his own residence in his latter years.

The classical traditions and taste that marked the architectural aspects of improvement in Exeter after 1769 reached their climax about 1825. In 1823 the building firm of Rowe completed Pennsylvania Terrace (now Pennsylvania Park) for the Quaker banker Joseph Sparkes. In a commanding position on the hills north of the city and with a magnificent view, Pennsylvania Terrace became one of the most admired tourist attractions of Exeter. With Pennsylvania Crescent, completed about the same time, it is a fine example of the development of Regency architecture for the wealthier citizens of a provincial capital. The construction of Pennsylvania Terrace and of William Hooper's Chichester Place on Southernhay virtually ended the classical inspiration of the great years of Exeter's domestic architecture. The last major essay was Northernhay Terrace, designed by the architect John Lethbridge and constructed by Thomas Cole. Not all the houses were completed when Thomas Cole went bankrupt in 1827. One was inhabited by the artist James Leakey and another was the home of the attorney James Brutton, who also bought nine of the other incompleted houses on Cole's bankruptcy. But Northernhay Terrace never reached the front rank of the city's desirable residences and architecturally was no more than routine work.

In 1837 the Hoopers bought more of the Baring estate of Mount Radford for the very large sum, by contemporary standards, of £16,730.[20] On 1 September they began construction with the first stone of 'a line of cottages' in what is now St Leonard's Road. Attractive and unpretentious, destined to be the stronghold of a prosperous middle-class conservatism throughout the nineteenth century, St Leonard's presaged the cosy villadom of Victorian England. Under William Hooper's son Henry the firm continued to prosper, constructing, with much else, the Higher and Lower Markets, their bills figuring prominently in the financial embarrassments of the reformed corporation after 1835.

The boom in house construction which began in the 1770s and intensified after 1800 was an offshoot of the expansion of the national economy as a whole, intensified by the stimulation provided by lavish government expenditure during the wars of 1793-1815. As the local directories testify, the genteel new houses were occupied by professional men, clergy, doctors, surgeons, lawyers and bankers, and especially by retired officers of the services. Exeter could not match the social attractions of Cheltenham, to which George III gave such encouragment, and lacked the mineral waters from which the Cotswold spa derived its reputation. But living was cheap and the flourishing medical profession made the most of the Devon air; the 'salubrious' air of Heavitree in particular was alleged to have earned the recommendations of 'the most eminent physicians in the country'.[21] The rural surroundings were much admired. Visitors and new residents were assured of congenial society. In 1819 houses offered for sale by Mathew Nosworthy were commended for 'the respectability of their neighbourhood, their extreme pleasantness, the salubrity of their situation and their internal conveniences'.[22] In the time of the Regency a galaxy of retired admirals and generals, mostly of the Hon. I.C.S. and not particularly distinguished, lived in the new houses of Southernhay and Bedford Circus. Old Admiral Sweeny, Rear-Admiral of the Red, retired to Sydney Place in St Thomas after seventy years in the Navy. Colonel John Macdonld, son of the celebrated Flora, lived in Summerlands Place. He was prominent in religious and philanthropic activities and was given an impressive funeral service at the Cathedral, many shops being closed, on his death in 1831.[23]

The occupants of the new houses for the most part shared the growing awareness of social responsibility with its religious basis influenced by both Evangelicalism and Dissent. Among them were the 'respectable citizens' whose meetings held at the Guildhall to discuss matters of public interest were so frequently reported in the press. They included successful well-educated men who formed the first serious opposition to the traditional authority of the Chamber. When in 1809 the Chamber contemplated new legislation for paving, lighting and otherwise improving the streets, to replace the Improvement Act of 1806, the parish vestries, that is the leading ratepayers, appointed their own committees to consider the matter. The mayor refused to co-operate. Accordingly in November a meeting was held at The Hotel under the chairmanship of S.F. Milford, banker and until recently a member of the governing body of the Unitarian chapel, George's Meeting. The main objection to the draft legislation was that it made insufficient provision for participation by the prosperous citizens. Milford offered to withdraw the opposition if the justices, that is the aldermen, undertook to seek provision for the election of improvement commissioners from among the ratepayers and to exclude themselves, *ex officio*, from office. The Chamber, divided over the issue and worried about the cost of a contested bill in parliament, came to terms. The improvement commissioners were to include all members of the Chamber except the magistrates, as well as representatives of the Dean and Chapter, together with thirty-six elected commissioners, each of whom should own property of an annual value of £50 or personal estate valued at £2,000. They were given wide powers including the levying of rates and were authorised to borrow up to £6,000 on the security of the rates. The justices were to retain the duty of hearing appeals in quarter sessions. Henceforward elections to the improvement commission were conducted with keen interest since, like those to the Corporation of the Poor, they afforded an opportunity for active citizenship which the Chamber had confined to a limited class. Respectable citizens were given an opportunity to apply the spirit of improvement to such matters as the construction and alteration of streets and sewers, the naming and numbering of streets, the regulation of the unloading of carts and wagons and the prevention of nuisances. It was an important step towards the association of the ratepayers with what would be accepted as the functions of municipal government.

Milford congratulated his supporters on their success after an arduous struggle. The bells of the cathedral and the parish churches rang to acclaim the elections held to choose the thirty-six improvement commissioners and Milford's health was drunk amid plaudits at a convivial dinner. Exeter's citizens of unimpeachable respectability and affluence had won a round in the battle for municipal reform in the year when Wellington was retreating towards Torres Vedras. Moreover the leadership in Exeter was falling into the hands of the heirs of Old Dissent. Like most of his contemporaries Milford was a prolix orator but when he announced that the Improvement Act of 1810 opened a new era in Exeter he was stating an undoubted fact. It was a sign that educated citizens outside the circle of Exeter's establishment would no longer tolerate the assumptions on which the Chamber had based its authority since 1688.[24]

The 'exhilarating hand of improvement', as a local directory expressed it in 1822, inspired by the growing moral and religious earnestness of the age, was further epitomised in Exeter by the demolition of the South Gate prison and the construction of the new church of Holy Trinity in 1819–20. The Chamber itself encouraged and assisted both projects. Indeed it had discussed the state of the prison in February 1803, and at a special meeting in September 1817 it was agreed that it was 'highly inconvenient' as well as too small. The mayor, Samuel White, was requested to discuss the matter with some of the respectable inhabitants.[25] But it was the oratory of S.F. Milford that mobilised the middle-class conscience. A disciple of the prison reformer John Howard, Milford assured a meeting in the Guildhall in October 1817 that he had visited most of the gaols of England and that the South Gate prison was 'the most disgusting and disgraceful in the kingdom'. Howard's own scathing comments had been published in 1779 and were re-affirmed by James Neild in his *State of the Prisons in England, Scotland and Wales* of 1818, with the hope that 'so opulent a city' would build a new gaol. A proposal to this effect received firm support. By May 1818 the relevant legislation had passed through all its stages and within two years a new gaol had been completed, on the site now occupied by the Rougemont Hotel. It provided separate accommodation for minor offenders, debtors and felons, and for the segregation of men and women.[26]

On the day that the prisoners were moved to their new quarters a large congregation attended, in the June rain, the laying of the foundation stone of the new church of Holy Trinity and heard Milford claim that if the old churches had been enlarged, or new churches built, the gaols would not be 'so disgustingly and portentiously full'.[27] It was still assumed that England was a Christian country, but it was also becoming clear not only that tens of thousands of people never went near a church but that they had no church to go to if they wished. The Exeter parish churches were for the most part in no condition to attract the hungry sheep. St Olave's had been closed for fifty years before it was at length repaired and reopened in 1815. All Hallows on the Walls had been demolished in 1770. St Martin's was in a dangerous state of disrepair. The parish churches of St David, St Stephen and, till its rebuilding, Holy Trinity were little better. All Hallows Goldsmith Street was so badly dilapidated that, with the consent of the bishop, it was scheduled for demolition under the Exeter Market Act of 1820.[28] But help was at hand. Throughout the city the wealthier parishioners rallied to improve the opportunities for religious observance at a time of social and economic turbulence which to many suggested the dissolving throes of the social and moral order. In 1819 the vestrymen of St Mary Arches were driven to declare that they would not be found slumbering at their posts when menaced by 'the continued efforts of Infidelity and Sedition'. St Sidwell's was restored in 1812 at a cost of £8,599 and its reopening was a social event, the church being thronged by a congregation eager to hear the famous soprano, Angelica Catalini, who commanded high fees. Bishop Pelham (1807–20), though usually to be found in London acting host to the Prince Regent and the highest society, found time to dedicate the little church of St David after it was rebuilt in 1817. In 1820 the parishioners of All Hallows Goldsmith Street defied the Chamber and insisted on restoring instead of demolishing their neglected church which survived till 1906.[29]

At the same time there were signs that what would be regarded as aspects typical of Victorian England were appearing. In 1801 the mayor and magistrates, 'taking into consideration that it is their indispensable duty to

give all the weight that can be derived from their official character to the
support of Religion', urged their fellow citizens to observe Good Friday and
by 1804 it was observed with satisfaction that on that day shops were shut
and parish churches were full. There was too renewed emphasis on
decorum. In 1819 the mayor, Thomas Floud, announced his resolve to end
the 'most shameful and lawless practice' of throwing water over passers by,
both men and women, on the Thursday of Easter week. The Sunday School
movement took root in Exeter from 1790, St Sidwell's parish church setting
the pace, and all denominations agreeing on the necessity of inculcating the
children of the poor with the knowledge of their duty towards God and
Man, and on the need for useful accomplishments such as reading. A public
meeting was held to discuss the distribution of bibles to the 'lower orders'.
There was, inevitably, sectarian competition.

In 1825 a meeting of citizens at the Guildhall, where they were addressed
by Bishop Carey, bore witness to 'the importance of furnishing to our
poorer brethren the opportunity for attending Divine worship'. Evening
services were introduced at about this time and became both a religious
duty and a social occasion for those with suitable clothes.[30] When St
Sidwells and Mary Arches introduced evensong in December 1819 both
churches were over-crowded. Collections to assist the Sobre and
Industrious Poor were becoming a regular event. Prosperous citizens were
also solicited for subscriptions for French refugee clergy, for wounded
seamen, for Spanish patriots and, at the end of hostilities, for war-
devastated Germany. Indeed Alexander Jenkins was not unjustified when
in the preface to his history of Exeter, published in 1806, he dwelt with pride
on the charitable activities of his time.

The Methodists too were beginning to prosper after seventy years of bare
survival. In 1810 the Wesleyan community purchased the old Mint chapel
and enlarged it to accommodate a congregation of seven hundred though in
1815 there were still fewer than three hundred Methodists in Exeter.[31] In
the same year the Baptists constructed their fine chapel in Bartholomew
Street at the expense of a son of Sir Francis Baring. But it was the
Unitarians of George's Meeting, descendants of the heroic age of
Presbyterianism, many of them extremely literate and successful
businessmen, who were the most active and influential in public life outside
the closed circle of the Chamber.[32]

In the years after Waterloo, the moral and religious aspects of
improvement became paramount; religious observances and charity
became essential for all who wished to be regarded as members of
respectable society. In this respect as in others county society gave the lead
to the city, organising the West of England Institution for the Deaf and
Dumb at a meeting in The Hotel in 1826 with Sir Humphrey Davy of
Shobrooke in the chair and, after promoting the construction of the new
Subscription Rooms in Southernhay, using them for the first time in 1820

for the annual meeting of the Devon and Exeter Society for promoting Christianity among the Jews under the enthusiastic sponsorship of Sir John Kennaway. In 1828 Sir Thomas Acland presided at a meeting of the Devon and Exeter Bible Society which discussed the pacification of Ireland with Protestant Holy Writ.

But if county society retained its prestige in post-war Exeter it maintained its social standards in appropriate settings. Samuel Foote, on acquiring The Hotel in 1813, embellished its assembly room, ball room and card room. Here in 1822 the county assembled in the old style, Morley and Clifford, Northcote, Acland, Carew, Pole, Chichester and Palk. In the much-admired Egyptian Hall of The Hotel the friends of Sir Thomas Acland assembled to discuss politics. The New London Inn at East Gate, rebuilt in the Georgian style in 1794 and much admired by Robert Southey, was a convenient rendezvous for county business. Here, in 1822, representatives of the gentry of Devon and Somerset met to devise measures for the protection of the red deer of Exmoor, then being harried towards extinction on account of the temporary lapse of organised hunting. The Devon and Exeter Horticultural Society was launched in 1829, almost inevitably inspired by a previous meeting in the Guildhall, and Lord Clifford became its first president. Gardening was becoming popular and was assured of a respectable status, ladies anxious about the proprieties being informed that for females gardening was 'an agreeable and rational occupation'. In 1816 Dutch bulbs were advertised in the Exeter papers.[33]

Nor were the citizens without their diversions. The Theatre situated at the southern end of the modern Bedford Street, was rebuilt and improved after a severe fire in 1820. Audiences after the war were enjoying productions founded on the novels of Walter Scott, *Rob Roy, The Antiquary, Kenilworth,* or, as in 1822, were 'electrified' — the term was then in use — by blood and thunder melodramas such as *The Vampire.* Tender consciences to whom the theatre was suspect were assured that the melodrama was evidence of the established truth that to the wicked increase of power is increase of wickedness. To secure the approval of respectable circles amusements had to be 'rational' and, if possible, instructive. Little allowance was made for the need of the working man to escape from the usually harsh realities of daily life and there was wisdom in the remark of the eccentric saddler, John Cooke, who in opposing the foundation of the Mechanics and Tradesmen's Institute declared 'take way men from their enjoyment of cakes and ale and you will take away their seven senses.'

Respectability in the 1820s was struggling with cruelty and violence such had endured for centuries and the existence of which did much to explain the growing insistence on chaperonage for girls and women. In 1823 Maria Holcombe of Cullompton who had the temerity to abandon her baby outside the new Southernhay Place was committed to hard labour as a rogue and a vagabond though as by the time she appeared before the

Assizes she had already suffered two months' hard labour in detention she was released. For her sisters with means contemporary advertisements offered 'temporary retirement' and medical attention in a villa safe from intrusion or inquiry.[34] In the vicinity of the expensive new church of St Sidwell mob law was invoked against erring wives or husbands by the custom of Skimmington Riding which Thomas Hardy was to describe in *The Mayor of Casterbridge*. Ratepayers in parish vestry meetings called for a more effective police force, but firmly refused to pay for it.[35] The night watch was still composed of ostlers, gardeners, shoemakers, braziers and others much addicted to drink and liable to intimidation by roughs, and even by respectable businessmen, as Mark Kennaway found to his embarrassment when he had to prosecute on behalf of the Improvement Commissioners.[36] The daily round in Exeter, however, was unshadowed by the disorders experienced elsewhere in the decades after Waterloo. In 1817, when there were serious riots in Manchester, Huddersfield and Nottingham, the Recorder of Exeter congratulated the grand jury on the good behaviour of the city.

The Devon and Exeter Savings Bank, founded with the support of Bishop Pelham in 1816, was inspired by the Protestant equation of hard work and thrift with moral worth. At the time of the bank's foundation S.F. Milford estimated that unmarried labourers and mechanics earning 15*s.* and 23*s.* a week would have no difficulty in saving 5*s.* and 10*s.* a week respectively and that if they were married their accumulated savings at compound interest would be a safeguard against 'wretched poverty' in the event of sickness and unemployment. Judging by examples of wages at this period few men could have relied upon earning these rates, or upon making regular payments, even if they postponed marriage and exercised a rigid austerity. But by 1827 deposits amounted to £643,000 and there were 18,700 individual accounts. The largest number of accounts were in the names of 968 male and 3,122 female domestic servants, most of whom must have been provided with board and lodging and clothes by their employers. But even agricultural labourers and husbandmen numbered 1,943, and labourers employed in trade and manufacture some three hundred.[37]

Between 1811 and 1821 the population increased from 18,896 to 23,479, that is by 23.8 per cent. Between 1821 and 1831 there was a further increase of 20 per cent. Some compensation for the loss of the cloth industry was found in the demand for the new houses, and also in work on the extension and improvement of the canal. Except in severe weather there was therefore employment for masons, plasterers, carpenters, bricklayers and allied trades, who together now formed the largest single element among Exeter's working class. Towards the end of the 1820s the full daily wage for a skilled carpenter ranged from 3*s.* 6*d.* to 3*s.* 8*d.* a day, though for rougher work, such as setting up a fence in the Bonhay, the pay was 3*s.* 4*d.* Bricklayers were paid between 3*s.* 6*d.* and 3*s.* 9*d.* (At Manchester about this time bricklayers and carpenters were paid just over 4*s*.) Plasterers engaged in work such as plastering and white-washing at the Guildhall received 3*s*. 6*d*. Plumbers working for Richard Rouse at the Corn Market in 1828, 'drawing off water', were paid 3*s*. a day. The assistants of carpenters and plasterers were paid 1*s*. 6*d*. a day but bricklayers' assistants received as much as 2*s*. 4*d*., which was also the rate paid for removing the posts of drying racks in the Bonhay — the memorials of a decayed industry — and for 'wheeling out stones'. In general therefore a skilled craftsman was paid 18*s*. to 22*s*. 4*d*. a week, provided employment lasted the full six days. Much depended on the circumstances of the work; a carpenter who, for instance, was paid 1*s*. 10*d*. 'making a stable door' may well have had no further work that day, or even that week. Labourers working for Francis Perryman, mason, at the Double Locks in 1827 received only £6 6*s*. for fourteen weeks' work, that is 9*s*. a week.[38]

Henry Ellis the jeweller, with his flourishing High Street shop and a wife and four children, claimed in 1822 that £3 a week for household expenses 'provided everything in abundance and comfort'. This was the weekly wage of his assistant after sixteen years' service and was the sole source of income for the support of the man and his family. He was discharged for intemperate habits and on that account is unlikely to have been regarded as one of the 'deserving poor' whom the charitable preferred to assist.[39] Strikes and illegal combinations, ill-organised and with no strike pay, though minuscule in scale, testified to the existence of hardship. In 1822 a strike in the boot and shoe-making trade led to the imprisonment of eight cordwainers. At least one master shoemaker was put to the expense of obtaining blackleg labour from London which, he complained, he had to send home without employment. Helliers struck for higher wages in 1823 and were defeated by labour from Bristol. Journeymen tailors, carpenters, masons, helliers and papermakers struck for higher wages in March 1825 and some concessions were made to 'the best workmen'.[40]

In 1823 the carpenters appeared at the Guildhall to answer charges that they had entered into an illegal combination for an advance of wages but the mayor, George Galloway, contented himself with warning them to behave more cautiously in future.[41] A shadow of the nightmare of plots and insurrection worrying Lord Liverpool's government fell on Exeter when, in 1819, one James Tucker of South Street was charged with 'vending blasphemous and seditious documents', including pamphlets accusing the Manchester magistrates of murder for the Peterloo Massacre of that year. Tucker admitted that he had sold one hundred pamphlets and claimed that he could have sold many more from his shop 'The Black Dwarf', named after the newspaper of the Devon-born Radical pamphleteer Richard Carlile.[42] In consequence respectable Exeter noted, with some satisfaction, that Tucker was one of the first occupants of the new prison. Woolmer's *Gazette* found it 'melancholy' that even in Exeter some persons encouraged such publications.

For those in employment the situation was eased by the downward trend of prices. In May 1821 the quartern loaf was sold at $8\frac{1}{2}d.$, the lowest price since 1804. The price of coal too fell sharply. When seventeen sail of Sunderland colliers were due at Exmouth in 1821 the price of coal on board ranged between 12*s.* 6*d.* and 13*s.* 6*d.* a quarter, compared with 24*s.* to 26*s.* in 1813. Meat prices fell to low levels in 1822 when beef ranged between 4*d.* and $5\frac{1}{2}d.$ per lb, mutton between 3*d.* and $4\frac{1}{2}d.$, pork between 3*d.* and $4\frac{1}{2}d.$ In 1825, however, beef, mutton and pork were all sold for between 5*d.* and 6*d.* a pound and subsequently for between $6\frac{1}{2}d.$ and $7\frac{1}{2}d.$[43] Fluctuations of this scale were a serious matter for labourers and artisans though probably most of them, in so far as they ate meat, would rely on cheap Saturday night purchases when butchers cleared stock before the days of refrigeration. The bulk contract purchases of the Corporation of the Poor at the end of 1825 on the whole reflected the downward trend in prices. Butcher's meat in September 1825 cost the corporation 39*s.* 11*d.* per cwt. instead of 41*s.* 4*d.* as in 1817, flour 43*s.* 6*d.* a sack compared with 46*s.* 6*d.*, but cheese and butter were both more expensive at 29*s.* per cwt and 10*d.* a gallon instead of 26*s.* and $7\frac{1}{2}d.$ In general market prices had settled to the level which would be maintained into the 1830s. Farmers were correspondingly unhappy. In February 1822 the depression of the Exeter corn market was said to have 'exceeded all former precedent'. In March 1826 it was 'more completely stagnant' than at any time within memory. In the countryside landlords reduced rents and meetings were held to discuss the Corn Laws. By 1831 labourers at Swimbridge in north Devon on 8*s.* a week would mutter confusedly about laying gentlemen's heads on the block.[44]

In Exeter, however, the future seemed bright. In 1817, two years after the formation of the Exeter Gas company, the whole of Fore Street and High Street was illuminated by gas light. Tradesmen were hastening to adopt the new method of lighting and coke was becoming available as a cheap alternative for coal. 'Nothing could be more gratifying', declared the *Flying Post* in 1824 'than the progressive advance of the prosperity of this country'.[45] To secure a share for Exeter the Chamber had already embarked on a major scheme for the improvement of the canal.

By a resolution of 12 May 1819 the surveyor, James Green, was 'desired to make a correct plan of the canal to enable him to make an estimate of the cost of such works as he may consider desirable in order to make Navigation as complete as possible'.[46] At first a limited improvement was contemplated. By 1826, however, it was decided, with the powerful support of the engineer Thomas Telford, to extend the canal a further two miles to Turf, to deepen it throughout to fifteen feet and to provide, in Telford's words, 'for the purpose of perfect navigation . . . regular and extensive quays at Exeter'. The Chamber, though worried by an intimation that there was a debt of £20,000 due to the city charities, adopted Telford's plans.[47] By the autumn of 1827 the extension was completed and celebrated with cannon-fire, bands and fireworks. Four members of parliament sailed in a procession of decorated barges. But a reminder of the perennial navigational difficulties of the Exe estuary was the delay by wind and tide of the schooner which should have entered the new lock at Turf. The whole project was completed by the opening of the New Basin in 1830. It was then, at a celebratory dinner, that Alderman Sanders extended Exeter's welcome to 'the commerce of the world'.[48] The commerce of the world would decline the invitation. Indeed Alderman Sanders admitted to the parliamentary commissioners in 1835 that if the true expenditure had been foreseen at the outset the Chamber would not have undertaken the project, 'even for the citizens of Exeter'.[49] The Chamber was left with an additional debt of £95,000, and in 1845 the control of the canal would pass into the hands of the city's creditors.

Exeter opinion applauded the Chamber's initiative, but the year 1825 had seen the opening of the Stockton and Darlington Railway. In 1826 the steam packet *Sir Francis Drake* had demonstrated the potentiality of the new source of power by carrying the Royal Mail, coach, passengers and baggage, from Plymouth to Falmouth in four hours less than the journey by road. In 1827 the shareholders of the Grand Western Canal between Devon and Somerset had recognised that nearly 80 per cent of their capital, over £200,000, had been spent without any prospect of a return. Landed and commercial interests in Exeter and its neighbourhood began to make plans the same year for the construction of a railway line from Exmouth to Exeter; and a company was formed, with a capital of £40,000. Estimates and plans were rudimentary, and there were acrimonious disputes over the route, but these activities foreshadowed the approaching new era in transport.[50]

In the meantime the Chamber embarked on the last of its major schemes for the improvement of the city, a scheme which roused heated opposition. In November 1818 the Chamber had resolved that markets in the street caused great inconvenience and a committee was accordingly appointed to study the problem. Members were 'desirous of paying every attention to the wishes of their fellow citizens' and discussions were arranged. In January 1819 it was decided to approach Parliament for the necessary legal powers.[51] The core of the Chamber's proposals was the construction of a new market, primarily a pannier market, between Gandy Street and Goldsmith Street. The cost was to be met by loans, or by a tontine, loan charges being met from rents and tolls; a representative of the Equitable Assurance Company was paid £5 for advice on methods of financing the project.[52] The interests of shopkeepers were to be safeguarded by prohibition of the sale of manufactured articles in the market. Stalls for the buchers, always a turbulent element, were to be leased at a reduced rent.

The proposals aroused violent controversy. Traders in High Street and

Fore Street feared loss of business. Many vociferously rejected the need for any change, bearing in mind the potential cost to the ratepayers. The proposals were denounced as ruinous. Rival committees were formed in support of alternative sites. The Chamber, 'having reason to believe that their original intentions . . . were not correctly understood', issued explanatory handbills and emphasized that the proposals would not involve a rate. They continued to fight for the original plan, a new market on the eastern site (the future Higher Market), 'thinking it right to be explicit and distinctly state that they will not apply for any other site'. But in June 1820 the Chamber's representatives in London were authorised to offer a compromise; powers would be taken to provide two markets. On this basis the first Exeter Market Act was enacted in July 1820 with schedules listing the property to be expropriated at the two sites but for the most part concerned with the eastern or higher site.[53]

Opposition continued. Crowded Guildhall meetings were harangued by the men who would become prominent local Reformers: J.D. Osborn, once a young apprentice debating history and philosophy in the circle of Henry Ellis and his friends, now a prosperous glass and china merchant; Samuel Maunder, boot and shoe manufacturer; Mark Kennaway, destined to be elected to the city council in 1837, and to be the ablest and most eloquent member of the city's Liberal Party. S.F. Milford spoke for the last time at a Guildhall meeting on the subject. For the first time he was told to sit down. The dispute had widened to challenge the Chamber itself. 'In some minds', declared Osborn, 'there existed feelings adverse to that body.'[54]

The rival market committees eventually reached an agreement between themselves. Towards the end of 1833 the Chamber issued an appeal 'to the good sense and dispassionate consideration of their fellow citizens'. Two new markets would be constructed; one on the western site, the Lower Market, would incorporate the existing corn market; a new market, the Higher Market, would be constructed on the eastern site. In March 1834 a new market act was obtained stating unequivocally that the Chamber was 'willing and desirous to provide two markets'.[55]

The battle had raged for some fifteen years. It was inspired by calculations of the effects on property values of the choice of one site or another, by arguments over costs and, in great measure, by opposition to the Chamber itself. In 1842, when the accounts were at last set in order, the outstanding market debt was reckoned at £103,000. The Lower Market, designed by the distinguished Cullompton-born architect Charles Fowler, remained in use till its destruction by enemy action in 1942. The Higher Market, designed by the Exeter-born George Dymond, was completed by Fowler on Dymond's death in 1835. Its facade remains, thanks to restoration in the 1970s, a survival of 'one of the best market buildings of its date in England'.[56] The silencing of S.F. Milford in the Guildhall and the decision to erect the markets in the classical architectural tradition make a fitting epilogue to the reign of the spirit of improvement which began in 1769.

NOTES

1. *History of Exeter*, pp. 212-3.
2. R. Southey, *Letters from England*, edn of 1814, p. 27.
3. J. Bowring, *Autobiographical Recollections*, p. 40.
4. *Woolmer's Exeter and Plymouth Gazette*, 19.2.1831.
5. *FP*, 1.12.1791, 5.1.1797, 25.2.1802.
6. *Athenaeum*, no. 2181, 14.8.1869, p. 203.
7. DRO, ECA, Act Books, 9.3.1769.
8. *ibid.*, 24.3.1775.
9. Jenkins, *History of Exeter*, p. 220; DRO, 76/20, p. 65.
10. DRO, ECA, Act Books, 8.11.1774.
11. *FP*, 12.8.1812.
12. Thomas Sharp, *Exeter Phoenix*, 1946, p. 28.
13. DRO, L 1258M/LL/3/2: Bedford Papers, building contract 1825.
14. *FP*, 23.11.1820.
15. *History of Exeter*, p. 357.
16. DRO, 60/5/2: particulars of sale of the Colleton estate.
17. *FP*, 28.1.1796.
18. DRO, 1926/B/B/E/5/21/1-3: building lease for what would be Baring Crescent.
19. *FP*, 6.3.1831.
20. DRO 67/9/1: abstract of title referring to indenture between John Baring and William Hooper.
21. *Gazette*, 15.7.1831.
22. *FP*, 2.9.1819.
23. *ibid.*, 24.5.1831.
24. *ibid.*, 4.1.1810, 11.1.1810, 1.4.1810, 14.6.1810; DRO, ECA, Act Books, 14.11.1809, 23.12.1809, 22.2.1810, 28.4.1810; 46 George III, cap. 39.
25. DRO ECA, Act Books, 15.9.1817, 24.9.1817, 21.1.1818.
26. John Howard, *State of the Prisons*, 1784, pp. 386-7, James Neild, *State of the Prisons*, 1812, pp. 209-10. See also W.J. Forsythe, *A System of Discipline: Exeter Borough Prison 1819-63*, Exeter 1983.
27. *FP*, 20.6.1819.
28. B. Cresswell, *Exeter Churches*, passim.
29. *FP*, 18.3.1817, 2.10.1817; 1.6.1820, DRO, ECA, Act Books, 13.1.1822. For Bishop Pelham see *FP*, 21.5.1818.
30. *FP*, 14.2.1825; 2.12.1819.
31. Elijah Chick, *History of Methodism in Exeter*, pp. 105-6.
32. A.A. Brockett, *Nonconformity in Exeter*, especially Chaps xii and xiii.
33. *FP*, 19.3.1829; 5.2.1816.
34. *ibid.*, 21.8.1823.
35. *Western Times*, 16.9.1837; *FP*, 30.8.1827.
36. *FP*, 17.12.1829, 14.1.1830; 7.12.1825.
37. *ibid.*, 7.12.1825, 3.3.1828.
38. DRO, ECA, Receivers' Vouchers, 1822-3, 1826-7, 1827-8. For rates in Manchester see G.D.H. Cole and R. Postgate, *The Common People 1746-1946*, 1961 edn, p. 206.
39. DRO, 76/20, ii, p. 244.
40. *FP*, 5.12.1822, 27.2.1823, 6.3.1823, 31.3.1825.
41. *ibid.*, 6.3.1823.
42. *ibid.*, 30.9.1819.
43. Details from local newspapers.
44. *FP*, 13.1.1831.

NOTES *continued*

45. *ibid.*, 12.8.1824.
46. DRO, ECA, Act Books, 12.5.1819.
47. *ibid.*, 15.5.1825, 13.6.1826.
48. *Western Times*, 17.9.1831.
49. DRO, ECA, Municipal Corporations Commissioners, proceedings, 1833, 5th day, fo. 55.
50. *FP*, 13.6.1826; 21.6.1827; 31.3.1827; 31.3.1825.
51. DRO, ECA, Act Books, 11.11.1818, 28.1.1819.
52. *ibid.*, 22.12.1819.
53. *ibid.*, 20.11.1819, 26.1.1820, 12.6.1820; 1 George IV, cap. lxxviii.
54. *FP*, 28.10.1824, 24.2.1825.
55. 4 & 5 William IV, cap. viii: 'an Act for Removing the Markets held in the High and Fore Streets and other places within the City of Exeter'.
56. N. Pevsner, *South Devon*, 1952, p. 45. For the aftermath see my *Victorian Exeter*, p. 45.

Plate 4. Interior of George's Meeting House, South Street, completed 1760. The elaborate canopy of the pulpit is probably late seventeenth century and may have come from the older James's Meeting House erected in 1687. Photo National Monuments Record.

Plate 5. Southernhay House, Southernhay East, builder Mathew Nosworthy, c. 1800. Photo A. Payne.

Plate 6. Chichester Place (now Terrace), Southernhay East, builder William Hooper, completed 1825. Photo S.J. Hobson.

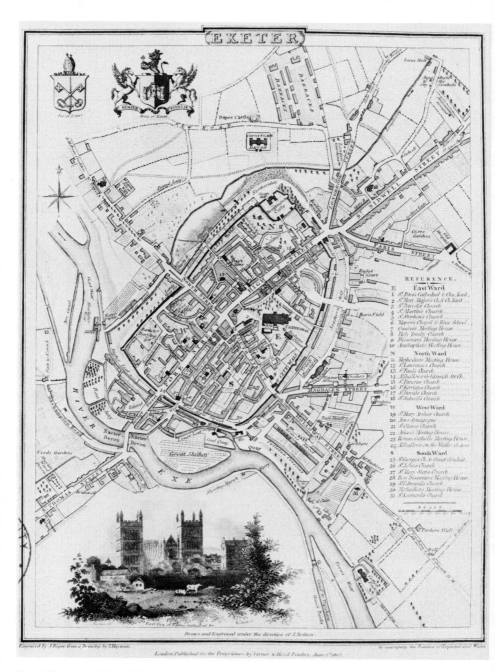

Plate 7. Exeter in 1805 by I. Hayman.

Chapter Nine

The Eve of Reform: Exeter in 1831

In 1845 a report on Exeter appeared in one of the great nineteenth-century publications seeking to influence parliament and public by means of massive concéntrations of selected facts.[1] The report was in fact written by Dr Thomas Shapter, M.D. (Edin.), elected to the Chamber in 1833 and later re-elected to the reformed corporation. A man of culture and with an enquiring mind, Shapter was deeply interested in the relationship between environment and health. He was one of that select band of medical men who used statistical evidence to enforce public awareness of the inter-relation between dirt, disease and poverty. Born in 1808, Shapter was a prominent figure in early Victorian Exeter. He became mayor of the reformed Corporation in 1847, by which time he was one of the 'nobs', as the *Western Times* termed them, of the local Conservatives. He died in 1902, blind and virtually forgotten in Exeter.

Shapter described the Exeter of 1831, at the time of his arrival to set up in practice, as no longer a manufacturing city; in fact it could have hardly been described as such for some forty years, the woollen industry having virtually disappeared. The population 'as regards employment, had no very distinctive character . . . a collection of gentry, tradespeople, artisans, and the ordinary admixture of the poor'. Sinks and water-closets had come into general use but Exeter was still badly drained and ill-supplied with water, and 'in the poorer parts of the city much that was objectionable remained.'[2]

As at the end of the seventeenth century, in the early nineteenth the well-to-do parishes were those clustered about High Street at the top of the central ridge: St Martin, Bedford Precinct, St Petrock, St Stephen, St Lawrence and All Hallows, Goldsmith Street. In these parishes, Shapter found, the average annual mortality rate was 1.28, or half that of the poorest parishes, St Edmund, St Mary Major and St Mary Steps. The poor parishes, the breeding-ground of cholera and once the heart of the industrial city, contained a crowded population of artisans, particularly shoemakers and labourers, a population notably in need of poor relief. The great houses of Tudor merchants had been converted into overcrowded tenements with eight to ten persons inhabiting one room. In this area 56 per cent of those who died were under the age of fifteen years.[3] The parish of St Mary Major contained 388 inhabited houses but barely 30 per cent were liable to rates, in St Mary Steps the proportion was 17 per cent. In comparison 80 per cent of the inhabited houses of St Lawrence were rated, 83 per cent in St Stephen and in St Martin 100 per cent.[4]

Shapter seems to have attached no great importance to the disappearance of Exeter's ancient commerce and industry. The population was increasing, its 'personal comforts publicly considered and provided for while the whole aspect of the city was being improved'. In the opinion of some of its citizens Exeter at this time was a 'centre of fashion and gaity . . . a rising and flourishing city'.[5] There was certainly 'fashion and gaity' up to a point, though balls and assemblies were no longer attracting the distinguished names they had done on occasion during the Napoleonic wars. Lady Paterson, at that time living in Baring Terrace, was impressed by the company she met at a dinner given by Bishop Phillpotts, but her husband, General Sir William Paterson, made it clear that he found more congenial society at Cheltenham.[6] The Patersons evidently could not afford a carriage and their residence in Exeter points to the popularity of the city with retired people of moderate means seeking congenial society.

Since 1760 the more prosperous businessmen and professional men had escaped from the smells and noise of the more crowded areas of the city and had sought the fresh air and the view of the new genteel residences amid the society of their fellows. There was a natural desire for improved amenities and this encouraged the snobbery such as Dickens caricatured when Mr Pickwick, in the reign of William IV, was informed at Bath that tradespeople were 'quite inconsistent with Paradise'. There were houses in Bedford Circus and others on Southernhay, 'most genteel, fitted up with mahogany doors and skirtings' for which the price asked was as much as one thousand guineas. Besides his construction, never fully completed, of the family residences in the Barnfield, Mathew Nosworthy, with the collaboration of Mr Dix, the fuller, had built the fine terrace known as Dix's Field. The respectability of these houses was not, of course, diminished by doctors' surgeries and lawyers' offices, or by their use as lodgings suitable for occupation by titled visitors, and occasionally as town houses for county society.

In the crowded city within the walls there was still space by modern standards. Many of the older houses retained gardens and small orchards, as the advertisements of properties for sale would make clear for another generation. These larger properties still inhabited by tradesmen and professional men were set in the midst of brutalising slums. The cholera epidemic of 1831 would reveal all too dramatically the conditions in the poorer areas of the city, in the tenements and the decaying mansions of Tudor Exeter. A visit to a house on Stepcote Hill, occasioned by a report of putrid fever in 1802, revealed a mother, three adult daughters and a boy of thirteen living in a single, windowless room with light and air admitted by the door. A similar investigation found a family of eight living in a single room. In airless lanes, courts and alleys pigs still scavenged among heaps of offal and ordure. In May 1800 the Chamber was impelled to issue yet another stern order that 'No inhabitant should place in the streets any Ashes, Dirt, Dung or Filth on any pretence whatsoever.' It is unlikely that such admonitions were obeyed.

In retrospect it can be seen that in 1831 Exeter's claims to be 'a centre of fashion and gaity' were ceasing to be valid. The railways were approaching and London would soon become speedily, and cheaply, accessible. In the England of William IV for a city to rise and flourish depended on self-confident entrepreneurs such as, in Disraeli's literary imagination in *Coningsby*, would confront Norman manners with Saxon industry. At election times an Acland of Killerton, a Northcote of Pynes, a Quicke of Newton St Cyres would still ride into Exeter supported by cavalcades of friends and tenants. They were men of high standards of personal conduct. They headed subscription lists for the relief of distress, for the construction of schools and churches and for impoverished clergy. With Bishop Phillpotts they assembled at the Devon and Exeter Institution in 1832 to honour the memory of Sir Walter Scott. Directly and indirectly they set the standard for the respectable of Exeter; but they were not the life-blood of, and could not create, a flourishing city as the term would be understood in Bolton or Manchester or Newcastle-upon-Tyne. Their allies were the cathedral clergy and the parish priests, reflecting the class and the society in which they were set, men who stood firm against Reform and the menace, as the *Exeter and Plymouth Gazette* put it, of the 'restless and turbulent spirit of Ultra-Radicalism'.[7] Among all Exeter's Anglican clergy only Dr Carwithen, master of St George's Masonic Lodge, voted for the Whigs.

Exeter in 1688 had been in the forefront of the emerging England of expanding trade and commerce. In 1831 the city's importance depended on the contribution of its two Members of Parliament to party politics at Westminster. No merchant of Exeter could now aspire to this honour. The role of the periwigged merchants, whose cargoes had once been carried to the ports of Europe from Rotterdam to Leghorn, had been replaced by the bankers in black silk stocks, men who, in general, held aloof from overt participation in city affairs. By 1831 the leading bankers were all Anglicans connected by politics and social ties with Tory circles in church and society. The fortunes of the Sanders family had their origins in Dissent, but it was as a wealthy Anglican that the social position of the banker J.B. Sanders was proclaimed by a brief visit of the Duchess of Clarence at Stoke Hill in 1828. His son, E.A. Sanders, was then at Harrow and throughout Queen Victoria's reign he was the justly respected link between the old county society and city Conservatism.

The Exeter Bank, controlled by the Sanders family, financed the

Chamber, of which Alderman Robert Rogers Sanders was a prominent member. It was R.R. Sanders who raised the antique banner of the Chamber when he explained to the parliamentary commissioners in 1833 that the Ever-Faithful city would not admit Dissenters to its governing body, despite the removal of legal restrictions, and in so doing he repeated the words of the Earl of Bath in 1688. The Sanders family was related by marriage to Ralph Barnes, the Bishop's Registrar and Chapter Clerk and was connected with Henry Blackall, three times mayor and philanthropic churchman. Four members of the family, headed by E.L. Sanders the banker, voted for the unsuccessful Tory candidate in the parliamentary election of December 1832.[8] They were the heirs of the merchants who had ruled Exeter in the seventeenth century though they had become the epitome of middle-class respectability. They were professional men rather than 'in trade'; R.R. Sanders, as a successful wine-merchant, like successful brewers, was in an occupation regarded as socially superior.

In the Chamber itself the professions rather than trade had become dominant and medical men in particular had reached their zenith in the city's public life. In 1831 five members of the Chamber were doctors or surgeons. They included John Haddy James, 'James of Exeter', who had served with credit as assistant surgeon in the Life Guards during the Waterloo campaign and later became a distinguished member of his profession; another was Philip de la Garde, opthalmic surgeon and last mayor of the old regime. Among their colleagues was Edward Woolmer, printer and proprietor of the *Exeter and Plymouth Gazette*, a devoted upholder of the connection between Church and State as the foundation of the social order. Other members were Paul Measor the postmaster, whom the Reformers regarded, wrongly, as a sympathiser, Henry Leslie Grove, collector of customs, and William Kennaway, wine merchant, who won universal approval for his conduct as mayor during the cholera epidemic of 1832, a moderate Tory whom some termed a Whig. A genuine 'tradesman' was old Reuben Phillips, the druggist, freeman in 1769, elected to the Chamber in 1784 and a survivor from the age of Lord North. He died in 1833, aged 87, living to the last in his premises in High Street. In 1831 the members of the Chamber, in so far as their personal characters were concerned, were beyond reproach. But, whereas in Stuart times their predecessors for the most part represented the men who created and maintained the thriving industrial and commercial city, by the 1830s they represented the more restricted circles of the professions and gentility.

The Chamber in its last years wrestled with the problems caused by a growth of over 60 per cent in the population between 1801 and 1831. The increase was impressive though not remarkable. The population of Leicester, almost exactly the same as that of Exeter in 1801, had grown to 40,000, but had not lost its former basic industry. Exeter would now live by supplying goods and services to a countryside of dwindling economic significance. The heavy expenditure on canal improvements had been a brave and unavailing attempt by the old regime to resurrect the past.

The population in 1831 consisted of 12,683 males and 15,559 females. Of the 6,573 males aged twenty years and over 3,655 were reported as employed in retail trade and handicraft, principally as boot and shoe makers, carpenters and joiners and tailors. 617 men aged twenty and over were classified as capitalists, bankers, professional and 'other educated men'. These, some two per cent of the city's population, provided the city's ruling class. Among them were the 'professional gentlemen' who were given pride of place in contemporary directories: forty-three surgeons and apothecaries, sixty-two barristers and attorneys, forty-nine Church of England clergy.[9] There were also twelve Protestant Dissenter clergy, men who, then and later, were not regarded by purists as worthy of inclusion in 'good society', though they were usually widely respected, well-educated and influential; all who voted were firmly in support of parliamentary and municipal reform.

In 1688 the Chamber had been a true reflection of a thrusting commercial and industrial city; in 1831 its members represented a city which was not without a touch of the social snobbery satirised by Dickens in the *Pickwick Papers* set in the reign of William IV: 'Stationer! No, no; confound and curse me! No trade', as Mr Smangle said to Mr Pickwick in the Fleet Prison. There was a wide gulf between the social circle of members of the Chamber and the smaller shopkeepers and tradesmen, and particularly the Dissenters who, in 1831, were demanding the right to take part in the government of the city. These social divisions lay beneath the decorum and respectability of the quiet cathedral city throughout the nineteenth century. In 1857 they were to give rise to a revolt against the 'nobs' of the Conservative Party, the squires, bankers and doctors. In 1880 there were allegations of hostility against Churchmen, and in 1889 that the 'trading classes were being held up to derision'.[10] Irritating social jealousies and conventions gave an edge to the strife between Churchman and Dissenter, Whig and Tory, in the era of Reform.

Despite its limitations the Chamber at this time had declared its faith in the future of the city in a manner reminiscent of its predecessors of the 1690s. Had circumstances remained as they had been in the reigns of William and Mary the expensive improvement of the canal would have reinvigorated the city. The census of 1831, however, sharply defined the problems faced by most of the towns and cities with rapidly growing populations but with which Exeter, then relapsing into the status of a large market town, was ill-fitted to deal. The census of 1831 confirmed the virtual disappearance of the cloth industry and recorded no more than sixty-fiive fullers and twelve dyers. The various branches of the building industry on the other hand gave employment to some eight hundred men aged twenty and over. According to the census reports the number of inhabited houses in the city rose from 2,692 in 1801 to 4,056 in 1831. But by 1831 the period of building activity derived from the prosperity engendered by the Napoleonic Wars was ending; similar activity, in a different form, would not be seen again in the city for fifty years.

The coach industry based on the horse had reached the peak of its development: the railway would not reach Exeter until 1844. No less than 125 men were recorded as coach owners, drivers and grooms. Including blacksmiths, carriers, saddlers, harness-makers and the like, many of the 142 servants and most of the 122 hotel or innkeepers and beer retailers, the transport industry could well have provided a livelihood, and occasionally wealth and status, for some five hundred males. The census of 1841 records eighty-three coachmen, guards and postboys and also twelve female hotel or innkeepers.

The published census records of 1831 omitted female employment other than to record for Exeter 1,879 female servants among a total female population of 15,559. In 1841 there would be 116 charwomen, 263 laundry-keepers and washerwomen and 2,265 domestic servants. Wages were low and many servants were overworked, but domestic employment at least provided clothes, board and lodging and, with a good employer, an education in domestic management that was useful on marriage. Henry Ellis jr, who a this time was beginning to prosper, now employed two servants from Buckland Brewer at £3 a quarter with, of course, board and lodging. His female shop assistant was paid twelve guineas, later increased to fourteen.[11] His wife, in the early years of married life, took an active and efficient part in the management of the shop.

Female employment by the early nineteenth century made an important contribution to the economic life of the city and undoubtedly assisted families who, if the wages of men alone are considered, theoretically must have found life impossible. By 1841 there were 557 milliners and dressmakers, 95 nurses and 72 schoolmistresses or governesses. Millinery and dressmaking could be notorious for sweated labour but some women, like Mrs Colson, had founded important and long-established businesses, while others prospered in the dress trade. Though business generally was a man's world, one of the twelve female hotel and innkeepers in 1841 was Sarah Street who acquired The Hotel in 1826. After the Duchess of Clarence had expressed approval of her accommodation in the following year, Mrs Street had the satisfaction of naming her establishment The Royal Clarence.

Exeter's position in the communications system of the South West remained an enduring asset. In 1831 forty-four coaches left the city each day on three days a week and thirty-four on the remaining three days.[12] There was, of course, no Sunday traffic. The major destinations were London, Bristol, Bath, Brighton and Birmingham, and the western ports of Plymouth and Falmouth. The New London Inn was the hub of this traffic at the point where the major roads converged outside the site of the former East Gate. Sarah Street, on taking over The Hotel, announced that for the convenience of her clients there would be no coach traffic at night. From the New London Inn the Royal Mail left daily at 9.45 in the morning and was scheduled to arrive in London at 6.30 the following morning, passing through Sherborne, Shaftesbury and Salisbury. The Telegraph coach, patronised by leading Reformers such as Lord Ebrington and Edward Divett (MP for Exeter 1832–64) picked up passengers at the Clarence and left the New London Inn at 1.45 in the afternoon to reach London at 9 the following morning.

Most of the carriers still worked from South Street, especially from the Mermaid. Russell's big warehouse was there and his wagons went to Falmouth, Southampton, Salisbury and London. His 'van' undertook to complete the journey to London in thirty-six hours and three days a week left the Mermaid for Plymouth with goods and parcels for the Belfast steam packet. The founder of the firm, Robert Russell, had died in 1822, aged sixty-four, and by then had invested in banking. For the seaborne trade there were still twenty-three vessels trading between Exeter and London, five of just over one hundred tons, one of 74 tons and the remainder between 80 and 92 tons.

Other business activities included brewing, tanning, milling, glove-making and printing. In the Bonhay were situated the establishments of brass and iron founders such as George Bodley, ironmonger, improvement commissioner and patentee of the Bodley Stove, and William Huxham, both of whom founded flourishing and long-lasting firms. According to the census of 1831 fifty-eight men were employed in the manufacture of machinery; there were also seventeen ironfounders and twenty ironmongers. The firm of S. & W. Kingdon appears in the local directory as iron and brass founders though they were originally ironmongers; they were large-scale employers.

It was indeed a varied economy with a large proportion of small one-man businesses such as the 357 boot and shoe makers, 102 bakers of bread, gingerbread and fancy cakes, and 228 tailors and breeches makers. It was also well provided with trades and professions catering for the prosperous higher classes of city and country. There were twenty-nine booksellers and, according to the directory, eighteen artists, among them the gifted William Traies and James Leakey. For those who could afford them drapers such as Messrs Colson and Sparks bought furs in London, and milliners like Mrs Higgs, of 196 High Street, ventured in person to Paris for the latest fashions.[13] Henry Ellis, the jeweller, found that engraving had become an important part of his business, especially the engraving of crests and arms on plate; in 1831 he sold plate and other articles to a retired judge of the East India Company's service for £300. He also noted that the officers of the garrison were good customers. By now his net assets amounted to £13,000, a satisfactory situation which, like so many of his contemporaries, he attributed to 'rising early, and late taking rest, and eating the bread of carefulness'. Not till 1834 did he feel justified in taking a glass of wine after dinner.[14]

Exeter had been carried through the turbulence and economic crises of the years after Waterloo by the traditions and habits of the past. Devoid of the opportunities for growth, the city relied upon the assets that had attracted Dr Johnson's friend Mrs Piozzi some fifty years before. Contemporary guidebooks and directories made the most of them.[15]

Stimulated by the demand for comfortable houses in neat rural surroundings and within easy reach of shops and social attractions the parishes beyond the walls were now growing fast on a scale that would not be seen again till the introduction of cheap transport by means of the tram. The population of St Sidwells had increased from 2,707 in 1801 to 6,602 in 1831, that of St Davids from 1,853 to 3,078. In St Sidwells the number of inhabited houses had grown from 450 in 1801 to 1,070 in 1831; an increase of 138 per cent compared with 50 per cent for the city as a whole. In St Davids the increase in the same period had been from 313 to 529 and in Holy Trinity from 279 to 440. The population of St Leonards, a hamlet of 133 inhabitants in 1801, and not yet included within the city, had grown to 467 by 1831. Doctors were promoting Heavitree for its salubrious air and house agents and builders were expatiating on its wide views and genteel environment. Its population increased by 40 per cent between 1821 and 1831 and according to the census of 1831 the same number of families as lived in Crediton employed twice the number of domestic servants.

The demand for building land on the edge of the city was eliminating orchards and market gardens, as it would do throughout the century; in the neighbourhood of the modern York Road in 1831 William Ford, nurseryman, sold off his trees and shrubs.[16] Eldon Terrace, Clarence Place, York Terrace and Nelson Place had just been constructed in the vicinity of Longbrook Street. Sidwell Street was now built up on both sides as far as Black Boy Road, with offshoots such as Belmont Terrace, St Anne's Place and Hampton Buildings. In Heavitree new houses forming Stafford Terrace, Mont le Grand and Regent's Park provided some delicate touches of Regency taste in the form of plastered entrances and elegant tympanum wreaths.

But above all modest houses beyond the walls were being built for clerks, small shopkeepers, milliners, and widows with a small competence. For such as these King William Terrace, with no claim to architectural distinction, had recently been completed in St Sidwells. Its construction had been undertaken by Robert Fisher, joiner, who paid £550 for the site and then borrowed working capital from the grocer, William Luke, on the security of the houses to be erected.[17] Communities of artisans and shopkeepers had appeared too at Little Silver, close to St David's Church, and off Sidwell Street–Blackboy Road at Coburg Place and Salem Place. All these small houses were comfortable and well-designed by the standards of the day. In 1832 plans were broached for the construction of two hundred labourers' cottages, two storeys in height, in 'an open and healthy situation' on the edge of the city.[18] These cottages were designed for working-class families and were to have proper drainage. The plans were not carried out in full but they presaged Exeter's Newtown, the building of which began at the end of the 1830s.

Building and ancillary activities provided an extensive range of employment, though in the cold winter of 1829–30, when snow had interfered with outdoor work, parochial clergy and churchwardens had to be mobilised in the customary manner to solicit contributions towards the relief of distress. On that occasion £900 had been collected to provide bread and cheap fuel. Poor Law experts, wrestling elsewhere with the problems of massive unemployment and mounting expenditure on relief, noted with satisfaction that Exeter had been 'exempt from any marked local vicissitudes during a long series of years'. In the year 1830–31 outdoor relief distributed by the Corporation of the Poor amounted to what was described as the very large sum of £4,761 spent on over nine hundred adults and over five hundred children, some five per cent of the total population. Of these only about one hundred received relief on account of unemployment, or inadequate employment, 70 of them being over sixty years of age.[19] Not more than twenty individuals received relief to support large families, a form of relief which was widely regarded as subsidising improvidence at the expense of the ratepayer. According to the directory some four thousand children were receiving charitable education of a sort, one thousand in Sunday schools.

The higher echelons of local society enjoyed the last rays of the Georgian sunshine. Christmas balls and assemblies were as well-attended as ever and the season received additional éclat from the three concerts given by the renowned violinist Niccolo Paganini who was engaged through the good offices of the cathedral organist James Paddon. It was at this time that Richard Ford, writer and traveller, wrote

> This Exeter is quite a capital, abounding in all that London has except its fog and smoke. There is an excellent institution here with a well-chosen library in which I take great pastime and am beginning my education.[20]

The city was well-served by four local newspapers. Edward Woolmer's *Exeter and Plymouth Gazette*, established in 1790, was Tory and later became a pillar of Victorian Conservatism. Woolmer was opposed to parliamentary reform, not so much in principle but on account of the fear, encouraged by the more extreme reformers, that it would be followed by radical attacks on all the institutions of Church and State. The *Western Luminary*, like the *Gazette*, was High Church and opposed to Reform. Describing itself as a family newspaper *The Luminary* was somewhat dull. The paper's claim on the interest of posterity lies primarily in the appointment as editor in 1832 of

George Hogarth, later the father-in-law of Charles Dickens.[21] The older
Trewman's Flying Post aimed at the agricultural interest, in religion it was
Low Church and no admirer of the High Church Bishop Phillpotts (1830–
69). But the *Western Times*, established in 1828, became in the hands of
Thomas Latimer, the most readable and hard-hitting supporter of Reform
and later of the Liberal Party.[22]Latimer himself had much of the engaging
forthrightness and prejudices of Cobbett: he was well styled 'the Cobbett of
the West'. Fearlessly denouncing injustice and 'jobbery' whenever he
suspected them, he gave local politics something of the high drama of
Homeric battle. His gift for the trenchant phrase and epithet, with due
allowance for his prejudices, still gives flesh and blood to the plain-speaking
paladins of Exeter's politics. His feud with Bishop Phillpotts was notorious
and was not always justified.

These newspapers, appearing weekly and sold at 7*d.*, gave ample
coverage to national politics and foreign affairs with the help of extracts
from the metropolitan press. They are still indispensible for their vivid
reports of local events and personalities. From them the protagonists in the
hard-fought issues of the day, municipal and national, sometimes
homespun, often verbose and opinionated, emerge from the reports as
living men. The great traditions of the Victorian press, its enterprise, its
responsibility to an informed public, were foreshadowed at Exeter in 1835
on that epic occasion when Lord John Russell was howled down and
defeated in the election for South Devon amid rain and hail and Thomas
Latimer of Exeter's *Western Times* shielded from the downpour the notes of
the young Charles Dickens.[23]

The old order was busy erecting the framework of the Victorian and
twentieth-century city. In November 1831 the annual general meeting of
the turnpike trustees, with Sir Thomas Acland and the Hon. Newton
Fellowes prominent among them, began discussions on the reconstruction
of the northern approaches to Exeter. In the same month notice was given of
the intention of the Improvement Commissioners, with the backing of the
Chamber, to apply for a new act which would include powers to open a new
road from High Street to the intended road near the county gaol. These
activities were the genesis of the New North Road, constructed in 1834, the
smoothing of the steep contours of St David's Hill and the spanning of the
deep combe of the Longbrook in 1835 by means of the Iron Bridge. The
'new road' from the High Street eventually took form in 1839 as the modern
Queen Street. There were the usual allegations of jobbery; nevertheless it
was an imaginative and well-conceived programme.

However Thomas Latimer had arrived in Exeter to tell the receptive
readers of the *Western Times* that municipal bodies were antiquated and
should be rooted out, that no corporation in the kingdom needed this
'correcting influence' more than Exeter.[24] He was right in general but
wrong in singling out Exeter. The Chamber was conscientiously proceeding

with its programme of capital development, the port, new markets and, in conjunction with the Improvement Commissioners, a radical overhaul of the road system. Indeed a fleeting endorsement of expenditure on the canal appeared in August 1831 in the form of a brig of 200 tons burden which entered the basin with a cargo of hides and skins twenty-eight days out from Montevideo. Members of the Chamber and their circle continued to advance their own money. Edmund Granger was receiving five per cent on a loan of £12,000 and Henry Blackall on £1,000. Sanders & Co., of the Exeter Bank, advanced £10,000.[25]

The Chamber's accounts at this time underline not only the financial strain of maintaining and modernising the canal but also the dependence on canal revenue. The Chamber was gambling heavily on Exeter's future as a port. In the financial year 1830–1, when Edward Woolmer was Receiver, revenue and expenditure amounted to £10,843 and £10,751 respectively; Quay Profits amounted to over half the gross revenue, £6,005 out of £10,842 in 1830–31, £7,083 out of £10,287 in 1831–2.[26] The Chamber was undoubtedly attempting to live within its means. According to the accounts of 1831–2, salaries, including payment of the wharfinger, his clerks and canal personnel, amounted to £968, or a mere eight per cent of the total expenditure for that year. The mayor himself now received only £200, one-tenth of the salary of the mayor of Bristol. The so-called 'regalia' expenses amounted to £226 16s. 8d., of which £129 was the Chamber's contribution, which it shared with the county of Devon, to the cost of the Judges' Lodgings. The two permanent committees, for finance and navigation, features of the administrative machine since 1815, together cost £81. The remainder of the expenditure under this head were vestigial survivals, such as £2 14s. 6d. for the annual mural walk, including £2 2s. for the grammar school boys declaiming before the mayor; £9 16s. for the refreshments of the procession round the city boundaries; £2 16s. to the cathedral ringers on the mayor's 'chusing day'. 'Necessary Expenses' included traditional Christmas expenditure amounting to a modest £13 16s. 6d., of which £10 5s. was spent on wood, straw, candles and cakes; and £1 18s. 6d. on an honorarium to the staffbearers 'for staying up on Christmas Eve and for refreshment'.

Tradesmen's Bills and Necessary Expenses accounted for an expenditure of £2,675, or just over one-quarter of the total expenditure. £1,586 was paid from revenue this year towards the cost of canal extension work. There was also a payment to the Improvement Commissioners representing a contribution for two years to the cost of the city watch. The remainder consisted for the most part of payments to masons, helliers and bricklayers for repairs and maintenance of city property, including relatively large items such as £34 13s. 1d. for repairs at Blackaller Weir, £71 18s. 9d. for mason's work at Cowley Bridge and £48 8s. 1d. for repairs to the Cowley Bridge road. But the main item of expenditure consisted of debt charges of all kinds, these amounting to over forty-seven per cent of the total.

Revenue amounted to a total of £7,858, three-quarters being derived from quay profits, town duty and Topsham quay. Butchers' rents, markets, produce stalls and cattle market tolls contributed £879. Income from drying racks in the Shilhay was reduced to a derisory £1 15s. Excluding a revenue item of £1,000 entered under the heading 'Principal debt borrowed', the Chamber's income to all intents and purposes was made up of receipts from port facilities and markets, these amounting to £8,737 out of £9,368. The Chamber had therefore borrowed heavily in order to improve these major revenue-earning assets.

'Police expenditure' — the term police in the 1830s did not imply the existence of a modern police force — was limited, besides the contribution towards the cost of the city watch, to £207 spent on the salaries of the sergeants-at-mace and staffbearers whose duties included those of a rudimentary permanent police force. Sanitation and streets were the responsibility of the Improvement Commissioners. Poor relief was in the hands of the Corporation of the Poor, supplemented by private citizens at times of particular hardship. The water supply, uncertain and inadequate, was leased as a long-term concession.

The growing assault on the established order was aimed at all three of Exeter's corporations. The Chamber, the Corporation of the Poor and the Improvement Commissioners were the targets of oratory and of slashing articles in the *Western Times*. The newspaper conceded that the Improvement Commission 'was the best of the bad corporations with which the city is afflicted', but even elected commissioners were accused, in the customary general terms, of connivance with the Cathedral Chapter and the Chamber 'in any job which the Church and Corporation are ready to join in'. The annual dinner given to the Guardians of the Poor by their clerk was subject to waspish innuendo in August 1831: 'We are not allowed to know much of the proceedings of this junta, who lock themselves up when they appropriate our money; but we suspect, and with reason too, that Mr Gattey would hardly open his cellars to them for nothing.'[27]

The new bishop, Henry Phillpotts, who had made his official entry into the city in July 1830, managed to concentrate on himself the hostility towards the Established Church which was an important element of the reform movement. Phillpotts was High Church in a diocese strongly Evangelical and Low Church. His preferment to Exeter was widely supposed to be the reward of switching his considerable talent for controversy from opposition to support of Catholic Emancipation in 1829. Although by no means an out and out opponent of reform his logic and dialectical skill were wielded without discretion or sense of proportion.[28] In the Lords he urged the peers to reject the Reform Bill and confidantes to leave the consequences to God. His statement that what was wrong with the constitution was not the political influence of the aristocracy but the publicity given to parliamentary proceedings by *Hansard* was unlikely to make the new bishop *persona grata* to Latimer and his colleagues.[29] 'Chamber and Church', declared Latimer in December 1831 'have too much influence. We know that these bodies have always been in opposition to the general feeling of the people.'[30] The Reformers should not be judged too strictly by their oratory or by the language of contemporary journalistic warfare even though the latter, in the case of the *Western Times*, was being conducted by a gifted journalist of undeniable probity. But clergymen such as the Rev. Jonas Dennis feared that 'under the mask of reform, Revolution was not stalking but running through the land'.[31]

In the autumn of 1831 there was some excuse for the alarmist views of the Rev. Dennis. In Derby and Nottingham soldiers were called out to face the mobs. At Bristol in October a crescendo of mob violence included large-scale arson and looting and the destruction of the bishop's palace. In the same month, when city society was venturing on the newly introduced mazurka, fears were expressed that the Bishop of Exeter's palace would suffer the same fate as that of his colleague of Bristol. The yeomanry were ordered out at Tiverton. The Whig, Lord Ebrington, arrived at Exeter with his yeomanry in preparation for the traditional excitement on November the Fifth. Lord Rolle's yeomanry under Colonel Buller took up station in the barracks above Howell Road. But no mob emerged from the slums of the West Quarter for the cause of Bread and Reform. The Bishop, supported by Sir Thomas Acland and the Mayor, presided at the annual meeting of the Society for Promoting the Education of the Poor and of the Society for Building and Enlarging Churches and Chapels. In November Captain Brandreth and Mr Bush, 'two gentlemen of considerable intelligence' according to the *Flying Post*, arrived to make inquiries into the situation in Exeter, the numbers of freemen, houses and inhabitants, for the purpose of Reform.[32]

NOTES

1. PP *State of Large Towns and Populous Districts*. Commissioners' Second Report, H.C. 602, 610, 1845, xviii, Appendix II, pp. 351-80.
2. *ibid.,* p. 357. Shapter's other publications included *Medica Sacra*, 1834; *Observations on the Leprosy of the Middle Ages*, 1835; *Geology of Exeter and its neighbourhood*, 1838 and his better-known *History of the Cholera in Exeter*, 1849.
3. *State of Large Towns*, tables xv and xix. Cf W.G. Hoskin's map of poverty in Exeter in 1671-2 in *Industry, Trade and People*, p. 113.
4. PP *Municipal Corporations Boundaries*, H.C. 238, 1837, part i, xxvi.
5. *State of Large Towns*, Table v and *Flying Post*, 28.10.1831, 12.8.1824.
6. DRO, MS 36, Lady Paterson's Diary, 1831-5.
7. E.R. Norman, *Church and Society in England 1770-1970*, p. 47 and *Gazette*, 28.4.1832.
8. *List of Voters at the Exeter Election . . . December 10-11 1832*, Exeter 1833, p. 34.
9. T. & H. Besley, *Exeter Itinerary and General Directory*, Exeter, 1831.

NOTES *continued*

10.   *Western Times*, 14.3.1857, 28.3.1857; *FP*, 9.11.1889. On these divisions see also my 'Society and Politics in Exeter 1837-1914' in H.J. Dyos (ed.), *The Study of Urban History*, 1968.
11.   DRO, 76/20, ii, p. 359; iii, p. 221.
12.   Besley, *Exeter Directory* 1831.
13.   *FP*, 15.9.1831, 16.5.1833.
14.   DRO, 76/20, iii, pp. 77, 185.
15.   e.g. Besley, *Guide and Itinerary*, 1836, p. 31.
16.   *FP*, 20.10.1831.
17.   DRO, D7/594/4, abstract of title, and D7/596/2, mortgage, of King William Terrace.
18.   *FP*, 23.8.1832.
19.   PP *Poor Laws, Report of the Commissioners*, H.C. 44, 1834, xxvii, p. 232 (report by Capt. Chapman).
20.   R.E. Prothero (ed.), *The Letters of Richard Ford*, p. 135. The reference is to the Devon and Exeter Institution in Cathedral Close.
21.   J. Forster, *Life of Charles Dickens*, 1872, i, p. 78.
22.   R.S. Lambert, *The Cobbett of the West*, 1939, passim.
23.   *ibid.*, pp. 70-72.
24.   *WT*, 5.11.1831.
25.   DRO, ECA, Receivers' Accounts, Book 200, 1832-3.
26.   *ibid.*, Book 195, 1830-31.
27.   *WT*, 8.10.1831; 27.8.1831.
28.   E.R. Norman, *op. cit.*, p. 88. See also R.N. Shutte, *The Life, Times and Writings of . . . Henry Philpotts*, 1863 and G.C.B. Davies, *Henry Philpotts, bishop of Exeter*, 1954.
29.   *Hansard*, Series III, xxviii (March 1832), cols 279, 287.
30.   *WT*, 3.12.1831.
31.   *FP*, 16.6.1831.
32.   *ibid.*, 31.11.1831.

Chapter Ten

Cholera and Reform 1831-1835

The main structure of Exeter's life, erected in the era of the 'Glorious Revolution', was dismantled amid the controversies that culminated in the Reform Bill of 1832, itself swiftly followed by consequent reform in Church and State. Between August 1830 and January 1835 the city enjoyed the turmoil of four general elections, three of which were fought over fundamental issues, the reform of Parliament, the future of the Established Church and the reform of municipal corporations. The passions and copious oratory excited by differences over high policy were fed by the long-lasting jealousy and resentment aroused by the exclusive nature of the governing circles of the city that had prevailed since the revolution settlement of 1688–9; and debate was given a sharper edge because the principles evoked in support of parliamentary reform found practical expression at that time in local issues directly affecting the ratepayers. The dispute over Exeter's new improvement act, which became law in 1832, and over the siting of the new markets, provided ample opportunities for verbal onslaughts on two favourite targets of the Reformers, the Chamber and the Cathedral Chapter. The noise of these particular battles was still reverberating when the cholera epidemic of 1832 brought Exeter face to face with the stark problems of public health in a crowded city.

There were few out-and-out opponents of parliamentary reform; for most the question was not one of principle but of degree.[1] On the political battlefield, however, there was no place for refinements. The *beau ideal* of the independent county member, Sir Thomas Acland of Killerton, was a prominent casualty in 1831 when the Whig, the Hon. Newton Fellowes of Eggesford, 'blew his hunting horn and called his pack together'. Acland had declared in the House of Commons that Reform was expedient but, as he explained to his Devon neighbours, he feared that 'in pulling about the building too rashly, the foundations of the old walls may give way'.[2] Dissenters were united on behalf of Reform, seeking to remedy grievances which were as much social as legal or religious; in April 1835 the Exeter Dissenters' Committee requested all Dissenters to vote for the Whig, Lord John Russell.

The first election in the series, in 1830, was occasioned by the death of George IV. The sitting members were Samuel Trehawke Kekewich of Peamore, and Lewis William Buck of Daddon, near Bideford. Both were

Tory. Kekewich stood down. The Whig, James Buller of Downes, a member of one of the traditional political families of the West Country, was requested to 'maintain the unsullied Loyalty and uncompromising Independence of the Citizens of Exeter'.[3] Buller's supporters, according to the requisition requesting him to stand for election, were primarily Tory. Among them were Edmund Granger; the banker, E.L. Sanders; Mark Kennaway, the future leader of Exeter's Liberals but in most respects conservative; Edward Woolmer, the newspaper proprietor; the surgeon Samuel Barnes, later a Conservative alderman; the artist John Gendall; the ironmonger, Samuel Kingdon, who would be the first mayor of the reformed corporation and also Stephen Brunskill, that remarkable example of private enterprise on his way up from journeyman tailor to the ownership of Polsloe Park and the acquisition of a fortune.[4] The Exeter election was uncontested. The Devon county election on Rougemont was particularly rowdy. At a convivial celebration at the New London Inn to celebrate the return of Lord Ebrington at the head of the poll, the company drank the health of Dissenting ministers engaged in the Whig cause, and also that of 'The people, source of all power'.[5]

The Duke of Wellington's government, formed after the general election of July, resigned in November 1830. The Whig leader, Lord Grey, came to power after over twenty years in the wilderness. The tempest of Reform burst with dramatic suddenness.

The following election, in May 1831, was fought squarely on the issue of Reform. The first Reform Bill[6] had been introduced into the Commons by Lord John Russell in March and had proved more drastic than had been expected or feared. The second reading scraped through with a majority of one vote and the bill succumbed in committee. Parliament was dissolved in lively circumstances. The government had been defeated by a wrecking procedure — the so-called Gascoyne amendment — that the total number of members for England and Wales should not be reduced. It had been supported in the House by Lewis Buck, MP for Exeter, as well as by fifteen of the twenty-six members for Devon. Buck accepted the principles of the Bill, 'in so far that much of Reform was necessary', but in his view the proposed electoral qualification was too low and some details would never receive his support.[7] The banker J.B. Sanders, seconding Buck's nomination at Exeter, provoked uproar by making too explicit the misgivings of Buck and his supporters. The proposed £10 franchise would destroy 'the wholesome and legitimate influence of property'. It would 'place the elective franchise in the hands of those who had always used it to abuse it'. Buller, who had not voted for the Gascoyne amendment in April, announced his 'zealous support' for measures calculated to strengthen the constitution. His support in practice was not notably zealous.

In 1831 the Whigs brought forward a third candidate in the person of Edward Divett of Bystock, near Topsham. The initiative was taken by Divett's brother-in-law, Captain T.W. Buller RN, of Whimple, and the formal nomination as a candidate was proposed by Captain Truscott, RN, the chairman of the Exeter Reform Committee.[8] Naval officers at that time tended to be less conservative than their colleagues in the army. Divett was well-calculated to appeal to a large section of nineteenth-century Exeter. Cool-headed, an efficient businessman, he was a friend, and later the business adviser, of the millionaire ironmaster Sir John Guest. A firm supporter of Reform, an opponent of restrictions on middle-class talent, he did not indulge in the rhetoric that aroused the worst fears of county rectories or ancient guildhalls. He had no time to canvass but he made an encouraging impression. In May 1831, 909 electors voted. Buller headed the poll with 752 votes. Buck received 548, representing the hard-core of opposition to Reform. In the circumstances Divett did well to receive 379 votes.[9] At the county election on Rougemont Lord Ebrington and Lord John Russell were returned without a contest owing to Acland's retirement.

Divett's supporters, close on one-third of the electorate, represented a resurgence of the ancient Whig vote that had existed in Exeter throughout the eighteenth century and in the circumstances of the 1830s was finding allies. This vote had declined to its lowest level in 1818 when 293 electors had voted for the only genuine Radical who stood for the city in the nineteenth century, Exeter's neighbour, Thomas Northmore of Cleeve. Northmore voted for Buller and Divett in 1831 in the respectable company of Sir George Bampfylde of Poltimore, Squire John Quicke of Newton St Cyres and Exeter's Dissenting minister, the Rev James Manning. Their example was followed by shopkeepers and artisans, helliers, joiners, plasterers and porters, and by some who still styled themselves yeomen.

The Chamber, its employees and dependents, supported Buller and Buck, a cautious policy which did not involve die-hard opposition to Reform. Ten of the fifteen city constables whose votes can be traced followed the same line. Of the thirty-two Anglican clergymen who voted eleven gave plumpers for Buck, thus expressing total opposition to Reform, an attitude which was not without relevance to Whig toasts to Dissenting ministers. Eighteen clergy, like the Chamber, voted for Buller and Buck, two for Buller and Divett. In contrast the Improvement Commissioners, whose appointments had long provided an opportunity for public service to men traditionally excluded from the Chamber, provided fourteen votes for Divett. Among Divett's supporters was the future staunchly Conservative 'Iron Sam' Kingdon. The builders Henry and William Hooper, both of whom became pillars of Exeter's Conservatives, voted for Buller and Divett. The Hoopers were among the citizens who had long chafed against the exclusive membership of the Chamber and were practical Reformers who would vote plumpers for the Conservative candidate, Sir William Follett, in the general election of 1835.

In March the Chamber had petitioned against the Reform Bill as 'a most extensive and dangerous alteration in the Established Constitution of these

Realms'. For the record it was claimed that members 'did not pretend to exercise any Political Influence over their fellow citizens'. Certainly no formal resolution was approved, as it had been so often in the past, to support any individual candidate with their votes and interest. Strong objection, however, was taken to indications that the freemen would be deprived of the right to vote. Mass admissions to the freedom by some corporations had become notorious — the borough of Maldon in Essex had admitted one thousand during an election in 1826 — but Exeter had long given up the practice. During the hotly-contested elections of 1802 and 1818 there had been 123 and 113 admissions in Exeter, but only five on each occasion were admitted 'by order of the Mayor and Chamber'.[10] The Reform Bill eventually retained the right of the freemen to vote subject to certain conditions.

It may be assumed that in Exeter freemen in reduced circumstances were liable to influence by authority or to other inducements. The right to vote was a valuable possession and, judging by the voting lists, for some it was the most valuable property an elector possessed in the year of an election. In the general election of 1832, the first after the Reform Bill had been passed, and when the Conservative opposition was regaining strength, 418 freemen voted in a total vote of 2,055 and provided 272 plumpers for the Conservative, Follett. Eighteen inmates of the almshouses and three recorded as 'in the workhouse' voted, as freemen, for Buller and Follett; this was the orthodox Conservative line followed, among others, by men such as Aldermen Blackall and Sanders, the wharfinger Henry Campion and the gaoler John Gulley.[11] 'The corporation', wrote Thomas Latimer in the *Western Times*,

> with their town-serjeants, staff bearers, tradesmen and their workmen, and, worst of all, the inmates of the almshouses, of which they are patrons, have hitherto presented a most powerful barrier to the free expression of the popular opinions of the citizens.[12]

The barrier was not as powerful as Latimer implied but undoubtedly it had long existed.

In October 1831 the Reform Bill was rejected by the House of Lords. There followed widespread and riotous demonstrations throughout the country accompanied by arson and destruction of property. Country houses were put in a state of defence. Exeter reacted less dramatically. The inhabitants of the West Quarter showed no inclination to burn the Guildhall. Instead the mayor, William Kennaway, presided with dignity over a public meeting which debated with much heat a petition to the King.[13] A speaker with the temerity to claim that the Bill had been 'notably resisted', that passions had been engendered by 'an infuriated press', was howled down. Mark Kennaway, always a conservative Reformer, and later a very conservative Liberal, doubted whether the £10 franchise was a satisfactory test of property justifying the franchise. He suggested, amid noisy disapprobation, that the level should be raised to £12 or £13. A denunciation of the bishops provoked 'great uproar, cries of shame, hisses, violent and menacing gesticulations and cheering'. The petition was approved by a large majority.

The national political crisis ended in June 1832. On the night of 5 June the Telegraph coach clattered up to the Old London Inn with the news that the bill had been passed. The reaction was restrained. A few windows were broken, but there were no illuminations. Tories in Exeter received the news with resignation. Woolmer's *Gazette,* though disturbed by 'the restless spirit of ultra-Radicalism', expressed confidence in the good sense and moral integrity of the British people, despite some fear that in the larger towns the £10 vote would place too much power in the hands of democracy. The newspaper trusted that the act would have the effect of 'tranquilizing the public mind' and expressed the hope that the very names of Whig and Tory would perish.[14]

The precise size of the Exeter electorate on the eve of the Reform Act has never been exactly determined. According to the parliamentary returns the probable number of voters in 1831 was 'about 1,300 in a total male population of 12,683'. According to local sources the electorate at the time of the election in July 1831 comprised 991 resident voters and 134 out-voters, a total of 1,125.[15] The freemen in particular were an unknown quantity and their number could have been ascertained only by an analysis of the city records. The Reform Act of 1832, passed only after much amendment, compromise and manoeuvres, was not based on accurate electoral statistics; it is probable that the lower figure of 1,125 was the more accurate. The pre-reform electorate included a democratic element, in the modern sense, of about one-third, in the persons of mechanics, artisans, labourers and small shopkeepers, horn workers, umbrella makers, braziers and the like, who voted as freeholders or freemen.

After the Reform Act it was necessary to register the new electorate. The electoral area of the city parliamentary borough was doubled, being extended from 2,400 to 4,600 acres. Registration of voters, involving scrutiny and challenge of their qualifications, proved a new and lively exercise in political warfare and, in view of the legal technicalities involved, the new democracy enhanced the income and influence of the political attorney. In Exeter the state of play, claims admitted or dismissed, was followed with lively interest in the local press. It was a great day for the Liberals, in October 1835, when they objected to the registration of eighteen voters in the Close and seventeen were expunged, two cathedral dignitaries among them. The parliamentary commissioners investigating the city for the purpose of municipal reform stated that 2,952 electors were registered; this figure was repeated by the Select Committee on parliamentary expenses in 1834.[16] According to local figures there were

2,333 registered voters at the time of the election — the first after the Reform Act — held in December 1832, and this is likely to be approximately the correct figure.[17] It was more than double the electorate of May 1831, the last under the old system. In this reformed electorate something of the order of four hundred can be regarded as working-class, mechanics, artisans, a few labourers, waiters and the like, some of whom owed their franchise to the retention, after much controversy, of the ancient freemen's right to the franchise.

On the result of the general election of December 1832 depended the course and extent of future change in Church and State: Church reform, the power structure and administration of municipal corporations, the grievances of Dissenters over such matters as church rates and the obligation to be married in the parish church. At Exeter Lewis Buck declined to stand. His vote for the Gascoyne amendment had cast him in the role of an enemy to Reform. Divett experienced no electoral difficulties. His position on reform had been firm. His assurance, in December, that he was 'no lover of speculative reform', accorded well with cautiously progressive opinion in the city. He looked forward to economy and the removal of the abuses of the Church. Provoking from his audience cheers, and uproar, he declared that there should be no more non-resident rectors and starving curates, and that the system of ecclesiastical courts should be 'completely broken down'.[18]

James Buller offered himself again and the third candidate was the accomplished William Webb Follett, of a Topsham family, a renowned speaker and a brilliant lawyer, who sought the support of 'every independent man of all parties'. Claiming to be neither Whig nor Tory, neither a Conservative nor a nominee of the Chamber, he would give the Reform Act a fair trial but noted that 'there was a restless spirit abroad which, if not checked, might endanger the constitution'.[19] Buller headed the poll with 1,615 votes. Divett was returned with 1,120 votes and henceforward would be Liberal member for Exeter until his death in 1864. Follett, after being shouted down by Divett's more enthusiastic followers, obtained 985 votes. He attributed his defeat in part to partizanship on the part of the revising barristers who had begun work in November to register electors in accordance with the qualifications specified by the Reform Act.[20]

Despite Follett's claim to be no Conservative, among his supporters were the men who would control Exeter's Conservative party for the ensuing forty years. Among his plumpers were John Gidley, town clerk 1835–65, and John Daw the attorney, later an influential and discreet Conservative political agent and twice mayor of the reformed corporation. He was supported by bankers such as Henry Collins and E.L. Sanders, by freemen among the landed gentry, Sir John Duckworth, Sir Lawrence Palk and Sir Stafford Northcote; by Henry Hooper the builder, later the rough and tough Conservative political boss; and by that model of Methodist probity the grocer John Dinham.

The Reform Bill had adapted the parliamentary system to meet the aspirations of the prosperous middle-classes. Life went on as usual but within six weeks of the arrival of the news that the Bill had been passed Exeter received a drastic reminder of the perils lurking in the insanitary and overcrowded cities. This was *Cholera morbus* which had spread westwards from its reservoir in India through Russia to reach Sunderland in October 1831, Plymouth and Exeter in July 1832. Dr Thomas Shapter has left us a vivid account of the course of the epidemic in Exeter, a tale of conscientious hard work, of heroism and panic and administrative inadequacy.[21]

The causes and morphology of the disease were then unknown. Shapter himself expressed the hesitant opinion that the disease might have been due to 'aerial influences, but capable under peculiar and rare conditions of being transmitted from man to man'.[22] It was the unknown aspect of the disease and its unpleasant features that caused terror, and in contrast emphasised the courage of those such as medical men, clergy and their assistants whose duties exposed them to the disease. In the event, as Shapter demonstrated, the disease fell most heavily upon the over-crowded and insanitary areas of the city and no doctor or clergyman who worked in these areas was infected. Cholera was bred in dirt, in the human body and its discharges. It flourished in that other Exeter which existed beside the cathedral city of genteel society, schools and churches, a city described in Besley's *Guide and Itinerary* of 1835 as one of the healthiest and most desirable cities in the kingdom. So it was for the more fortunate of its residents.

After the first appearance of this particular epidemic in England the government recommended that a local Board of Health should be established in every town and should incude the magistrates, parochial clergy, medical practitioners and representatives of the principal inhabitants. At Exeter it was decided, after a public meeting, that the Board should include the Mayor and magistrates, the Bishop and another member of the Chapter, nine doctors or surgeons, representatives of the Corporation of the Poor and of the Improvement Commission, and a clergyman from each of the four quarters of the city. This Board was authorised to form local committees and to collect funds by public subscription for the sanitary measures deemed necessary; the guardians of the poor were also requested to take such measures as were required. On 7 November 1832 the central Board of Health in London expressed 'great satisfaction' with the prompt manner in which their recommendations had been carried out.

In fact the Exeter Board had not been constituted in due form. It was therefore necessary to have its proceedings and policy endorsed by another public meeting in December 1832. Further difficulties arose because orders made by the Privy Council referred to individual parishes and not to unions of parishes such as had been formed in Exeter in 1698. In August 1832 John Gidley, secretary to the Board and future town clerk, waited upon the under secretary at the Home Office to explain the situation. He was referred to the Privy Council Office where learned counsel admitted the existence of great impediments due to the defective state of the law. In the meantime on 19 July the first cases of cholera had been reported in Exeter.

Before the epidemic ended 402 people died, 335 in August when the epidemic was at its height.[23] That summer fear of death fed on ignorance and credulity.

> The medical attendants . . . were accused of inducing the unknown symptoms, and even of being the murderers of the prople; drunkenness prevailed; derisive, blasphemous and wanton songs were sung; rioting and opposition to the enactments of the law took place.[24]

At length the city was reduced to an awed silence. August 22 was set aside as a day of public humiliation and prayer; the churches were gratifyingly full. In the minds of many was David's vision of the angel of the Lord, his sword stretched over Jerusalem. 'The people', in Shapter's words, 'became appalled, and repenting, appealed, by public humiliation and prayer, to the Great Disposer of all events, to stay the pestilence.'[25] By mid-September there was evidence that the epidemic was receding.

The eighteenth century had bequeathed no administrative machinery to deal with such a crisis. The public authorities in Exeter, the Chamber, the Guardians of the Poor and the Improvement Commissioners, all were bound by the terms of their charters and the strict terms of the acts of Parliament that gave them their existence and powers. The new Board of Health was no more than an impromptu committee of the leading citizens, such as had always assembled from time to time to debate matters of public importance, and now met daily as the crisis deepened. As finally constituted the board consisted of fifty-seven individuals, some, like the bishop, virtually in an sleeping capacity. It included the eight aldermen-magistrates and two other representatives of the Chamber; fourteen medical men; all the parochial clergy and Dissenting ministers; Mark Kennaway, clerk to the Improvement Commissioners; J.D. Osborn, the Reformer; William Hooper the builder; James Golsworthy the proprietor of the water works; representatives of the Improvement Commissioners and of the Corporation of the Poor.

The board had authority but no funds, since it was assumed in London that funds would be raised by means of the parochial assessments for poor relief. But the authority for poor relief was the Corporation of the Poor, and then only for purposes prescribed by statute. Moreover there was a marked lack of cooperation between the board and the corporation; as Shapter put it, there was 'something like a feeling of jealousy'. Cooperation between the board and the Improvement Commissioners was more cordial and the latter appointed a powerful sub-committee with authority and funds to cover or clean open drains, construct sewers and to clean the streets in general. In St Sidwells, a vestry meeting decided to form its own board of health, a proposal approved by the authorities in London without consultation with Exeter; but the St Sidwells board, like the Exeter board, had no power to raise money except through the Corporation of the Poor and so its activities 'did not extend beyond whitewashing a few houses and removing some pigs'.[26]

Emergency operations to clean the streets demonstrated the inadequacy of the water supply system. There were lengthy negotiations with the proprietor, James Golsworthy, who explained that the demand was such that he was unable to supply his private customers or to fill the cisterns at the public baths, the hospital and the gaol. Plans for an emergency hospital were obstructed by vigorous local opposition due to fear of contagion, with the consequence that it was not till the epidemic was subsiding, in September, that the site could be selected, and the hospital fitted out, in time for the reception of one family. The siting of a cholera burial ground in particular aroused, in Shapter's words, 'torrents of ill-feeling and abuse', and there was riotous opposition from the parishioners of St Davids before a plot of ground was finally consecrated in a corner of Bury Meadow.[27]

In such circumstances it is remarkable that so much was done. The Board of Health, after a hesitant start, raised over £4,000 by subscription from the more prosperous citizens. Streets and houses were fumigated. Measures were taken to destroy or sterilise the clothing of victims and to remove bodies for burial. Food and clothing were distributed. The crisis was faced with courage and devotion. The mayor himself, William Kennaway, won a deserved reputation for his handling of the crisis as mayor an chairman of the Board of Health.

To some the cholera appeared to confirm the connection between godly habits, especially temperance, and worldly survival. It certainly emphasised the relationship of dirt, disease and water supplies. The inadequacy of the city's water supplies was plainly demonstrated and it was therefore decided by a public meeting to establish a public water company with shares of £25 each, a decision supported by a wide range of Exeter's respectable society with the chancellor of the diocese, Canon Martin, taking a leading part. Despite some opposition the necessary act of parliament was obtained in May 1833. Pynes Mill was purchased from Sir Stafford Northcote for £3,000 and the proprietor of the existing supply, James Golsworthy, an ardent Reformer, was bought out. A reservoir was then constructed at Dane's Castle, in the northern suburbs behind the county gaol, from which, it was claimed, water could be supplied to the upper storeys of buildings in the highest parts of the city.

In the meantime the Improvement Commissioners obtained their comprehensive new act of 1832 which gave them a wide range of powers until, in 1867, the recrudescence of cholera and the noisome defects of the city's sanitation were followed by the reluctant surrender of the commissioners' powers to the city council. The stimulus provided by the cholera died down. Thirty years later some influential Exonians were protesting against pressure to reform administration hallowed by time, and their leading spokesman disagreed with the suggestion that infant mortality and defective sanitation might be related.[28]

The controversy over the new improvement act reached its height in February and March 1832. The Improvement Commissioners themselves were conciliatory but there were heated exchanges at meetings in the Guildhall suggesting that the interest of ratepayers who supported parliamentary reform, and would soon win the right to be elected to the city corporation, would not always coincide with the public weal. The commissioners, declared J.D. Osborn, were asking for powers

> at variance, as the inhabitants conceived, with that protection of property and those just rights, of which no man without cause should be dispossessed, in that it deprived him of due control over the amount of assessment to which it was sought to make him subject . . . This power the inhabitants were determined no set of men should have.[29]

The high level of principle, with its echo of disputes with Stuart kings, was not always maintained. The Guildhall echoed with substantial charges of insincerity and corruption while the Improvement Commissioners were dismissed as 'imbecile and ignorant'.[30] Prominent builders such as Robert Cornish and Henry Hooper turned up with retinues of stalwart employees to vociferate on behalf of the commissioners. 'Everybody must see', declared the *Western Times,* that plans then under consideration for the construction of the future Queen Street were intended to 'improve the property of the Chamber and [that of] some of its members', a remark reflecting the ancient distinction between the Chamber and the citizens.[31] Some of the more ardent members of the opposition sought to ensure that the proposed legislation would make a clean sweep of the existing membership of the Improvement Commission.

There now remains no evidence to prove or disprove the allegations of corruption and self-interest. Neither is unknown in twentieth-century local government and the probability is that neither was absent in the 1830s. Certainly in Exeter the reforms of the period did not inaugurate the 'pure government' which the Reformers predicted with such confidence. The arguments over the city's new improvement bill derived their heat primarily from the more general onslaught on privilege and the old order, on the power and select nature of the Chamber. Despite last minute attempts to block the bill it was passed with the assistance of the city's two Members of Parliament. It provided for the retirement and election of all elected members of the commission by rotation, thus ensuring continuity of experience. The *ex officio* membership of the Chamber, which had aroused so much opposition, was reduced from eight to six. The bill authorised the immediate raising of a further £6,000 for improvement works but thereafter the raising of further sums would require the assent of two-thirds of the full membership at a special meeting. Proceedings henceforth were to be held in public, thus providing the newspapers with material for lively reports of rowdy debates.[32]

The reconstituted Improvement Commission began work in February 1833, and members were at once in dispute over major planning decisions such as the relative priority of North Street and Sidwell Street for development. The decision was of some importance to property owners and to builders such as Henry Hooper whose workshops and power-centre as a rising local politician were in St Sidwells.[33] Nevertheless it was in the early years of the new commission that the construction of the modern approaches to the city on the North began. In August 1833 part of Bury Meadow was acquired from the Corporation of the Poor for the construction of the road junction where later the statue of General Sir Redvers Buller in martial splendour would proclaim Devon's support of a local general in defiance of the War Office. In March 1835 the recently constructed Canal Basin received 200 tons of ironwork from Newport, Wales, for the construction of the Iron Bridge which was completed in December of the same year and still carries traffic from the site of the old North Gate across the deep Longbrook valley.[34]

The improvement bill controversy at Exeter was a probing attack on an outwork of the old regime. It was followed by the major assault on the citadel itself. The new Whig government prepared for the reform of the municipal corporations by assembling the evidence to support an indictment before the bar of public opinion. In September 1833 the Chamber received the Secretary of State's circular requiring details of the appointment of members of corporations. Very shortly afterwards Henry James and Edward Rushton arrived at Exeter on behalf of the commission of inquiry. After a slight contretemps, due to faulty staff-work, the inaugural meeting was held in the Guildhall, on 1 November, a day which, the *Western Times* announced, would be long celebrated 'as that on which the Sesame of Reform threw open the long-closed doors of this very closed Corporation'.[35]

The Chamber sensibly resolved to give full cooperation. All members of the Chamber's staff were formally authorised to answer any question put to them.[36] The Commissioners in their turn were tactful and were careful to explain that the inquiry involved no charges against any individual member of the Chamber. Allegations of corruption and self-interested were relegated to a conveniently vague past when, according to John Terrell the attorney, 'persons of low degree' were sometimes admitted to the Chamber. Terrell acknowledged that the contemporary members of the Chamber would not place their private interests before the public welfare.[37] The Commissioners themselves kept a firm hand on the proceedings; when J.D. Osborn launched into the technical aspects of the canal extension he was reminded that the problem was within the competency of the engineers. Inevitably much was made of the canal expenditure. Alderman Sanders was driven to admit that if the full cost had been foreseen the Chamber might not have undertaken the work.[38] He also admitted that, notwithstanding the removal of legal obstacles in 1832, no Dissenter had yet been elected to the Chamber.

When the report was published the criticism amounted to little more than that 'the Corporation of Exeter, being self-elected and conducting their affairs in private, have not gained the confidence of the inhabitants.'[39] This was incontestable. The Chamber was the product of conditions very different from those of the 1830s. The report on Exeter contained no reference to political malpractices. In contrast the report on Tiverton commented severely on the 'pernicious effects arising from the connection between a corporation with the right to return members of parliament and an influential nobleman'.[40]

No evidence had come to light of the misappropriation of public funds for the use of individual members, nor of 'partiality and unfairness' in the letting or sale of property. The debts however were an embarrassment, amounting as they did to over £141,000, of which £105,827 represented expenditure on the canal and the quay. Clearly this expenditure had been based on inadequate estimates and had not been properly controlled; as the commissioners pointed out, 'the impropriety of contracting a vast share of the overwhelming debt' belonged to the existing Chamber. The mass of unaudited accounts apparently escaped notice: at one of the first meetings of the reformed city council William Kennaway, expressing his reluctance to reflect on his former colleagues, admitted embarrassment over the existence of unaudited accounts amounting to between £60,000 and £70,000.[41] Of far greater significance was the fact that conditions in Exeter supported the charge that 'The Corporation look upon themselves, and are considered by the inhabitants, as separate and exclusive bodies.'[42]

In its final months the Chamber continued to fulfil its functions with dignity. The proceeds from all sales of property were at least hypothecated for the reduction of debt. The Higher and the Lower markets were begun and the Hoopers, who erected both, were given a lease for the construction of the impressive warehouses still standing on the quay. The Chamber's last political gesture was in character; it was an address to the King welcoming Peel's abortive government of December 1834, and expressing confidence that the new Prime Minister would take measures for 'the benefit of the State and the preservation of the Established Church'.[43]

On 12 December 1835 the Chamber met for the last time. The common seal was affixed to recent appointments: the recorder, the coroner, and John Gidley as committee clerk and curator of charities. He would be the first town clerk of the new era. Tribute was paid to the existence of 'cordial kindness and cooperation' between Guildhall and Cathedral, to the 'Honor, Integrity and Ability' of the Chamber's officers.[44] The last heirs of the Glorious Revolution of 1688 then laid down their offices and with them faded the colour and ceremonial that had reminded Exonians of an historic past. Such things could not be measured on the Utilitarian scale, they were dismissed as 'silly pageantry . . . for the prattling tenants of the nursery'. One of the new councillors, the Wesleyan, J.C. Sercombe, quoted St Paul, with premature satisfaction: 'the fashion of this world passeth away'.[45]

The pattern of Victorian politics was forming. The terms Liberal and Conservative were coming into use. The first use of 'Conservative' as a political term in Exeter appears to have been on 17 May 1832 when the *Flying Post* reported a political meeting at the New London Inn under the heading 'New Conservative Meeting'. In December 1832 William Follett told a meeting in the Guildhall that he was not a 'Conservative'. The term 'Liberal' appeared in 1833 when the *Flying Post* on 29 August discussed the candidature of Sir James Hamlyn Williams of Clovelly Court on behalf of the 'Liberals in North Devon'. In 1835 both Buller and Divett stood for re-election at Exeter. Follett also renewed his candidature and topped the poll with 1,425 votes. Divett was returned with 1,176 votes. Buller, in third place, withdrew, shortly to become father of Devon's Boer War hero.

For local electoral purposes the act of 1835 divided Exeter into six wards, each returning six councillors. The councillors in turn elected twelve aldermen. The act itself was an essential measure of modernisation if the administration of the old boroughs was to be adapted to the facts of contemporary life. The Whigs hoped it would have the additional advantage of eradicating Tory influence from the boroughs; in this respect however, it was a marked failure.

The contest for the first election on 26 December 1835 was presented by the Liberals as a fight between Right and Wrong, between a party alleged to be seeking to 'perpetuate the corruptions on which they had so long gorged' and the other 'animated by genuine patriotism' demanding the 'purification of our ancient institutions'. It was fought on party lines; one Liberal councillor regretted that he saw all too clearly 'the bane of party'. The result was disappointing for the Liberals. The Conservatives received a majority of votes — 3,232 to 2,309 — with eighty per cent of the electorate voting. Eighteen councillors were elected for each side. One of the new Liberal councillors, John Dymond, was a Quaker whose conscience could not accept the prescribed oath on assuming office. The Conservatives were therefore given a majority of one.[46]

The Conservatives — who may have represented Wrong but who were tactically the more adept of the two sides — promptly secured the election of Samuel Kingdon, a reformer but no Liberal, as chairman of the new Council, pending the election of aldermen and the subsequent election of a mayor. They then used their majority of one to elect five Conservative aldermen and one Liberal, the former mayor, William Kennaway. The fashion of this world had not passed away.

At the ensuing by-elections the Liberals secured a fleeting majority of elected councillors, but after 1840 the Conservatives would control the city Council, with one brief interlude, for the next sixty years. The Municipal Corporations Act changed the form of local government but it did not change Exeter's basic character. The election of 'Iron Sam' Kingdon as first mayor of the new regime summarised in personal terms the effects of the act. Kingdon had been active in public life since his election as a member of the Corporation of the Poor in 1807 but as a Unitarian he could not then be considered for membership of the Chamber. At the time of his election as mayor the Unitarians of George's Meeting had firmly resolved that the popular doctrine of the Trinity was incompatible with scriptural doctrine of the Unity of God. The _Western Times_ commented sardonically, therefore, on his worship's attendance at a Unitarian service to listen to a 'truly heretical discourse'.[47] Samuel Kingdon was one of the new men who would reinforce Exeter's conservative ruling class. He had no great reverence for ancient ceremony and traditional practice but he steered the Council through a difficult first year and earned the presentation of plate from his supporters.

Ratepayers were now eligible for election to the new city Council without distinction of creed or class. The press was admitted to Council meetings and while the city's Victorian newspapers were vigorously partisan they were also outspoken and kept the public well-informed on the views and idiosyncracies of their councillors. The opposition to the association of the city sword with a Dissenters' meeting house was overcome at last; among the men of the new regime who entered the Guildhall William Nation, banker, William Snell, grocer and, a later replacement, William Drewe, wine merchant, were all Unitarian.[48] J.C. Sercombe, grain merchant, was a Methodist. The first Council election in December 1835 marks the end of eighteenth-century Exeter.

NOTES

1. N. Gash, _Aristocracy and People_, p. 149.
2. _Flying Post_, 17.3.1831; _Hansard_, Series 3, lxviii, col. 624.
3. _FP_, 8.7.1830.
4. Brunskill was reported to be worth £250,000 at his death: _Western Times_, 10.1.1857.
5. _FP_, 19.8.1830.
6. The first Reform Bill was introduced on 1.3.1831, to be defeated in committee. Parliament was dissolved. The second was introduced on 24.6.1831, was carried in the Commons and defeated in the Lords, an event followed by serious riots. The third bill was introduced on 12.12.1831 and pased on 4.6.1832.
7. _FP_, 28.4.1831, 5.5.1831.
8. For Divett's relations with the Guests see Earl of Besborough (ed.), _Lady Charlotte Guest, Extracts from her Journal_, 1950.
9. 'List of Voters at the contested election of 28-30 April 1831', in T. & H. Besley, _Exeter Itinerary and General Directory_, 1831.
10. DRO, ECA, Act Books, 26.3.1831. For admissions to the freedom, Rowe and Jackson, _Exeter Freemen 1266-1967_.
11. T. Besley, _A List of Voters at the Exeter Election on December 10th and 11th 1832_, Exeter, 1833.
12. _Western Times_, 10.9.1831

NOTES *continued*

13. *FP*, 20.10.1831.
14. *Gazette*, 21.4.1832, 18.4.1832, 9.6.1832.
15. PP *Return of Freemen and Voters 1831-32*, H.C. 112, 1833-4, xxxvi and Besley, *Directory*, 1831.
16. PP *Select Committee on Election Expenses*, H.C. 591, 1834, ix, appendices A and N. *White's Directory* of 1850 stated that while in 1836 the number of registered voters was 3,488, the true figure, after allowing for double entries, was about 2,800.
17. Besley, *List of Voters . . . 1832*.
18. *FP*, 13.12.1832.
19. *ibid.*, 5.7.1832, 31.12.1832.
20. *FP*, 13.12.1832. For an interesting 'score-board' of objections see *ibid.*, 8.10.1835.
21. T. Shapter, *History of the Cholera in Exeter in 1832*, 1849, reprinted 1971, was described in the *British Medical Journal*, April 1933, as 'one of the best descriptions extant of an historical epidemic'.
22. *ibid.*, 1971, p. 230.
23. *ibid.*, pp. 208-9.
24. *ibid.*, 216 and chapter xiv generally.
25. *ibid.*, p. 235.
26. *ibid.*, pp. 60-61.
27. The modern park known as Bury Meadow is a remnant of the old Bury Meadow, ten acres of good grazing which extended from the modern Elm Grove Road to St Davids Church. The name 'Bury' had nothing to do with cholera burials: W.G. Hoskins, *Two Thousand Years in Exeter*, p. 141.
28. See my *Victorian Exeter*, pp. 122-24.
29. *FP*, 16.2.1832.
30. *ibid.*, 23.2.1832; 1.3.1832, 8.3.1832, 25.3.1832.
31. *Western Times*, 9.6.1832, 23.6.1832; 26.11.1831.
32. 2 & 3 William IV, cap. Cvi.
33. *FP*, 13.3.1833, 15.3.1833, 5.9.1833. For the end of Henry Hooper's public career see *Victorian Exeter*, pp. 113-4.
34. *FP*, 9.3.1835.
35. *WT*, 2.1.1833.
36. DRO, ECA, Act Books, 23.9.1833.
37. DRO, Municipal Corporations Commissioners' Proceedings, 1833, 3rd day, fo. 37 and 5th day, fo. 55. These were taken down by Thomas Latimer, an expert stenographer.
38. *ibid.*, fo. 37.
39. PP *Municipal Corporations in England and Wales*, 1st Report, H.C. 116, 1835, xxiii, Appendix, p. 498.
40. *ibid.*, p. 630. The nobleman was Dudley Ryder, first Lord Harroby.
41. *ibid.*, 498, 493-4 and 498.
42. *ibid.*, p. 498 and *WT*, 23.1.1836.
43. DRO, ECA, Act Books, 8.4.1835.
44. *ibid.*, 12.12.1835.
45. *WT*, 15.1.1836.
46. *FP*, 31.12.1835; *Gazette*, 2.1.1836, 16.1.1836; *WT*, 31.12.1835, 7.1.1836.
47. *WT*, 9.1.1836, *FP*, 17.9.1835.
48. See G. Kitson Clark, *The Making of Victorian England*, p. 161, for the significance of Unitarian mayors after 1835.

Chapter Eleven

The Ever-Faithful City

Victorian England regarded Exeter as a picturesque city with a colourful past, a diminished status and a propensity to rowdiness. The members of the British Association, in 1869, found it, in contrast to Liverpool, a place of 'silence and past memories'.[1] Exonians themselves looked back with regret for a vanished golden age, unspecified in date, in fact an amalgam of the city of Queen Anne and the Regency. Growth ceased 'many generations since' remarked the *Flying Post* in 1881.[2]

While the development of seventeenth-century Exeter, with its vigorous economic growth, 'epitomised the economic history of England as a whole',[3] by the time the new industrial England was taking shape after 1800 Exeter was no longer the capital of a region described by Defoe as 'full of great towns, and those towns so full of people, and those people so universally employed in trade and manufactures'. By 1850, when the first excursion train from Birmingham arrived at Exeter, the county's reputation for most people was becoming that of a land of cob walls and thatched cottages, cream teas and Widecombe Fair. It was a reputation enhanced in Edwardian England by the advertisements of the two competing railways, the L.S.W.R. and the G.W.R.

Exeter's prime, remembered with nostalgia in the late-Victorian city, belonged to the England of small-scale industry, country produce and horse transport. At the time William of Orange entered Exeter, in 1688, the prosperity of Devon derived from wool was reaching its climax after some five hundred years of growth and development ending, in the last decades of the seventeenth century, with the pre-eminence of the manufacture of serge. Exeter accordingly had prospered, as an industrial city, particularly for the finishing processes of the cloth industry, as a financial centre and as a port. The city was ruled by a self-confident and able merchant class which had successfully piloted Exeter through the hazards of civil war and religious strife under the Tudor and Stuart monarchs. The Chamber had joined with zest in the Cavalier reaction after 1661 and on the eve of the reform of the 1830s Oakapple Day was still being celebrated by a procession of the Chamber and Incorporated Trades to a service at the Cathedral followed by a convivial dinner at the Half Moon. In 1688 the Earl of Bath reported on the joy with which the city sword, borne before the mayor on ceremonial occasion, was rescued from a conventicle when James II's policy of packing the governing bodies of parliamentary boroughs was abruptly reversed. Henceforward, until 1835, Exeter's Guildhall was barred to all but orthodox Churchmen.

The Chamber of Exeter was an exclusive club, self-elected and jealously maintaining its status and privileges, its members closely linked by family relationships and business interests. In the earlier years of the eighteenth century many of them were successful, and often wealthy, businessmen, accepting the risks, and enjoying the profits, of overseas trade in an age of maritime warfare and privateering. Their interests were the interest of the city. Their weakness was the barrier, political, social and religious, between themselves and their Anglican circle and the Dissenters and their Low Church sympathisers.

There is no evidence of abuse of power that might have exceeded the latitude allowed by their contemporaries: nor could the partisan investigation of the Whigs in 1833 provide any. The Chamber was not, in practice, an autocratic authority. On matters outside the competence conferred by charter and tradition the Chamber wisely consulted representatives of the respectable citizens. During the controversies of the 1830s the Reformers made free with allegations of corruption and self-interest, and it is not unlikely that members of the Chamber in the age of Walpole were less discreet in the pursuit of their own interests than they became in the nineteenth century. The reference in 1833 to 'persons of low degree' having once upon a time been admitted to the Chamber,[4] is an indication, however, of a further barrier that had been erected between Chamber circles and many of the undoubtedly respectable citizens. In the second half of the eighteenth century the Chamber, by and large, had come to represent gentility as the term was understood in the world of Jane Austen, and not the trading element, which when the economic tide had run in its favour, had created the city admired by Celia Fiennes and Daniel Defoe.

By the second decade of the nineteenth century no appeals to the 'Glorious Revolution', to the sanctity of tradition and the time-honoured relationship of Church and State could meet the charge that the Chamber was unrepresentative and uncontrolled by the citizens. Outside the society of Guildhall and Cathedral were god-fearing, earnest and often wealthy citizens, some, as Unitarians, the heirs of seventeenth-century Presbyterians, others hard-working shopkeepers, serious minded men demanding as of right a share in the administration of their city, and in the parliamentary franchise. The Reformers of the 1830s were men such as those described by Henry Ellis as apprentices eagerly debating constitutional and moral issues; their views were shaped by romantic visions of an Anglo-Saxon England governed by conclaves of free citizens.

For the *Western Times* the Reform Bill would elicit 'a perfect representation of popular opinion'. For J.D. Osborn the Municipal Corporations Act would ensure that 'the institution of municipal government, which was once the pride and boast of our citizens, would once again be restored to that state of vigour which the great men of the early ages of English history intended it to be'.[5] Their aspirations enriched city life but were not notably realized in the Victorian city.

The Chamber in 1835 could not be defended on any ground of utility or constitutional theory. But by then no action of Parliament or of the city's own Reformers could restore Exeter's national importance as it had been in the days of William of Orange and Queen Anne. Maritime trade, as it developed in the eighteenth century, required better facilities than could be provided by the estuary of the Exe and, on land, easier access to more profitable markets than could be provided by the limited consumer society and the poverty-stricken agricultural workers of Devon. The Chamber in its final years undertook improvements on a scale comparable with that of the great reconstruction of the canal in 1697-1700. The effort of the 1820s was courageous but out of time. By 1800 the successful descendants of the immigrants once attracted to the city by its thriving economy and overseas connections had turned their attention to international finance and banking. Improved communications and business enterprise elsewhere brought competition which Exeter was unable to meet, and the city's business largely depended on the distribution of goods from beyond Devon.

The loss of the city's basic industry coincided with a substantial growth in population. In the first half of the eighteenth century Exeter's population had been static, but towards the very end of the century the city was experiencing the remarkable growth of population that was a feature of Western Europe at this time. The real expansion came only after the Napoleonic Wars. Between 1811 and 1821 the population increased by 24 per cent. In the following decade it increased by 21 per cent. Writing of the city of 1831 Dr Shapter commented that Exeter had no more than 'the ordinary admixture of the poor'.[6] The Poor Law Commissioners observed in 1834 that Exeter had 'been exempt from any marked local vicissitudes during a long series of years'.[7] Exeter indeed had not experienced vicissitudes on the scale experienced by contemporary towns and cities in the Midlands and the North, but there had been times of severe distress. In late-Georgian and Regency Exeter probably at least one-third of the total population had a struggle to exist from day to day, hoping to be spared the accident of misfortune which would tip the balance decisively against them.

But the full consequences of the loss of the cloth industry and of the rise of population were not experienced until the reign of Queen Victoria. For a time the French war of 1793–1815 resulted in the brief flowering of Exeter as a social capital with the amenities required by genteel consumer society, and also in the city's longer-term popularity as a place for retirement. Building became a major source of employment. The demand for goods and services and comfortable, easily-maintained houses, for opportunities for social display and for entertainment, provided a living, and indeed moderate wealth, for innkeepers, jewellers, furriers and milliners, booksellers and above all the builder-architects.

During the long war naval affairs and overseas campaigns brought a constant flow of distinguished visitors to a city firmly astride the main road between London, Torbay, Plymouth and Falmouth. Royal dukes, admirals and generals enjoyed the hospitality of Exeter's leading inns. Births, marriages and deaths in the local press testify that many of Exeter's younger sons were seeking adventure and fortune overseas and so, in the case of those who survived, in Kitson Clark's phrase, were 'graduating into gentility'.[8] The old trade and industry had vanished but Exeter shared in the profits of war and expanding empire. Moreover with the increasing commercialisation of leisure,[9] tourism and retirement had begun to exercise what would later become a major factor in the South West's economy. In the vicinity of Exeter, Sidmouth and Exmouth were already being developed for those with the means to afford enjoyment of climate and scenery in the company of congenial society. Torquay was becoming popular with wealthy visitors and W.C. Pollard, of North Street, published in 1827 his *Directions for visiting the most picturesque spots on the Eastern and Southern Coast from Sidmouth to Plymouth.*

Amid the social unrest, hunger and rioting of the decades after Waterloo, the county's capital remained quiet. The urban radicalism that was appearing elsewhere towards the end of the eighteenth century had received virtually no response in Exeter. Criticism of the authority of the Chamber during the controversy over the Improvement Act of 1810 was organised by members of the respectability of the city. The local papers were congratulatory on the city's tranquillity and supported subscriptions to funds for the relief of distress in Northern England or Ireland. At a time when men drilled by torchlight on northern moors and burning ricks flamed in the southern counties the only drama in Exeter was provided by the illegal, but theatrical, ceremonies, duly suppressed, of an incipient trade union.[10] In a small city standing apart from the new industrial England the old social discipline remained effective.

Public decorum, though not always achieved, had become a necessity for all who claimed to be respectable. Even the neighbouring squires rode into Exeter to discuss the distribution of bibles, or the affairs of the Devon and Exeter Institution rather than, as their predecessors had done, to bet on cockfighting contests at the Globe. Among the civic establishment there was an atmosphere of moral earnestness that bordered on spiritual pride. Men such as Dr Macgowan, Liberal mayor in 1838, held themselves to be 'honoured instruments under Providence for the succour of a benighted world'.[11] It was an attitude that did not always encourage charity towards those whose views differed over religious principles and observances, but there was a growing sincerity in the attempts made to alleviate the hardships and distress of contemporary life. The Exeter Dispensary, opened in 1818 and supported by subscriptions, was reported to have admitted 1700 patients by 1835. The West of England Eye Infirmary was modernised and handsomely rehoused at the top of Magdalen Street in 1830. The Mendicity Society provided a night's lodging for over 1200 men, women and children in 1827. Churchman and Dissenter laboured to provide a modicum of education for the children of the poor, not without the stimulus of sectarian rivalry.

There was indeed every reason to regard Exeter itself as part of a benighted world. Yet Dr Shapter, in describing the Exeter of 1831, wrote that:

> Instead of the decline and ruin of the town we find the population increasing, their personal comforts publicly considered and provided for, and the whole aspect of the city undergoing a change for the better.[12]

Exeter would not boast the new textile mills and factories which aroused the admiration and awe of visitors to the Midlands and the North, but the generations who lived in the city between the last decades of the seventeenth century and the 1830s had already left their architecture to testify to their achievements and aspirations. By this architecture they can claim to be judged, by the Canal, Sir John Elwill's house in Pinhoe, the terraces of Southernhay and Lower Summerlands, the villas of Heavitree, the facade of the Higher Market and the great warehouses on the Quay. For today's citizens it is no bad heritage.

NOTES

1. *Athenaeum*, No. 2237, 10.9.1870.
2. *FP*, 27.4.1881.
3. W.B. Stephens, *Seventeenth Century Exeter*, p. 163.
4. DRO, ECA, Commission for Municipal Corporations, 1833, proceedings on third day, p. 37.
5. *WT*, 15.8.1835.
6. PP *State of Large Towns and Populous Districts*, Second Report, H.C. 602, 1845, xviii
7. PP *Administration and Operation of the Poor Laws*, H.C. 44, 1834, xxvii
8. G.Kitson Clark, *The Critical Historian*, 1968, p. 154.
9. P.J. Corfield, *The Impact of English Towns 1700-1800*, 1982, p. 52.
10. See W.G. Hoskins, *Two Thousand Years in Exeter*, pp. 99–100 for the raid on an illegal oath-taking ceremony at the Sun Inn.
11. *FP*, 28.10.1830.
12. PP *State of Large Towns and Populous Districts*, Second Report, H.C. 602, 1845, xviii.

Bibliography

MANUSCRIPTS

DEVON RECORD OFFICE
A EXETER CITY ARCHIVES
  Act (or Minute) Books of the Chamber, 1684-1835
  Receivers' Account Rolls, 1689-1713
  Receivers' Accounts (Books 29-202), 1712-1835
  Receivers' Vouchers and Tradesmen's Bills, 1715-1834
  Miscellaneous Books, including 159A, Rate Assessment, March 1690
  Miscellaneous Papers, including Polls for the Election of Mayor, 1735, 1736, 1738, 1740, 1760 and 1768
  Corporation of the Poor, Court Minute Books from August 1698
  Commissioners for Municipal Corporations, Proceedings at Exeter, 1-6 November 1833
B OTHER RECORDS
  Miscellaneous Deeds, Leases, etc. concerning property in Exeter
  2065M/SS2/16-18 Buller Papers, Election Account Book
  76/20 Memoirs of Henry Ellis, 3 vols, 1790-1859
  MS 36 Diary of Lady Paterson, 1831-5

British Library, Department of MSS, Add. MS 41805

PRIMARY PRINTED SOURCES

NEWSPAPERS
A DEVON LIBRARY SERVICES, WEST COUNTRY STUDIES LIBRARY, EXETER
  Trewman's Exeter Flying Post, from December 1770
  Exeter Evening Post, from July 1765
  Exeter Mercury or West Country Advertiser, 1763 to July 1765
B DEVON AND EXETER INSTITUTION
  The Exeter Mercury, September 1714 to September 1715
  The Protestant Mercury or The Exeter Postboy, October 1715 to September 1717 (with gaps)
  The Exeter Post-Master or the Loyal Mercury, 1720 to 1725 (with gaps)
  Brice's Weekly Journal, April 1725 to June 1729
  Farley's Weekly Journal, May-June 1725, May-June 1726, 19 April 1728
  Woolmer's Exeter and Plymouth Gazette, 1792-3, 1798-1800, 1809-
  Flindell's Western Luminary, 1813-26, 1828-
  Western Times, from 1831

LOCAL DIRECTORIES

Andrew Brice, *Grand Gazeteer*, Exeter 1759
Exeter Pocket Journal, 1797, 1801
T. & H. Besley, *Exeter Itinerary and General Directory*, 1828, 1831, 1835
T. Besley, *Guide and Itinerary*, 1836

CONTEMPORARY PERIODICALS

Annual Register, 1758-
Gentleman's Magazine, 1731-

PARLIAMENTARY PAPERS

Sessional Papers of the Eighteenth Century: Minutes of Evidence relating to Wool, 24 April 1800
Abstract of Answers and Returns made pursuant to an Act passed 43 George III
Return of Freemen and Voters, 1831-2, H. C. 112, 1833-4, xxxvi
Election Expenses, Select Committee Report on, H. C. 591, 1834, ix
Administration and Operation of the Poor Laws, Commissioners' Report, H. C. 44, 1834, xxviii
Municipal Corporations (England and Wales), Commissioners' First Report, H. C. 116, 1835, xxiii
Municipal Corporations Boundaries, H. C. 238, 1837, xxvi
State of Large Towns and Populous Districts, Commissioners' Second Report, H. C. 602, 610, 1845, xviii

OFFICIAL PUBLICATIONS

Journals of the House of Commons
Hansard
Private Acts of Parliament
Report of the Commissioners concerning Charities, Exeter 1825
Endowed Charities, County Borough of Exeter, 1909
Report of the Medical Officer of Health, Exeter 1911

PAMPHLETS AND BROADSHEETS

A WEST COUNTRY STUDIES LIBRARY
The Expedition of His Highness the Prince of Orange ... in a Letter to a Person of Quality, 1688
John Whittle, *The Exact Diary of the late Expedition of his Illustrious Highness the Prince of Orange ... by a Minister, Chaplain in the Army*, 1689
List of Freemen and Freeholders ... 1776

B DEVON AND EXETER INSTITUTION
The Substance of what Sir Bartholomew Shower spoke at the Guildhall Exon, 19 August 1698
Devon Election Addresses, 1789-90
Elections in the city of Exeter and county of Devon, 1816-18, Exeter 1818
T. Besley, *List of Voters at the Exeter Elections ... on December 10th and 11th 1832*, Exeter 1833

OTHER CONTEMPORARY PRINTED SOURCES

Andrew Brice, *The Mobiad*, 1770
G. Burnet, *History of His Own Times*, 2 vols, 1724
W. Carwithen (ed.), S. Isacke et al., *Account of the Legacies left to the Poor of Exeter*, 1820

John Cernick, *An Account of the late Riot in Exeter*, 1745
John Fisher (ed.), *Sermons on Several Subject*, Sherborne, 1741
W. Gilpin, *Observations on the Western Parts of England*, 1808
John Hooker alias Vowell, *The Antique Description ... of the City of Exeter*, Exeter 1765
John Howard, *State of the Prisons in England and Wales*, 1784
W. Marshall, *The Rural Economy of the West of England*, 2 vols, 1796
Hannah Moore, *Strictures on the Modern Form of Female Education*, 1811 edn.
James Nield, *State of the Prisons in England, Wales and Scotland*, 1812
Robert Southey, *Letters from England*, 1814
Charles Vancouver, *General View of the Agriculture of Devon*, 1808
J. Wright, *Sir Henry Cavendish's Debates of the House of Commons, 1768-71*, 1841

RECORD PUBLICATIONS

K. Balderston (ed.), *Thraliana*, 2 vols, Oxford 1951
C. Barrett (ed.), *Diary and Letters of Madame D'Arblay, 1778-1840*, 6 vols, 1904-5
Besborough, earl of (ed.), *Lady Charlotte Guest's Extracts from her Journal*, 1950
Graham Bush (ed.), *Bristol and its Municipal Government 1820-51*, Bristol Record Society, xxix, 1976
Calendar of State Papers Domestic
Calendars of Treasury Books
Calendar of Home Office Papers
S. D. Chapman (ed.), *The Devon Cloth Industry in the Eighteenth Century: Sun Fire Office Inventories ... 1726-1770*, DCRS, New Series 23, 1978
R. P. Chope (ed.), *Early Tours in Devon and Cornwall*, Newton Abbot, 1967
G. D. H. Cole (ed.), *Tour through the whole of Great Britain by Daniel Defoe*, 2 vols, 1927
Sir William Drake (ed.), *Heathiana*, privately printed, 1881
Historical Manuscripts Commission
    29 14th Report, App.II, *Portland III*, 1894
        15th Report, App.IV, *Portland IV*, 1897
    71 *Finch Mss* IV, 1965
    73 *City of Exeter*, 1916
W. G. Hoskins (ed.), *Exeter in the Seventeenth Century: Rate and Tax Assessments 1602-99*, DCRS, New Series 2, 1957
W. G. Hoskins (ed.), *Exeter Militia List, 1803*, Chichester 1972
C. Morris (ed.), *The Journeys of Celia Fiennes*, 1947
R. E. Prothero (ed.), *The Letters of Richard Ford, 1797-1858*, 1905
M. M. Rowe and A. M. Jackson (eds), *Exeter Freemen, 1266-1967*, DCRS 1973

SECONDARY WORKS

Alexander, J. J.   'Exeter Members of Parliament, part iv, 1688-1832', *DAT*, lxii, 1930
    'The Exeter Election of 1695', *DCNQ*, xvi, 1930-31, 231-5
Boggis, R. J. E.   *History of the Diocese of Exeter*, Exeter, 1922
Bowring, Sir John   *Autobiographical Recollections*, 1877
Brockett, A. A.   'The Political and Social Influence of Exeter Dissenters', *DAT*, xCiii, 1961
    Nonconformity in Exeter, 1650-1875, Manchester, 1962

Brushfield, T. N.   *The Life and Bibliography of Andrew Brice*, privately printed, 1888

Carlisle, N.   *Concise Description of the Endowed Grammar Schools of England and Wales*, 2 vols, 1818

Carswell, J.   *The Descent on England*, 1969

Chick, E.   *A History of Methodism in Exeter*, Exeter 1907

Clark, E. A. G.   *Ports of the Exe Estuary, 1660-1860*, Exeter 1960

Clark, G. Kitson   *The Making of Victorian England*, 1962

Cobbett, W.   *Parliamentary History*

Coleman, D. C.   *The British Paper Industry, 1495-1860*, 1958

Cole, G. D. H. and
  Postgate, R.   *The Common People, 1746-1946*, 1961 edn

Corfield, P.   *The Impact of English Towns, 1700-1800*, Oxford, 1982

Cranfield, G. A.   *The Development of the Provincial Newspaper, 1700-1760*, Oxford, 1962

Cresswell, B. F.   *Exeter Churches*, Exeter, 1908

Davies, G. C. B.   *Henry Philpotts, Bishop of Exeter*, 1954

Duckett, Sir George *Penal Laws and the Test Act*, 2 vols, 1882

Forster, J.   *Life of Charles Dickens*, 1872

Forsythe, W. J.   *A System of Discipline: Exeter Borough Prison 1819-63*, Exeter 1983

Freeman, E. A.   *Exeter*, 1887

Fritz, P. S.   *The English Ministers and Jacobites between the Rebellions of 1715 and 1745*, Toronto, 1975

Gash, N.   *Aristocracy and People*, 1979

Gidley, J.   *A History of Royal Visits to the Ancient and Loyal City of Exeter*, 1863

Gilboy, E. W.   *Wages in Eighteenth Century England*, Cambridge, Mass., 1934

Harte, W. J.   'Some data for assessing the population of Exeter at the end of the seventeenth century', *DCNQ*, xx, 1939, 210-14

Henning, B. D.   *The House of Commons 1660-90*, 3 vols, 1983

Holmes, G.   *The Trial of Dr Sacheverell*, 1973

Horwitz, H.   *Parliament, Policy and Politics in the reign of William III*, Manchester, 1977

Hoskins, W. G.   *Industry, Trade and People in Exeter, 1688-1800*, Manchester 1935, reprinted Exeter 1968
                       'The Inns of Exeter, 1686-1708', *DCNQ*, xx, 1939, 266-7
                       'The Population of Exeter', *DCNQ*, xx, 1939, 242-7
                       Two Thousand Years in Exeter, Exeter 1960

Isacke, S.   *Remarkable Antiquities of the City of Exeter*, 1724

Jenkins, A.   *The History and Description of the City of Exeter*, Exeter, 1806

Jones, J. R.   *The Revolution of 1688 in England*, 1972

Lambert, R. S.   *The Cobbett of the West*, 1939

Little, B.   *Portrait of Exeter*, 1953

MacCaffrey, W. T.   *Exeter 1540-1640*, Cambridge, Mass., 1958

Macaulay, T. B.   *The History of England from the Accession of James II*, 5 vols, 1849-61

Namier, L. and
  Brooke, J.   *The House of Commons, 1754-1790*, 3 vols, 1964

Newton, R.   *Victorian Exeter*, Leicester, 1968
                       'Society and Politics in Exeter, 1837-1914', in H. J. Dyos (ed.), *The Study of Urban History*, 1968
                       'Exeter 1770-1870', in M. A. Simpson and T. H. Lloyd (eds),

	Middle Class Housing in Britain, Newton Abbot, 1977
Norman, E. R.	*Church and Society in England, 1770-1970*, Oxford 1976
North, R.	*The Life of the Rt Hon. Francis North, Baron Guilford*, 1742
Oliver, G.	*The History of the City of Exeter*, Exeter, 1861
	Biographies of Eminent Exonians (newspaper cuttings) in Devon and Exeter Institution
Pares, R.	*King George III and the Politicians*, 1959
Parry, H. Lloyd	*The History of the Exeter Guildhall*, Exeter, 1936
	The Founding of Exeter School, Exeter, 1913
Patterson, A. T.	*The Other Armada*, 1960
Pickard, R.	*The Population and Epidemics of Exeter in pre-Census Times*, Exeter 1947
Polwhele, R.	*The History of Devon*, 3 vols, 1797-1806
Portman, D.	*Exeter Houses 1400-1700*, Exeter, 1966
Powley, E. B.	*The Naval Side of King William's War*, 1972
Prince, J.	*The Worthies of Devon*, Plymouth, 1810
Russell, P. M. G.	*A History of Exeter Hospitals*, Exeter, 1976
Sedgewick, R.	*The House of Commons, 1715-54*, 2 vols, 1970
Shapter, T.	*The History of the Cholera in Exeter in 1832*, 1849, reprinted with Introduction by R. Newton, Wakefield, 1971
Sharp, T.	*Exeter Phoenix*, 1946
Sheldon, G.	*From Trackway to Turnpike*, Oxford, 1928
Shorter, A. H. et al. (eds),	*South West England*, 1969
Shorto, A. M.	*The History of Exeter*, Exeter, 1906
Shutte, R. N.	*The Life, Times and Writings of the Right Rev. Dr Henry Philpotts*, Otley, 1863
Simmons, J.	'Some Letters from the Bishops of Exeter, 1668-88', *DCNQ*, xxii, 1942-6, 43-8, 72-80, 108-12, 143-4, 153-5, 166-8
Stephens, W. B.	*Seventeenth Century Exeter*, Exeter, 1958
Sykes, N.	'The Cathedral Chapter of Exeter and the General Election of 1705', *English Historical Review*, xiv, 1930‧
	Church and State in England in the Eighteenth Century, 1934
Walrond, H.	*Historical Records of the First Devon Militia*, 1897
Wood, Francis	'The Social Identification of Merchants in Exeter, 1680-1760', unpublished MA thesis, Monash University, 1977 (copy in Devon and Exeter Institution)
Youings, Joyce	*Tuckers Hall Exeter*, Exeter, 1968

Index

All subject headings relate to Exeter unless otherwise indicated